PROFOUND IMPROVEMENT

CONTEXTS OF LEARNING
Classrooms, Schools and Society

Managing Editors:

Bert Creemers, *GION, Groningen, the Netherlands.*
David Reynolds, *School of Education, University of Exeter, Exeter, UK.*
Sam Stringfield, *Center for the Social Organization of Schools, Johns Hopkins University, USA.*

Erratum

Coral Mitchell and *Larry Sackney*

Profound Improvement: Building Capacity for a Learning Community

Title page

Where the text reads:

Coral Mitchell
Faculty of Education, Brock University, USA

it should read:

Coral Mitchell
Faculty of Education, Brock University, **Canada**

PROFOUND IMPROVEMENT

Building Capacity for a Learning Community

CORAL MITCHELL

Faculty of Education, Brock University, USA

AND

LARRY SACKNEY

Department of Educational Administration,
University of Saskatchewan, Canada

SWETS & ZEITLINGER
PUBLISHERS

LISSE   ABINGDON   EXTON (PA)   TOKYO

Library of Congress Cataloging-in-Publication Data

Profound improvement : building capacity for a learning community / Coral Mitchell
and Larry Sackney.
   p. cm. -- (Contexts of Learning)
  Includes bibliographical references (p.) and index.
  ISBN 9026516347
   1. Learning--Philosophy. 2. Constructivism (Philosophy) I. Mitchell, Coral, 1948- II.
Sackney, Larry, 1941- III. Series.

LB1060 .P79 2000
370.15'23--dc21

00-044658

Printed in The Netherlands by GPB Gorter BV, Steenwijk

ISBN 90 265 1634 7 (hardback)

Contents

Contents

Acknowledgements

This book has been the culmination of several years of work with one another, with school people in Saskatchewan and Ontario, and with colleagues from the University of Saskatchewan and Brock University. We take this opportunity to thank those individuals who have helped to shape our understandings of a learning community and who have shared different parts of the journey with us. At Brock University, Coral has been privileged to share research projects with Terry Boak, Joe Engemann, Kris Kirkwood, Jim Kerr, and Tony DiPetta. Each of these colleagues has brought a different perspective on education and on the notion of professional learning. At the University of Saskatchewan, Larry's ideas and thinking have been influenced by his colleagues Murray Scharf, Patrick Renihan, Keith Walker, Vivian Hajnal, Ken Jacknicke, Pauline Leonard, Lawrence Leonard, and Allan Guy. For both of us, retired faculty members at the University of Saskatchewan have been deeply influential in our professional and academic growth. Of particular note are Kevin Wilson, Dennis Dibski, Earle Newton, and Barry Lucas. The stories of all of these colleagues are closely intertwined with our own.

We are especially grateful to the people who have opened their schools for our research. They have been so gracious and willing to share their lives with us. Not only did they allow us to conduct our research in their schools, but they also willingly acted as our 'guinea pigs' from time to time. Our ideas (sometimes only half-formed – and often half-baked) were forged in the heat of their professional activity, and their stories are what make this book come alive.

Special thanks go to two colleagues who offered feedback on preliminary drafts of the manuscript: Keith Walker from the University of Saskatchewan and Ian Hall from Christchurch College of Education. Their encouragement has been more helpful than they can ever know, and their feedback is always welcome and valuable.

We have been fortunate to have ongoing contact and conversations with a number of academic scholars whose work has influenced our thinking. Of particular note are Karen Seashore Louis from the University of Minnesota, Ken Leithwood from the University of Toronto, Joe Murphy from Vanderbilt University, Adrienne Hyle from Oklahoma State University, and Patrick Duignan from the Australian Catholic University. These people have served as mentors and role models as we have struggled to shape the ideas that are presented in the pages of this book. Theirs are the shoulders upon which we stand.

The final copy would not have been possible without the expert assistance and guidance (along with superb technical support) of our editorial assistants. Thank you to Bret Maukonen and Lynne Maukonen at Brock University for copy editing, graphic presentation, and typesetting, and to Rodger Graham at the University of Saskatchewan for preliminary graphics. The final copy is as attractive and error free as it is because of their careful attention to detail. Any remaining errors are entirely our own fault. Thank you, also, to the editorial staff at Swets and Zeitlinger. Your quick attention to our requests for information made the cross-Atlantic process much less intimidating.

This book is based on many different research projects that have been funded through various agencies. Funds have been provided through research grants from the Social Sciences and Humanities Research Council of Canada, from Saskatchewan Education, and from TVOntario. Additional funds have been provided through contracts with many different schools and school systems in Saskatchewan. These contracts have been administered by the Saskatchewan Educational Leadership Unit at the University of Saskatchewan. We are grateful for the assistance of past and present associate directors of SELU, particularly Bill Stodolka, Barry Earl, and Dave Hawley. Our institutions, Brock University and the University of Saskatchewan, have been generous in providing funds for research assistantships and for publication costs. We gratefully acknowledge the support of each of these agencies and institutions.

Dedication

To Darlene Case and Kay Sackney
Thank you for your patience, your support, and your commitment
to this project and to our academic careers.
We couldn't have done it without you.

Introduction

This book is about the life world of school people as it relates to professional learning. That is, we are fundamentally concerned with human growth and development, human cognition and affect, and human interactions and actions in the context of a school community. This set of concerns is embedded within but distinct from what Sergiovanni (2000) calls the systemsworld and what Starratt (1996) calls the administered world. These latter terms relate to a deliberately constructed set of systems, roles, rules, procedures, and expectations that guide human behavior and that constrain human thought. In our view, this artificial construction has usually been at the center of educational discourse, a circumstance that has placed the humanity of school people at the margins of what matters. We place the human elements at the center of our discussion. Our concern here is with the less controllable aspects of human endeavor, the good and bad aspects of confronting what we do and do not know. It entails all the undercurrents of presuppositions and beliefs as well as the surface waves of knowledge and learning.

We believe that the undercurrents are deeply affected by our perspective of the social order, a perspective that is, in turn, deeply affected by our understanding of the physical order (Lakoff & Johnson, 1980). In the 1980s David Bohm, a theoretical physicist, advanced some rather novel ideas about the way in which he believed the physical world to be constructed. His idea was that the fragmented, part-to-whole perspective derived from Newtonian science did not accurately reflect the natural world. Rather, Bohm saw all the various bits and pieces of the physical world as unique expressions and manifestations of one unified whole and therefore as deeply and intimately connected. Instead of a fragmented world of parts, he saw a whole world of connections, relationships, and common origins. This wholeness worldview has in recent years been transferred from the physical world to inform understandings of the social and organizational worlds. This is the foundation from which the likes of Senge (1995) and Gozdz (1995) talk about the primacy of the whole in relation to organizational structures and cognitive frames. And this wholeness worldview is at the bottom of our own understandings about a learning community in schools. Although our way of writing may not adequately reflect that worldview, that is more a problem with the linear presentation of a written document than it is with the way we understand the concepts. Even as we present our ideas in fragments, we ask the reader to step back occasionally and to consider how the various fragments connect with and inform one another. Each part we present can only be understood in relation to its interactions with the other parts. The recognition of this principle will be helpful in understanding our arguments.

Our arguments also locate in a specific philosophical orientation. Beck and Foster (1999) argue that educational scholars have, from time to time, confused liberal and communitarian philosophies. This is especially the case, they say, in discussions related to the notion of community. They see the debate as hinging on the distinction between education as an arena for the development of the individual and education as an arena for the enhancement of the community. We do not see this as an appropriate distinction. At the risk of confusing the reader, we speak from each of these traditions at different times. That is, we believe that people are both autonomous, rational individuals (the liberal view) and that they are fundamentally social in nature, responsible for the well-being of others, and interested in the overall health of their social or organizational context (the communitarian view). Since we operate from a wholeness pespective, we cannot see any way out of this dilemma. At times the individual is the basic unit of concern, but at other times the collectivity is. The trick is to be aware of which element is being emphasized at any given time, to determine if this is the appropriate level for the exigencies of the moment, and to find ways to move seamlessly from one level of emphasis to the other.

Our way of configuring the learning community in this book synthesizes elements from the liberal and the communitarian traditions. We do not necessarily see our work as reconciling the two views (Beck & Foster, p. 343) but as integrating them into a cohesive framework that acknowledges the value of both the individual and the community. In our view, a singular liberal focus divorces individuals from the social context within which they live and work and can lead to isolation, alienation, fragmentation, irresponsibility, and arrogance. Similarly, a singular communitarian focus undermines the value of the person and can lead to groupthink, forced compliance, standardized practices, enforced obligations, public intrusion into private matters, devaluing of diversity, and a tyranny of uniformity. Neither of these worlds seems to be particularly enticing or sustainable. Taking the best of each world (rather than the worst, as has often been done in the past), 'we are closer now to knowing how to create an ecology of community that promotes the richest forms of individual human life and to knowing how to create an ecology of individual striving that promotes the richest form of community life' (Starratt, 1996, p. 93). Our own work in schools has suggested that, paradoxically, careful and thoughtful attention to community building has also allowed individuals to be more openly and freely themselves. That is, as school people have learned to talk openly with one another, they have become more aware of the deep value of diversity, and they have been able to affirm their own positions with greater coherence and confidence. This standpoint has enabled them more evenly to balance personal interests with the interests of others.

In terms of social constructions, our philosophy follows a communitarian more than a liberal ideal. That is, we do not see how a social contract, which spells out the rights and obligations of individuals in different social stations, can generate the sorts of common understandings, shared meanings, and close bonds that are constitutive of a learning community. Instead, we see community building as an organic, evolutionary process that entails the deep involvement of each individual in pursuit of ways and means to promote sustaining and sustainable processes, structures, tasks, and commitments. In Sergiovanni's (2000) terms, the social contract is replaced by a social covenant whereby 'connections are based on commitments, not trades' (p. 65). We do, however, believe that there can and should be limits on the construction of a community. From our standpoint, one limit will be to dispel standard forms and norms. The community we envisage is one that does not filter out or subvert difference. It is, rather, one that embraces diversity as a fundamental element that provides opportunities for growth and renewal.

We approach the notion of learning and schooling from a social constructivist orientation. That is, we try to deconstruct what things mean and how they got that way and to reconstruct what else they might look like. We do not see schools from an instrumental perspective but rather from a generative one. We do not believe that schools should serve externally determined goals and purposes. Instead, they should be structured such that the central purpose is the learning of the individuals who are engaged in the process of schooling. Whoever that might include. Although we focus our discussion in this book on the students, teachers, and administrators within a school building, we do not mean to exclude others who have vested interests in the quality of education going on within the school walls. The social constructions of schooling and of learning emerge from longstanding formal and informal negotiations and conversations among many interested parties. Our intent here is not to suggest that those outside the school walls are not part of the discourse but to concentrate on those people who live out a large part of their lives within the walls. From time to time, we do include other community partners in the discourse as it is appropriate to do so in pursuit of improved professional practice. Our position is that students and parents (and other interested parties) should be part of the discourse associated with teaching and learning. That is, students should not be seen as passive recipients of external knowledge, and parents should not be seen as extraneous to the entire process of schooling. In a learning community, students and parents make a meaningful and valued contribution to the discourse of professional practice.

We have been somewhat troubled that the literature which seeks to extend the learning community beyond the school walls is primarily concerned with the locus of influence and control over educational and/or integrated services. Beck and Foster (1999, p. 348) indicate that this literature base falls within three categories of concerns: (a) site-based management, (b) inter-agency services for high-need students, and (c) parental involvement in educational governance. Although these issues are certainly important, attending to them can serve to divert attention away from pedagogy and professional educational practice. That is the focus of our concern. We do not believe (nor does the literature confirm) that a shift in governance automatically translates into improved professional practice or improved student achievement. In this book we are first and foremost interested in the quality of the learning that happens within the walls of the school. From that perspective, we believe that teachers who are themselves learners and who are supported by a professional learning community can generate a more exciting, stimulating learning environment for the students in their classrooms. Consequently, we see a need for direct and explicit attention to the conditions that promote, support, and sustain professional learning among educators – both classroom teachers and school administrators.

From time to time in this book, we use different terms to refer to the professional staff in the school community. When we use the term *educators*, we are referring to teachers, school administrators, and system administrators. If a specific point is applicable to just one or two of these groups, we make that specification. Otherwise, we assume that our points should be applied equally to the professional work of classroom teachers, school principals and vice-principals, and supervisory officers. Similarly, when we use the term *leaders*, we are referring to anyone in the school community who undertakes leadership initiatives. This might include teachers, non-instructional staff, students, parents, other community members, and administrators. When we use the term *administrator*, we mean to include school principals and vice principals, department heads, and supervisory officers. When we speak about any one of these groups, we specify their role designation. In all cases where we refer to specific individuals from our research cases, we use pseudonyms.

We believe that the majority of teachers, school administrators, and supervisory officers are dedicated educators who do good work and who want to do better. We have worked with many educators at all these levels for many years, and we have been deeply impressed by the quality of these professional folk. We certainly acknowledge that some not-so-stellar educators do exist, and we also acknowledge that the efforts to improve have not always been successful. But our own experience suggests that these issues often result from systemic barriers as much as from any personal failure. Educators have not been able to do the things that we suggest in this book naturally or easily, but they have done them willingly when the cultural and organizational conditions give them space and permission to do so. We have been excited by the ways in which our ideas have breathed new life into certain schools, and we have been impressed by the dedication of the school people with whom we have worked.

Organization of the Book

In subsequent chapters we will blend theoretical concepts and practical examples in our discussion. We have chosen a more personal voice for this book. From that standpoint, when we talk about our research, we position it as practical examples rather than as cited references. The field-based examples are all taken from the schools and teachers with whom we have undertaken various research projects over the years. We do not rely on one or even two defining studies but instead share the voices and experiences of many professional educators who have touched our academic lives in a variety of contexts. This research has taken the form of school effectiveness reviews, professional interviews with educators, school improvement projects, doctoral and other academic research, school system reviews, professional workshops, graduate seminars, and consultancy projects. Where we have taken concepts and data directly from our formal research that has been previously published, we have cited the sources. Where we have taken concepts and data from informal field experiences or unpublished research, we provide the examples as unreferenced anecdotes.

We end this preface with a brief note on how the rest of the book will unfold. Chapter 1 sets out the foundation for the remaining chapters. In this chapter, we present some reasons for why we think the time has come to reconfigure schools as learning communities and we present some definitions and understandings about the learning community that are fundamental to the way we work with it in subsequent chapters. We offer a first look at a model that we have found to be useful for building the capacity for learning among teachers. The model consists in three mutually influencing and interdependent categories of capacity: personal, interpersonal, and organizational. In subsequent chapters, we expand this model in greater detail.

The purpose of Chapters 2 and 3 is to explore the section of the model dealing with building personal capacity. In Chapter 2, we discuss the search for personal knowledge. Building personal capacity means, first, confronting the implicit and explicit cognitive structures that shape and constrain educators' professional practice and learning and, second, articulating the professional theory-in-practice that has developed in conjunction with these cognitive structures. The search is both internal and external, with educators' deconstructing both their own professional narratives and the dominant narratives in the larger professional networks to which they are connected. This search yields insights into why teaching and learning unfolds as it does in certain schools and classrooms. It means opening the professional identity and expertise to reflective analysis, with the expectation that some adjustments to the narrative might be necessary.

Chapter 3 moves the individual from reflection and analysis into action. The primary assumption underlying this chapter is that teachers are creators of knowledge, not simply consumers of knowledge. Knowledge creation is a process of disciplined inquiry that seeks answers to current or long-standing problems of practice or to the deep mysteries of teaching and learning. In this chapter we position educators as both active creators of knowledge and facilitators of knowledge creation. That is, they ask questions of themselves, their colleagues, and their students, and they seek out new networks and experiment with new ideas. Through this process, they reconstruct their professional narrative and generate a foundation that can lead to profound improvement in teaching and learning.

In Chapters 4 and 5, we shift from personal capacity to interpersonal capacity. We advance the argument that professional learning is most likely to lead to profound improvement when individuals work collaboratively with supportive colleagues who are also engaged in continuous development. For this to happen, a culture of collegial relations and professional risk taking needs to be in place. That is, teachers need sufficient interpersonal skills to develop collegial foundations that can support professional learning. These collegial foundations entail affective conditions, cognitive processes, and group interactions. Chapter 4 deals with the affective and cognitive climate necessary to build a learning community. The affective climate entails building a culture of trust, respect, inclusion, caring, and support. The cognitive climate, on the other hand, entails building a culture where learning, growth, and professional development can be supported. Chapter 5 focuses on the group by examining how teams can be built and supported through collaboration. Particular attention is paid to collaborative cultures, which are the basis of effective learning communities. Interpersonal capacity increases in response to the development of a sustainable affective and cognitive climate and to the development of an effective collaborative culture.

Chapters 6, 7, and 8 deal with the third level of the model: organizational capacity. In Chapter 6, we discuss the ways in which organizational structures have typically served to isolate educators and to fragment the educational process. We argue that a learning community requires a different kind of organizational structure than has typically been the case in most schools. That is, structures need to honor connection rather than separation, diversity rather than uniformity, empowerment rather than control, and inclusion rather than dominance. Structures are both invisible, as in cognitive assumptions and attributions, socio-cultural conditions, and collaborative processes, and visible, as in the physical arrangements of location, space, time, and so on.

In this chapter, we present some strategies for creating socio-cultural conditions, structural arrangements, and collaborative processes that can serve to open doors and break down walls between, among, and within school people.

Chapter 7 argues that individuals in a learning community feel a deep sense of empowerment and autonomy and that they have a deep personal commitment to the work of the school. This means that leadership is concerned with making the 'good things' happen and that it is enacted throughout the school by a variety of individuals (teachers, administrators, staff members, students, and parents). Our position is that a school which functions as a learning community is leader-rich. In this chapter we advocate a number of strategies for building a leadership base that enhances and facilitates the development of a learning community. These strategies include such things as visioning and purposing, team building, facilitating communication, encouraging experimentation and risk taking, promoting rewards and recognition, facilitating staff development, reculturing, modeling self-learning, and creating time and space for learning.

Chapter 8 begins to pull the pieces together by presenting a sequence of steps for creating organizational conditions that can support and sustain a learning community. These steps are founded on our belief that the creation of a learning community is a developmental process that takes time and care. We argue that the first step is to engage the administrative cadre in the process, the second step is to create sustaining and sustainable organizational conditions, and the third step is to build a learning architecture in the school. We also argue that a learning community is a fundamentally human system that moves through cycles of progress and regress. The push and pull of professional learning can be expected to advance through successive iterations of three learning phases: naming and framing, analyzing and integrating, and applying and experimenting. The steps and the phases are systemic in nature, with each element building on and from all others, through multiple interdependencies and feedback loops, to create a synergy of enhanced capacity.

In Chapter 9, we return to our original thesis that building a learning community is a dynamic process that brings together the individual, the group, and the organization. We argue that tinkering with any one part of a system causes changes in other parts. A failure to realize the interdependencies that are involved in educational improvement can lead to fragmentation and unsustainable outcomes. Our retrospective look at the learning community suggests that it has often in the past been undertaken from a perspective that, in fact, fails to take into account the ways in which teaching and learning are embedded in a larger context. Our prospective look presents a new image of schools, one that is grounded in a wholeness perspective and that approaches school improvement and professional learning from a capacity-building model. Our position is that careful attention to the transition process is necessary if the organizational narrative is to be successfully reconstructed to reflect a wholeness perspective. We contend that this sort of transition is the best way to bring forth profound improvement in teaching and learning.

1

A Learning Community: Contextual Elements

One of the perplexities of education is whether schools as they are currently structured enhance learning or limit it. There is, of course, no doubt that schools were originally established to organize and facilitate the learning of children, but almost since their inception, their ability to do so has been called into question. This questioning has, from the early days of the 20th century, subjected schools and teachers to numerous calls for improvements of their performance. An even more curious aspect of this phenomenon is that the teachers, who stand to have a great impact on the learning of children, have been positioned in the debate as objects to be manipulated and controlled rather than as professional creators of a learning culture. This perplexity is central to the notion of the learning community.

The metaphor of the learning community assumes, first, that schools are expected to facilitate the learning of all individuals, and, second, that educators are ideally positioned to address fundamental issues and concerns in relation to learning. But these assumptions are perhaps the only thing about the learning community that we can say with any degree of certainty. In our own research, we have found the definitions of a learning community to lack clarity and agreement, and we have found even less agreement as to how to go about developing a learning community or as to whether a learning community is even worth the time and effort. This is perhaps to be expected, given the relative newness of the construct. We have been pondering these questions in our teaching and research for almost a decade, and our understandings about a learning community have undergone considerable evolution. We assume that what we present in this book is a limited perspective on the notion of the learning community and that our understandings will continue to evolve. The ideas that we outline herein can be juxtaposed with those that have come before and that will come after from other scholars and practitioners, ideas that will continue to shape the definitions and understandings of the learning community.

We open this chapter with some thoughts on the changing conditions within which schools are embedded – conditions that imply a need for a different approach to the mysteries, perplexities, and problems associated with teaching and learning. In the second section we turn our attention to some theoretical foundations that underpin the notion of the learning community and present some definitions, elements, and debates surrounding the concept. The third section provides an overview of the model that frames our understandings about a learning community. This model consists of three pivotal capacities that we believe need to be built if a school is to function as a learning community: personal capacity, interpersonal capacity, and organizational capacity. We close the chapter with a brief description of how we position the notion of the learning community in this book.

An Emerging Worldview

Manchester (1992) tells the story of Ferdinand Magellan who, in 1519, sailed west from Spain to find his way around the world. When his ship returned three years later, having circumvented the globe, the sailors were amazed to find that they had lost 24 hours during the voyage. Scholars scurried to address this dilemma. Their conclusion: the sun did not revolve around the Earth. Rather, the Earth and all the planets revolved around the sun. The premise upon which the medieval social order had been based was found to be false. Confusion reigned. Then, slowly, a new social order emerged, one in harmony with the belief that nature was like a gigantic clockwork with discrete sub-units functioning smoothly to create the larger whole. Thus was born the rational, analytical view of the world with which we still live today.

But that worldview no longer reflects contemporary images of our planet. In the 1960s, the Apollo astronauts boarded their spaceship to find their way to the moon. When they returned several days later, they brought with them pictures of the Earth from space. The Earth was seen not as borders, boundaries, and pieces but as a perfect and complete blue and white jewel shining radiantly against the black backdrop of space. That image brings forth a powerful response from most viewers. As in the 16th century, contemporary scholars scurry to understand this response. Their conclusion: the Earth is not divided into discrete sub-units separated by boundaries. Rather, it is a fragile ecosystem of dynamic relationships and interconnected patterns. A new social order, one in harmony with this ecological view of nature, is slowly beginning to emerge. But we are still in the state of confusion that typifies the transition period between different social orders.

In general terms, the educational order in most school systems more closely reflects the clockwork model than it does the ecological model. Starratt (1996), for example, contends that current educational practices have fragmented and trivialized learning and have separated school activities from the life worlds of students. Rather than school learning being a natural outgrowth of students' confrontation with the perplexities of their own lives, it has been managed, manipulated, controlled, organized, and constrained by adults who are, at best, out of touch with the realities with which students live. This condition, Starratt says, has created 'a massive alienation of young people from schooling' (p. 74). Furthermore, Beck and Foster (1999, p. 346) point out that the bureaucratic structures and standardized practices that typify contemporary schools do not adequately serve students who fall outside the 'normal curve' of learning style, academic achievement, or socio-economic status. Instead, schools 'have

actually decreased the quality of opportunities available to disadvantaged young-
sters' (p. 346). As things stand, then, school structures and practices that reflect a
clockwork view of the world are not natural, nor are they grounded in the realities of
individual lives, and they can lead to alienated and disadvantaged students. This is a
devastating indictment against schools and schooling.

Alienation is evident not just among young people, however. It is found also
among teachers and in public perceptions of schools. And it extends beyond the
school walls, with a deep anomie and disillusionment typifying much of contemporary
life. Anderson and Klinge (1995) have found that the fragmented and hierarchical
social order typical of many contemporary communities and businesses has led to
deeply entrenched social and economic problems. According to these authors, 'if we
continue on the path we are on, our businesses will continue to lose their competitive-
ness, our people will continue to lose their spirit and will, and our society will continue
to degenerate' (p. 359). This is a compelling and unsettling prediction.

From an ecological perspective, the tensions and confusions that have grown up
around a clockwork worldview are not sustainable. Things must change. One solution
that has been advanced in recent years is the notion of community, but it is community
with a difference. It is community that is grounded in a new way of understanding the
world. Anderson and Klinge (1995), for example, point out that the times demand a
complete shift in approach and attitude. They say, 'It is not about improving the
current path but rather about providing the basis for a totally new path – a path
grounded in the understanding of what it takes to create a healthy community' (p. 355).
Another argument comes from Gozdz (1995), who also calls for a fundamental shift in
perception: 'Businesses cannot sustain themselves as communities or as learning
organizations unless they become capable of embracing a paradigm of wholeness, a
paradigm compatible with a living systems perspective' (p. 63). In their emphasis on
healthy communities, these authors appear to be moving the discourse away from a
rational, analytical view toward a more ecological view of the natural, social, and
organizational orders. We have found this sort of concern for community to be a
central focus in much of the contemporary academic literature.

This concern appears to extend well beyond the academy. Zemke (1996), for example, argues that the search for community is endemic in contemporary society. It derives from a deep need to be part of something larger than oneself, to be part of
'something familiar, special and unique' (p. 25). This trend has inserted itself into
every aspect of the human enterprise in a host of ways – some prescriptive and
traditional, others vague and diffuse, and others evolutionary and organic. Regardless of the plethora of configurations and definitions, Zemke sees some commonalties:
permanence, belonging, meaning, and fulfillment – a sense that one is entitled to be
there, to contribute, to share in the joys, sorrows, successes, and failures of the community. From this perspective, people are engaged in a search for place, a search for
companionship, and a search for identity and belonging. They seek places and people
in which and with whom they can find relief from the alienating conditions of the
world.

The notion of community has also inserted itself into the educational discourse.
Use of the term in educational circles goes back to the early days of the 20th century
and the work of John Dewey, but only in recent years has it become central to the

discourse. Beck (1999), for example, found that 'the mid- to late 1980s and 1990s have born witness to a growing body of theoretical and empirical work concerned with understanding schools that function as communities' (p. 17). Although the educational discourse has defined and positioned community in many different ways, an underlying assumption is that when schools function as communities, the people in the building are better able to redress the alienation and anomie that saps energy and inhibits growth (Louis, Kruse, & Byrk, 1995, p. 16). From a community perspective, teachers and students are connected rather than isolated. They work *with* rather than *against* or *for* one another. They connect teaching and learning to the realities and mysteries of life. These conditions are more natural and more conducive to learning and growth than are conditions that organize and separate people into different physical and psychological spaces.

The notion of community also impinges on the isolation that has been such a part of traditional teaching and learning. For the most part, the loneliness of teaching locates not in relationships with students but in interactions with colleagues. As Lieberman and Miller (1990) point out, 'With so many people engaged in so common a mission in so compact a space and time, it is perhaps the greatest irony – and the greatest tragedy of teaching – that so much is carried on in self-imposed and professionally sanctioned isolation' (p. 160). The development of a professional community is one way to reduce the embedded isolation and loneliness. But careful attention needs to be paid to just what kind of community is being built. Hargreaves (1993), for example, argues that attempts to create professional learning communities among teachers may actually serve to mask differences or to drive diversity underground. His argument is that when any one 'correct' way is being advocated, the doors to true learning slam shut, and individual teachers are likely to retreat to their classrooms instead of being forced into educational practices that do not make sense for their students or for themselves. This is not the kind of community that holds the spirit or the promise of a learning community.

Louis, Kruse, and Bryk (1995, p. 15) argue that the failure to value diversity is at least partly due to the emphasis of contemporary liberal philosophy on the rights of the individual. That is, individuals are expected to advocate for their own wants and needs rather than to worry about their responsibilities toward others or to consider the worth of other individuals. In a world that is increasingly connected, diverse, and complex, this sort of philosophy seems somewhat misguided. This is not to say that individual rights are not important but that they must be situated within a particular social and, for our purposes, educational context. The students who are coming to school now are far more complex than were students in the past, and schools are now part of a larger set of services for children and families. What all of this means is that the teacher's world of work is far more complex than it used to be, and they cannot adequately deal with the tough problems and the deep mysteries of teaching and learning if they base their practice on individual interests and prerogatives. The world within which individual teachers and students live and move does matter. Other people and other agencies do matter. The metaphor of the learning community opens spaces for this kind of complexity and diversity to be acknowledged and honored and for connections to be forged among the people who make up a particular educational community.

At the same time that the notion of community has emerged in relation to organizational and cultural structures, changes have emerged in understandings about the nature of learning. One of the changes relevant to the notion of the learning community is the recognition that learning is, at its heart, a social as well as an individual phenomenon (Stamps, 1998). That is, people construct personal understandings and build personal knowledge bases at least partly through social interaction and social arrangements. This has, of course, always been true, but it has not always been evident in the clockwork structures and functions of schooling. Instead, students have been silenced and separated, and their only conversations have been with the content or the teacher. In recent years, however, the people who have traditionally been 'in control of things' have looked more realistically at human learning and have begun to recognize that those in formal positions of power must relinquish control over the individual's and the group's learning. To honor the social constructivist view of learning means to create conditions that will support and promote collective as well as individual learning and that will support individual learning that grows out of conversations with other learners.

Within the metaphor of the learning community, it is not only the learning of the children that is at stake. The learning of the teachers is also a primary concern. But professional learning is not an easy beast to tame, and the paradoxical and complex nature of education endows professional development with both promise and peril. As Bredeson (1999) points out, professional learning is embedded in a host of paradoxes that add layers of complexity and render the benefits of professional development somewhat problematic. That is, there is little agreement in the literature on exactly how to go about structuring professional learning or on how to connect it with improved professional practice. In the words of Louis, Toole, and Hargreaves (1999), it represents a 'wicked problem' that is 'inherently chaotic and unpredictable' (p. 256). An instructive way of addressing this wicked problem is found in Gherardi's (1999) distinction between learning in pursuit of problem solving and learning in the face of mystery. The first is more instrumental and cognitive, the second more natural and intuitive. In her words, 'Problem-driven learning was propelled by the aesthetic of the rational, while mystery-driven learning is sustained by the aesthetic of the relational' (p. 117). She claims that when professional learning is linked exclusively to problem solving and is pushed by institutional expectations, it loses its connection with the lives of the professionals and runs the risk of being unnatural and ineffective. By contrast, when learning is linked to the mysteries and perplexities faced by the professionals, it is embedded in the day-to-day context of the people and is more natural, effective, and durable.

Gherardi sees learning as 'an inseparable part of all organizational practices, and organizational learning is a heuristic device used to study how knowledge is socially constructed in organizing practices which do not halt at the organizational boundaries of formal organizations' (p. 113). In other words, professional learning happens all the time, but whether that learning leads to improved practice will depend a great deal on the extent to which the learning has taken place in the face of mystery. Furthermore, whether or not the learning leads to knowledge that will benefit other professionals in the school depends a great deal on what kind of professional learning community has been established within the walls of the school.

Convergence of these points – an ecological view of the natural, social, and educational orders; a turn toward community; the social aspect of learning; a concern for professional learning; and an awareness of learning in the face of mystery – signals the need for a different metaphor for schools and schooling. In the past we have relied on organizational metaphors and have thought in terms of structures, functions, procedures, rules, and roles. We suspect that these ideas will continue to rumble underground in educational circles for quite some time. But they no longer suffice for the needs of the day. Instead, we, along with others (e.g., O'Sullivan, 1999), believe that a new educational order is emerging, one that relies on metaphors of wholeness and connections, diversity and complexity, relationships and meaning, reflection and inquiry, and collaboration and collegiality. These are the ideas that underpin the construct of the learning community.

Some Terms and Conditions of a Learning Community

Over the past decade a considerable amount of attention, in both business and educational sectors, has been given to the notion of the learning organization. Our own understanding has moved from thinking about schools as learning *organizations* to thinking about them as learning *communities*. We believe that the two terms, although similar, are not synonymous. At the risk of sounding somewhat simplistic, we believe that the key difference lies in the definition of ends and means. In a learning organization, the ends of importance are organizational growth, productivity, efficiency, and effectiveness. The means are the people and the learning that they do in support of organizational goals. The goals are established by the gatekeepers of the organization, and learning is a tool to support organizational processes and efficiencies. Sense is meaningful if it contributes to the growth of the organization. By contrast, in a learning community, the ends of importance are the growth and development of the people. The means are the ways in which community members work and learn together. The goals are set through intensive and ongoing negotiation and discourse within the community, and learning is a natural process that is grounded in the realities and perplexities of human lives and that permeates every aspect of the community experience. Sense is meaningful if it makes sense to the members of the community, and there are likely to be multiple 'senses' co-existing peacefully (or not). Gozdz (1995) links the two notions by suggesting that a learning organization has community building as a core competence. That is, 'it has a central commitment and capacity to learn and grow, throughout its life cycle. It is a living community that learns' (p. 58). Even while we acknowledge this connection, we argue that the learning community is concerned with the human experience and that this concern is not necessarily evident in a learning organization. In a learning organization, the fundamental values and cultural beliefs are most likely to be defined by the organizational elite, whereas in a learning community, they will be defined by the members of the community, in negotiation with one another. From our perspective, the ideas associated with a learning community more closely reflect the kinds of conditions we think are appropriate for schools. We are not alone in this belief, and the term *learning community* is becoming the term of choice in the educational discourse.

In spite of its recent popularity, however, the notion of the learning community has not gone uncontested. One of the current debates in the educational discourse is the question of whether or not one ought to attach an adjective to the notion of community. Shields (1999) argues that attempts to do so positions the community as an instrument of something else rather than as a natural gathering of individuals. From her perspective, speaking of a *learning* community puts inappropriate weight on the learning tasks, leaves out large chunks of what brought the people together in the first place, and masks the diversity within the community. Leithwood (1999), on the other hand, argues that community is always attached to something else and is always associated with certain kinds of activities, actions, or tasks. An instructive way to address this debate is suggested by Starratt (1996). He argues that people build communities around some central feature that draws the individuals together – a common location, ethnic background, religious belief, or even a task function such as learning (p. 76). That is, people move into a community for various reasons – for safety, entertainment, support, relaxation, communication, learning, and so on. Attaching an adjective does not filter out all the complexity and diversity within the community. Instead, it specifies the central feature of a particular community. So one might talk about a religious community or a jogging community or a neighborhood community. In the context of education, the key feature is teaching and learning, and it makes sense to speak of a learning community in that context. The adjective does not necessarily position either the learning or the community in second or instrumental place. It does, however, highlight the central feature that has brought the people together in a particular place and time.

Our purpose in this section, however, is not to debate the issues or the constructs but to articulate our understandings of a learning community. The plethora of meanings given to the idea of community means that those who use it must carefully define what they are and are not talking about (Beck & Foster, 1999). This task is not an easy one. A case in point is Beck's (1999) discovery, in an extensive review of educational literature, of six different metaphors underlying discussions of community: ontological, psychological, behavioral, structural, political, and ethical. At times these metaphors were distinct and distinguishable and at others they were intersecting or nested. Beck contends that the multiplicity of definitions and metaphorical foundations does not necessarily constitute a confused picture of community but rather signals an inherent richness and complexity in the concept. She says, 'we need to be cautious about defining community as a variable or a construct characterized by a narrow or limited set of variables' (p. 36). We take her caution seriously and have struggled with finding ways to describe and define a truly complex phenomenon in one book. We acknowledge that our representation of a learning community in this book will be at best a partial representation.

A further complication is that, as Wyatt (1997) points out, 'Defining community is somewhat difficult because, to a large extent, what a community is depends on what its members intend it to be' (p. 80). Her point is that members create their own unique community and that the construction of the community is an ongoing process of active participation and intense communication. From that perspective, any definition we present will be situated in our own experiences with learning communities in schools. Because our understandings are deeply embedded in our own contexts, our definitions

will not necessarily make sense for anyone else. What we do anticipate, however, is
that each reader will shape our thoughts into new meanings that make personal sense.
The notion of creating meaning is, of course, one of the central features of a learning
community. Janov (1995), for example, says, 'Creating meaning is, for me, at the heart
of creating our organizations as learning communities' (p. 58). This idea is also reflected in Sergiovanni's (2000) description: 'Purpose and meaning are essential in
helping a school become an effective learning community – a community of mind and
heart' (p. 2). Starratt (1996) makes a similar observation: 'When we learn, we make
meaning. We do not learn information; we learn from information to make meaning. We
extract the meanings encoded in information and align that meaning with previously
constructed meanings' (p. 122). We understand this to imply that the tendency and
opportunity to create meaning, alone and together, will be found in a learning community and that the meaning of community will vary from school to school and from
context to context.

In spite of the problems with defining a learning community, however, some points
of convergence are becoming clear. We see these points as primarily two-fold: First,
communities entail some sort of 'glue' that holds the members together, whether that
is shared vision, common understandings, or a common goal. Second, members are in
close contact and communication with one another. That is, a learning community in
schools consists at least partially in pervasive values, enduring commitments, a sense
of belonging, a sense of togetherness, and caring interactions among and between
teachers, staff members, administrators, students, and parents (Beck & Foster, 1999).
In a learning community, each person is a worthwhile participant in the tasks, activities, and responsibilities of the community. Each individual works with others in a
spirit of experimentation and risk taking to improve the educational experience of all
individuals in the school. This is the task component. Furthermore, each person deserves the support and care of other school members. People work together in a spirit
of trust and mutual respect. This is the affective component. The conjunction of the
cognitive and affective aspects adds heart and passion to the work of teachers and
students alike. When school people demonstrate passion and fire for what they are
doing, that is a sign of a learning community.

This implies that a learning community has a value premise and a cultural orientation. What this means is that there will be certain norms, beliefs, assumptions, and
value systems that bind the educators, students, parents, and other community members together. In a traditional school, that implicit 'stuff' sits underground and silently
but powerfully affects the learning and actions of the individuals. In a learning community, it gets brought to the table, analyzed, critiqued, and changed, if the critique
indicates that change is desirable. In this way, learning and meaning-making happen
all the time, and they are not means to an end but are ends in themselves. People
construct their own knowledge bases through this sort of dialogue with belief systems, with information, with experiences, and with one another.

From this perspective, one of the recurring challenges is to identify the members of
a learning community – who's in and who's not. Merz and Furman (1997) distinguish
between two approaches to this challenge. The first approach focuses exclusively on
the people in the building. That is, community building is done with and by the teachers, school administrators, and (sometimes) the students. The second approach is

concerned with generating linkages and relationships among various stakeholder groups. That is, community building engages parents and other community members directly and continuously in the life and development of the school. This implies that there are different kinds of communities and that the boundaries one places around the rhetoric and the practice of community will shape to a large extent the kind of community that develops among a group of people. It will affect the people who are invited into the process, the kinds of problems that get addressed, and the nature of the processes that unfold and the discourse that goes on. In the traditional concept of community, all sorts of people are around, but physical and psychological constraints put boundaries around the communication and relations that go on in the community. For example, when we build a fence around our property, we shut out those on the other side of the fence. If we open our doors, strangers as well as friends can enter. This metaphor can be extended to schools. If we expand the boundary and open the doors, we will create a different kind of community than if we only include teachers and administrators. Our own orientation is toward expanding the boundaries and inviting students and parents into the school discourse, but we do not see our task as one of determining or even suggesting the boundaries of a community in and for any school. Rather, we see our task as providing concepts and strategies that can be used to enhance the professional work of any educational community, regardless of how it has been configured by the individuals in that context.

For us, a learning community consists in a group of people who take an active, reflective, collaborative, learning-oriented, and growth-promoting approach toward the mysteries, problems, and perplexities of teaching and learning. The learning of critical importance is that of the students, the teachers, and the school administrators. That is, in a learning community, the learning of the educators ought to receive the same sort of attention that the learning of the students does. We believe that teachers cannot give what they do not have and that teachers need the same kind of conditions in the staff room to teach well that students need in the classroom to learn well. It is one of the most devastating ironies of education that teachers are expected to provide a safe learning environment for their students within a teaching environment that at times is anything but safe for the teachers. This makes for a rather schizophrenic experience for the teachers, one that would not be tolerated in a learning community. Instead, teachers and school administrators would be supported and encouraged to learn within a spirit of trust and respect, for without trust, learning languishes.

The learning of professionals has been a hot topic at least since Schon's (1983) groundbreaking work on reflective practice but only recently has the social aspect of professional learning been recognized. Stamps (1998), for example, indicates that one of the greatest surprises of recent years for human resource officers has been the notion of 'informal workplace learning as a social phenomenon: the idea that humans learn within work-based groups called *communities of practice*' (p. 36, emphasis in the original). The importance of the community of practice has found its way into several recent works, including Wenger (1998) and Sergiovanni (2000). In fact, Sergiovanni positions the community of practice as *the* critical element in school development. He contends that 'developing a community of practice may be the single most important way to improve a school' (p. 139). The notion of the community of practice implies that, just as students learn from and with one another, so too teachers construct their knowledge upon the exemplars that they discover in their own practice and that they cull from their colleagues' practices. Exemplars emerge from effective strategies that resolve problems and from new understandings that illuminate mysteries. The problems and mysteries to be addressed are those that deal with the practice of teaching and learning, and the community is that which confronts those problems and mysteries. The nature of the discourse is a collegial problem-solving orientation and an orientation to learn in the face of mystery. As Gherardi (1999) points out, 'The knowledge problem that should therefore concern a community of learning-in-organizing scholars is the description and interpretation of the logic of practice and the practical knowledge embedded in practice as work, practice as language, and practice as morality' (p. 113). Although Gherardi gives primary place to the sort of learning that is driven by mystery, we believe that both sorts of learning, problem-driven and mystery-driven, are useful and that both sorts play a key role in a learning community.

The kind of professional learning that emerges within a community of practice is quite different from the more typical professional development opportunities that 'reinforce tinkering at the margins of teachers' work' (Bredeson, 1999, p. 22). Instead, it is the kind that is intended to generate what Bredeson calls 'critical competence, that is, teachers' consciousness of and critique of school practices and structures' (p. 22). It is the kind that can overcome what Argyris calls 'skilled incompetence' (Fulmer & Keys, 1998, p. 28), which occurs when individuals are unaware of the negative impacts and unintended consequences of their behavior. To us, it is learning that yields profound improvement. It delves into the heart of professional practice, into the assumptions, beliefs, and attitudes about students, about curriculum, and about teaching and learning that lie at the core of an educator's practice. It illuminates dark corners and reveals hidden alcoves of tacit practical knowledge, brings implicit elements into conscious awareness, and opens them to reflective critique. This is not to imply that all tacit knowledge is bad. Much of it is exemplary. But if it remains tacit, its effect on an educator's actions remains mysterious. Only by bringing tacit knowledge into the light of day can it be used consciously, critically, and reflectively. And it is the conscious, critical, reflective approach to practice that can lead to profound improvement.

Defining what is meant by a learning community is by no means the only challenge. Another thorny issue has to do with how to go about building one. Starratt (1996) contends that contextual circumstances shape the way in which a learning community develops and that there is no one model for this task. Instead, 'each school will have to invent itself as a learning community' (p. 82). As Beck and Foster (1999) point out, 'community does not simply emerge as well-intentioned people embrace new roles and values' (p. 353). In a recent interview, Argyris noted, 'It's as difficult to learn as it is to learn a poor game of tennis. The concepts aren't that complicated, but practice is what's needed' (Fulmer & Keys, 1998, p. 23). The practice involves an intense process of negotiation and professional conversation. It involves setting goals and aspirations through discourse among teachers, administrators, students, parents, and other interested parties. It means providing the conditions that will make the learning healthy and effective. The development of such a community depends on what Starratt (1996) defines as the principle of subsidiarity, that is, 'the authority to make discretionary decisions concerning the work is placed as close to the work as possible' (p. 121). The principle of subsidiarity rests on four conditions: '(1) trust, (2) knowledge of what the task is, (3) the capacity to carry out the task, and (4) a sense of the whole' (Starratt, p. 124). What all of this means is that, at the outset, the task requires a cultural transformation – one that does not demand homogeneity but that embraces diversity. A learning community is forged in the fires of conflicting beliefs as much as it is shaped in the shadow of shared norms.

Stamps (1998) argues that the growth and development associated with a learning community reflects an ecological metaphor where the system is self-regulating and self-sustaining. He warns, however, that ecosystems are fragile and that negative conditions can damage the system's ability to thrive or to survive (p. 34). The negative conditions have only recently begun to receive some focused attention. For example, Senge, Kleiner, Roberts, Ross, Roth, and Smith (1999) argue that learning and growth are organic outcomes of both reinforcing and limiting processes but that too much attention had been directed toward promoting growth and too little toward understanding limits (p. 9). The authors suggest that the limiting and reinforcing processes dance through cycles, with growth ebbing and flowing, depending on which process is ascendant at a particular time. From our standpoint, this ebb and flow moves through three spheres: the personal, the interpersonal, and the organizational. That is, the development of a learning community comes about through the interplay among personal abilities, interpersonal relationships, and organizational structures. Growth occurs as personal, interpersonal, and organizational capacities increase; it is limited as they decrease. We begin our exploration of these three spheres of capacity in the next section.

A Model for Building Capacities

In this book, for the most part, we locate principles and practices of the learning community within the cadre of educators. Our intention is not to exclude other members of the community but to emphasize the critical nature of professional learning. As Sergiovanni (2000) points out,

> Teachers count in helping schools be effective. But whether they will help students in a particular school or not depends on whether they are invested with enough discretion to act, get the support they need to teach, are involved in continuous learning, and are led by effective leaders. ... Building capacity among teachers and focusing that capacity on students and their learning is the crucial factor. Continuous capacity building and continuous focusing is best done within communities of practice. (p. 140)

Lambert (1998) points out that the notion of capacity building has a long-standing history in educational scholarship, harking back at least to the early 1970s. It is, from a relatively simple perspective, concerned with 'creating the experiences and opportunities for people to learn how to do certain things' (p. 11). She defines a professional community as one where 'teachers participate in decision making, have a shared sense of purpose, engage in collaborative work, and accept joint responsibility for the outcomes of their work' (p. 11). She positions these attributes as leadership skills. We argue, however, that they are fundamentally learning skills. Whether or not they are engaged in leadership tasks is a function of specific contexts and circumstances rather than a function of the skill set. To focus the discourse of capacity building on the notion of leadership, in our view, positions professional educational practice incorrectly. That is, it engages professional practice in the pursuit of *leadership* rather than in the pursuit of *learning*. Our view is that professional practice is all about learning. It is perhaps and at times concerned with leadership, but it is certainly and always concerned with learning. Linking capacity building directly to leadership functions is helpful when trying to build shared leadership but it is a limited approach and one that risks devaluing the professional practice of teaching and learning.

Since the early days of our work with learning communities in schools, we have been concerned with how one goes about making it happen. One of our frustrations with the educational discourse is that, when speaking about learning organizations or learning communities, scholars often speak about building capacity without explicating what kind of capacity or capacity for what. That is, there has been insufficient attention to what Starratt (1999) calls a 'curriculum of community' and what we might call a curriculum of capacity. The model we introduce in this section constitutes our initial foray into establishing such a curriculum. We construct a curriculum around building three pivotal capacities: *personal*, *interpersonal*, and *organizational*. Stamps (1998) provides some support for this kind of model. He observes that formal and informal learning in effective businesses occurs

> in four dimensions: *pragmatic* (job-related skills and knowledge); *intrapsychic* (personal coping skills and problem-solving abilities); *interpersonal* (how we interact, cooperate and share information with others); and *cultural* (understanding how the organization works, what things it approves of, what things land us in big trouble). (p. 34, emphasis in the original)

If the first two dimensions are collapsed into personal capacity, then Stamps' dimensions map well onto the three capacities we propose. Further support comes from Senge et al. (1999, p. 43), who list three reinforcing processes that can sustain profound change: enhancing personal results, developing networks of committed people, and improving business results. These reinforcing processes correspond with personal, interpersonal, and organizational capacities.

We propose a recursive model in which the three categories of capacity mutually influence one another, and growth in each category is built upon prior growth in itself and other categories, and builds a foundation for subsequent growth (see Figure 1). Boundaries between capacities are permeable, and borders are expandable. At times, circumstances will position one of the categories ahead of the others, and attention will focus on that kind of capacity for a while. At other times, the three capacities will nest within one another, and it will be difficult to tell them apart. Growth (and limits) will occur simultaneously in all three. Capacity builds not in a smooth, linear flow but in eddies and swells as well as in dips and depressions when no learning appears to be going on. The dips and depressions are opportunities to understand what individuals are trying to conserve, as this can give insights into why they do or do not embrace particular initiatives. According to Senge et al. (1999), 'Whether or not we value a particular balancing process depends on how much we value *what it conserves*' (p. 558, emphasis in the original). That is, growing seasons can yield the capacity to illuminate the mysteries of life and learning; non-growing seasons can yield the capacity to consolidate prior learning and to deal gracefully and effectively with difficult circumstances and conserving tendencies.

Even while the three categories are nested, mutual, and recursive, they also carry distinctive features. Stamps (1998), for example, argues that 'there are different kinds of learning and multiple factors that affect each of [the dimensions of learning]' (p. 36). The theoretical and practical structures associated with these differences and distinctions will be explicated in detail in subsequent chapters. The following paragraphs give us the opportunity to outline the core of each one.

Figure 1.1 Capacities for building a learning community.

Building personal capacity has to do with the active and reflective construction of knowledge. It begins with a confrontation with the values, assumptions, belief systems, and practices that individuals embrace. This is a profoundly personal and potentially transforming phenomenon. As educators come to grips with the implicit narratives that shape and constrain their professional practice and learning, they gain some sense of mastery over what they do know and what they need to know. This knowledge empowers them to begin a search for new knowledge and to reconstruct their professional narrative. Building personal capacity means that individuals have 'a caring attitude, conscientious stewardship, a calling for one's work, and creative energy' (Haskins, Liedtka, & Rosenblum, 1998, p. 37). A learning community emerges as individuals reflect on, assess, critique, and reconstruct their personal professional capacity and their capacity for collegial relations and collective practice.

Collegial relations and collective practice are the core of interpersonal capacity. Stamps (1998) argues that human relationships are critically important to creating a sustaining and sustainable workplace context. He says, 'Relationships, more than information, determine how problems get solved or opportunities exploited' (p. 37). Interpersonal capacity is also about creating collective meaning. As Janov (1995) points out, 'The communal nature of knowing depends on functional relationships that allow us to make meaning together' (p. 57). Another part of it has to do with

building the 'capacity for openness' (Senge et al., 1999, p. 244). This is critical because, as candor increases, sensitive issues become explicit. If people are unable to
deal with the attendant emotions that open and honest discourse is likely to engender,
then there is a gap between what is being said and what can be accommodated.
Building interpersonal capacity means that people work together on shared purposes,
they take individual and collective responsibility for the well-being and learning of
others, and they operate in a spirit of mutual respect and psychological safety. A
learning community emerges in response to sustaining and sustainable affective conditions, cognitive processes, and group interactions.

Organizational capacity is concerned with building structures that create and maintain sustainable organizational processes. Stamps (1998) warns that the ecological
model of learning 'doesn't square all that well with the traditional corporate model of
management and control' (p. 37). This is also true of schools. Typical school structures do not provide sufficient flexibility or autonomy for school people to approach
the mysteries and perplexities and problems of teaching and learning. Organizational
capacity entails creating a flexible system that is open to all sorts of new ideas, that
welcomes the eccentric and unusual as well as the tried and true. It is as much about
honoring diversity and embracing novelty as it is about opening doors and breaking
down walls. That means, as Hargreaves (1993) warns, that individualism and solitude
also need to be embraced, even in the midst of community and collaboration. Organizational capacity is about building a system that invests heavily in professional learning and relationship building (Haskins, Liedtka, & Rosenblum, 1998). At the school
level, it means placing 'professional development at the core of teacher work to ingrain
the value of continuous professional learning throughout teachers' careers' (Scribner,
1999, p. 261). A learning community is supported when organizational structures,
power dynamics, and procedural frameworks support professional learning for individuals and for groups.

The interpenetrations among the three pivotal capacities signify that 'creating and
sustaining educational communities requires attending to many different aspects of
life and work in schools' (Beck, 1999, p. 37). That is, one cannot build capacity in one
area and expect that to suffice. Rather, there needs to be direct, sustained, focused
attention on building capacity in all three areas. That will allow for synergy to develop
as each capacity builds from and extends the others. That is, increased capacity in one
category can exert pressure for improvements in the other categories of capacity.
Furthermore, Beck argues that 'there may be multiple points of entry into [commu-
nity]' (p. 37). From our standpoint, this suggests that the capacity of first attention is
probably context specific. That is, whether one starts to build personal, interpersonal,
or organizational capacity will depend on the needs of the people in each site, and an
in-depth analysis of the context will probably provide some clues as to where the most
leverage will obtain. One word of caution: starting with the least threatening capacity
is probably the most enticing entry point but is not necessarily the one that will lead to
the greatest improvement. At some point, school people need to tackle all three, even
the ones that feel uncomfortable or risky. Any one of the three levels of capacity
cannot work alone to bring about the kind of changes we envision. Without extended
personal capacity, educators may not be able to deconstruct the implicit elements of
their professional narrative or have access to new ideas with which to reconstruct it.

Without extended interpersonal capacity, the socio-cultural elements in a school may override any attempt to change the status quo. Without extended organizational capacity, teachers are likely to have little incentive or support to undertake the deep reflection, analysis, and reconstruction that can lead to profound improvement.

Positioning the Model: Addressing the Question, 'Why?'

There is overwhelming agreement that professional learning, although not a magic bullet, is directly and persistently linked to educational improvement and school development (Bredeson & Scribner, 2000; Louis, Toole, & Hargreaves, 1999). If that is the case, then there needs to be direct and persistent attention paid to the ways in which educators build the capacity to engage in professional learning. Saying that it must be so will not necessarily make it so, and sending teachers 'out for training' will not necessarily garner professional learning or generate change in educational practices. Instead, capacity needs to be built in relation to personal knowledge and capabilities, interpersonal relations and dynamics, and organizational structures and facilities. But when we talk about building personal, interpersonal, and organizational capacities, we are not talking about simply sharpening the edges of what we already do. We are talking about doing completely different things – and doing the same things completely differently. We envision a transformation of practice rather than a tinkering with practice. It is, at its best, profound improvement. It is a strategy for overcoming the tendency for educators 'to understand new things in the same old ways' (Sergiovanni, 2000, p. 146). And it means that 'individually and collectively held meanings experienced by teachers and students must change' (Sergiovanni, p. 147).

In this book we want to highlight the staff role of the teacher. Over the years our work with learning communities in schools has led us to develop a different mind set about teachers, one that places them in direct relationship with their colleagues. Traditionally, teachers have been seen, studied, and discussed in terms of their classroom role – what they need in order to teach children well. The model we present positions teachers in terms of their staff role – what they need in order to live, learn, and work well together (as well as alone). Previous models have looked at teachers as individuals rather than as members of a group, in which the individuals affect the learning and work of each other. Our model sees the teacher's work as a set of complex dynamics and interactions and the interplay of personal, collective, and organizational narratives. Highlighting the staff role of the teacher requires a different ideology based on different belief systems about what teachers can and should do in the school.

Although we have privileged educators in this discussion, we believe that the strategies and practices in the following chapters can be used with any number of stakeholder groups. We focus our discussion on educators because we believe that they cannot give what they do not have. That is, since they are the primary holders of educational expertise and knowledge and they are the first line of communication and interaction with students and parents, they hold the keys to extending the notion of community beyond the school walls. If they do not know how to do this for themselves and with their colleagues, then they have a decidedly limited foundation upon which to build a community with students, parents, and other community members.

What the educators learn needs to be transferred to the students and the parents so that they too can learn better. From this standpoint, the need for individual and collective professional learning provides a strong rationale for working to establish a learning community among educators. The creation of such a community for educators will help to give substance and grounding to the creation of a learning community for students. From that foundation, the learning community can be extended to parents and other members of the educational community.

2

Personal Capacity: The Search for Knowledge

A learning community is first and foremost about people, and it is with people that personal capacity is concerned. From the perspective of schools, personal capacity is an amalgam of all the embedded values, assumptions, beliefs, and practical knowledge that teachers carry with them and of the professional networks and knowledge bases with which they connect. Building personal capacity entails a confrontation with these explicit and implicit structures in such a way that teachers come to grips with the personal narratives that shape and constrain their professional practice and learning. This confrontation is necessary because new learning always accretes onto prior layers of knowledge and existing belief systems. If these embedded structures operate out of conscious awareness, then their influence on professional renewal is not open to scrutiny, and their tacit operation could undermine professional learning opportunities. Deconstructing the embedded layers frees teachers to reconstruct their professional narrative in the face of deep mysteries or difficult problems.

Deconstructing the foundation of one's personal capacity is, in essence, a search for one's theory of practice. It is both an internal and an external search. Members seek inside their hearts and minds for the tacit practical knowledge upon which they rely for their professional identity, and they search their networks for the explicit knowledge bases upon which they rely for their professional expertise. Identity and expertise, together, shape an educator's professional theory. Although there has been some debate as to whether teaching derives from theoretical beliefs or from practiced behaviors (Fang, 1996), we believe that people always hold some beliefs about what should be done, what should happen, or what is going to happen in most circumstances. For something as purposeful as teaching, to assume that educators approach their work without some professional theory is, to us, completely misguided. We believe that educators have a professional theory that includes explicit and implicit elements and that this theory shapes their capacity for personal professional action, for collegial practice, and for professional learning. From our perspective, building personal capacity begins with the deconstruction of that theory of professional practice. That is, it begins with the search for personal knowledge.

Internal Search

According to Argyris and Schon (1978), professional action is caught in the crossfire between espoused theory and theory-in-use. Espoused theory is the set of assumptions, beliefs, and values that people publicly declare. It is what they say they believe, what they advocate in open discussions, and what they promote in professional discourse. It usually consists of the 'best practice' or the standard rhetoric currently in vogue. Theory-in-use, on the other hand, is the set of assumptions, beliefs, and values that people do not necessarily declare but that they follow in practice. It is what can be seen underneath their decisions, actions, interactions, and reactions, and some of it might not always be stellar. The problem is not that these two sets of theories operate together but that they are often not aligned. When they are out of alignment, an individual's actions and statements are likely to be inconsistent or contradictory, and professional practice may consequently lack integrity or congruence. Lack of alignment between espoused theory and theory-in-use helps to explain why researchers have found that, for teachers, 'the relationship between beliefs and instructional practices varies from very consistent to very inconsistent' (Fang, 1996, p. 53). From this perspective, at least part of the inconsistency can be attributed to tacit theories-in-use that override espoused theories.

In our work with educators, we have come across numerous examples of a disconnection between espoused theory and theory-in-use. Perhaps the most devastating example is the case of one director of education in a small rural school division. Dick (a pseudonym, as are all names used in this book) had a reputation in the region as a director who encouraged and supported professional development. This reputation gave him considerable 'air time' at administrators' meetings, where he spoke eloquently about the need to develop a strong, professional teaching force such that teachers would be prepared to meet the special needs of high-risk students. But in his home district, this agenda took on a dark side.

When Dick first arrived in the school division, he found a cadre of strong, professional teachers who were using a variety of strategies to meet the needs of a variety of students. All of them were mid-career people who had built reputations as creative, innovative, and exciting teachers. Most of them were women. They became Dick's special project, and he set out to show them a better way. When some of them dared to question his strategies or to thwart his authority, he shifted gears and targeted them for disciplinary action. He placed them under surveillance by the principal, he questioned their professional judgement, and he impugned their reputation within the school district. These actions served to undermine their self-confidence and to curtail their professional activities. Eventually, some of the teachers bent to his will, others went 'underground,' and still others, tragically, lost their careers. Dick did not acknowledge his role in the loss of these teachers. Instead, he attributed it to a 'mid-career slump' that they were unable to overcome, in spite of his intense and personal interest in their professional development. Although Dick's espoused theory was to develop professional educators, his actions did not support this theory. Instead, they suggested that his theory-in-use was to develop disciples who would honor his expertise and who would bolster his personal reputation.

To be sure, Dick is one of the most extreme cases we have observed but he is by no means alone. We have seen discrepancies between espoused theory and theory-in-use in administrators who invite teachers, parents, and/or students to provide input into a particular decision when, in fact, the outcome has already been determined and the administrator stage-manages the discussion to ensure that the group arrives at the desired decision. We have seen discrepancies when teachers state a preference for collegial work but seldom attend planning or committee meetings. We have seen them when teachers say that they believe in the potential of all students to learn but they use an extremely limited range of instructional strategies. We have seen them in our own work when we embark on collaborative research, only to design the bulk of the research and to write the final report ourselves. In most cases, we have noted that the espoused theory positions the individual in a positive light but that the actual practices are somewhat less salubrious.

We have also observed discrepancies in which the theory-in-use outshines the espoused theory. One case in point is a teacher who told us that she ran a very teacher-directed and teacher-controlled classroom. When we went into the classroom, however, we noted that by far the largest portion of the day was under the direct control of the students. The teacher kept close track of everything that was happening and intervened when situations warranted it, but for the most part she gave the students freedom to control and direct their own learning. Her theories-in-use regarding teacher control and direction obviously differed considerably from what one would typically associate with those terms and from what she had originally described.

Addressing these sorts of discrepancies means confronting the contents of theory-in-use and espoused theory. But this is decidedly difficult to do if the theories remain unarticulated. Putting the theories into actual words may seem like a pointless exercise because, after all, we all know what we think. From our point of view, however, we only *think* we know what we think. Until theories of practice are visibly inscribed in some way, they are like so much air – they exert pressure and they take up space but they don't register on the senses and they can't be handled or manipulated. Thus the internal search begins by articulating both sets of theories.

Articulating one's professional espoused theory is a time-consuming but not particularly difficult task. It is a rather straightforward description of what people say in relation to their professional practice, their competencies, their attitudes, and their values. The content to be considered in this regard is likely to be context-specific, and different educators will probably define the content of professional theory differently, depending on what sorts of knowledge bases, conditions, or expectations currently impinge on their professional practice. As a starting point, an articulated theory might describe such things as students' learning styles, interests, and backgrounds; teaching and learning expectations; goals and purposes of education; instructional strategies and pacing; content scope and sequence; curriculum bases; evaluation purposes and practices; school and classroom organization; and classroom management practices. This list, which is derived from Shulman's (1987) categories of professional knowledge, is not intended to be an exhaustive or exclusive one, but it does signal some of the constructs that might be resident in an educator's professional theory. As Shulman defines these constructs, they refer almost exclusively to the *classroom* role of the *teacher*. The development of a professional learning community means that attention also needs to be paid to the *staff* role of the *educator*. This perspective requires an articulation of one's position regarding, *inter alia*, collegial practice, committee involvement, shared planning and decision making, and professional learning. It means, in effect, that educators need to inscribe their thoughts, feelings, and attitudes about what it means to be a teacher, to be a colleague, to be a leader, and to be a learner.

That is the easy part because it deals with what is in the mind of the individual. Articulating the theory-in-use is a different story because it deals with what is in the heart, and educators do not always or necessarily have ready access to this part of their professional narrative. In fact, Argyris and Schon (1978) contend that an individual's theory-in-use is always tacit. We assume, however, that it has both explicit and implicit aspects. The explicit part, or the 'known,' is open to examination and change. It is that part which aligns with espoused theory, where actual practices coincide with articulated beliefs. The implicit part, or the 'unknown,' remains out of conscious awareness but exerts a profound influence on an individual's decisions and actions. To get at the implicit aspect means measuring one's actions against the effects of those actions. It means that, at this stage of the personal search, educators need to look outward toward the effects of their actions on the people with whom they interact.

Critical reflection on practice is one strategy for exploring this unknown territory. It is intended to delve into the professional narrative from a number of perspectives and through a continuum of thinking levels (Mitchell & Coltrinari, in press). It begins with a simple description of existing practices, moves through an analysis and evaluation of the practices, and leads to a deconstruction of the professional assumptions, beliefs, values, and practices that are embedded in the professional narrative. This can be done in writing through reflective journals, in speaking through reflective conversations with colleagues, or simply in thinking by oneself. This sort of analysis, if done in a spirit of personal honesty and professional curiosity, is likely to reveal discrepancies between what was intended and what actually transpired. This provides a powerful metacognitive tool for blending these new insights with prior understandings in such a way as to reconstruct the professional narrative.

Descriptive reflection is the easiest and most common form of reflection and often is undertaken in relation to a compelling event, circumstance, situation, or interactive episode. It entails a brief outline of the events that transpired as the story unfolded. This is likely to begin with a simple recounting of what happened, who was involved, what was said and by whom, where the events occurred, and how they proceeded. To be more of a reflection and less of a description, this narrative should also describe the conflicts, successes and failures, emotions, and intentions embedded in the story. And, if it is to uncover theories-in-use, it needs also to describe how others have reacted or responded to the actions of the individual. Inscribing these details provides grist for the critical analysis that is essential if deep understanding is to occur.

Analytic and evaluative reflection involves examining the details from the descriptive analysis for discrepancies between intentions and effects and for recurring patterns of behavior. This reflection turns critical when it involves looking closely at the effects one has had on colleagues, students, parents, or other members of the educational community to see whether or not one's behaviors led to the anticipated or desired outcomes. Critical reflection entails writing out the attributions or assumptions that were being made about oneself and about others and carefully checking them for evidence of untested attributions or unfounded assumptions. It involves looking for patterns that seem all too familiar, for issues or problems that crop up regularly or periodically, and for elements of the story that have been a longstanding part of the person's history. And then it requires an evaluation of the desirability of the intentions, practices, effects, outcomes, assumptions, attributions, patterns, and histories that have been inscribed. This entails a deep and honest examination of the extent to which one's actions do, in fact, measure up to one's stated beliefs or if, instead, they reflect a set of attitudes or beliefs that may not be particularly appropriate or efficacious.

The evaluative phase holds both the promise and the peril of critical reflection. The promise is that it will lead to a deep intimacy with one's professional theory-in-use and an awareness of where that theory engenders warranted practice and where it needs to be reconstructed in order to improve professional capacity. But this is also the peril. Confronting unpleasant truths is at best disconcerting and can at times be completely devastating. Acknowledging that personal change is required can threaten one's sense of self and professional identity. When one's identity is deeply entrenched or when the individual is heavily defended against self-disclosure, then there are likely to be few uncomfortable revelations. In that case, evaluative reflection will probably not culminate in any real deconstruction of the professional narrative, and the promise will not be realized. But if there is sufficient psychological safety, and if reflection advances into deeper levels of analysis and critique, then educators are better equipped to make the sorts of changes in their theories-in-use that will increase their personal capacity and that will lead to profound improvement in teaching, learning, and leading.

Critical reflection is a complex, iterative process that can occur at different stages of professional action. Schon (1983), for example, distinguishes between reflection in action (critical analysis of events as they transpire) and reflection on action (post hoc analysis of events). The assumption is that novices will probably start with post hoc analyses and, as they gain competence with reflection, subsequently critique their actions as they happen. Most of our own experiences with professional reflection have been in workshops, interviews, and seminars, with the attendant time dislocation between the doing of practice and the thinking about practice. In those instances, it is always reflection on action, and we have little idea if the reflections represent actual narratives or if they increase personal capacity. We have been fortunate, however, to observe one principal reflecting in action.

The teachers in Alan's school had worked with us for almost a year experimenting with principles and practices of organizational learning. One outcome of that process was that they had developed a strong culture of shared decision making and collegial planning. In one planning session, which Alan was facilitating, intense arguments broke out over the procedures for a particular school-wide event, with Alan and one teacher lining up against four other teachers. This continued until a complete breakdown of communication seemed imminent. At that point, Alan said, 'Just a minute. Maybe we should go back and talk about what we're assuming should happen. Here's what I think, and then you tell me if you have the same assumptions.' When they had each laid out their assumptions, they were able to identify the places where they were and were not in agreement and to come to a satisfactory resolution. The description and analysis of assumptions turned out to be a compelling example of reflection in action. In this case, not only did Alan reflect on his own actions but he also opened a space for the teachers to do likewise.

This, of course, is not easy. In Alan's case, it came about after months of intense work on creating a learning culture and a professional community in the school. Professional thinking (as most thinking) is usually stuffed into a box constructed of habits, traditions, routines, and past successes. Breaking out of the box requires a prior recognition that what was assumed to be reality is no more than a habit of thought. This kind of awareness can be helped by the presence of what Carr and Kemmis (1986) call a 'critical friend' (p. 186). This is an individual with whom one feels comfortable and safe enough to engage in reflective conversation. It is an individual with whom one can share the embarrassments as well as the successes of professional practice. It is an individual who will challenge one's perceptions of reality in a spirit of trust, mutual respect, and deep personal regard. We admit that such friends are rare, but we have found such people when we have looked for them and when we have been willing to hear them. We have also served as critical friends to some of the teachers and administrators with whom we have worked over the years. Cindy is just one example.

Cindy taught middle-years students in an inner city school where teaching conditions were difficult and where students and teachers were transient. She had been instrumental in introducing a school-wide behavior management program and was deeply concerned that it be implemented in the 'right' way. Consequently, when the staff met to talk about issues with the program, her voice was the loudest, the most frequent, and the most insistent. Because she controlled group processes, outcomes usually reflected her wishes. This circumstance led to faithful adoption of the innovation by most teachers – and to a few disgruntled colleagues who refused to participate in the program or in collective processes. In several conversations with Cindy, we asked her to think about these conditions. In early conversations, she attributed a number of motives to her colleagues, none of which she had tested for accuracy. In subsequent conversations, as we asked her to probe further into the undercurrents of the situation, she gradually began to talk about the ways in which her own interaction style was limiting the opportunities for others to participate. At one point, Cindy said, 'Boy, it's hard to recognize things about yourself that you don't want to see, isn't it? If I could just learn to shut up and listen, I could learn a lot.' From then on, she was less strident in her interaction style and she inquired more frequently into her colleagues' points of view. Several of the disaffected teachers commented on the change in her behavior, and they began to participate in the behavior management program. While we acknowledge that Cindy may eventually have come to this realization on her own, our presence as critical friends certainly facilitated that realization.

The internal search, if conducted in a spirit of honest critical reflection, can yield a deep and satisfying connection with one's professional narrative. It can expose discrepancies between espoused theory and theory-in-use and it can target specific aspects of the theories for renewal. It can also highlight those aspects that deserve to be affirmed and validated. From this perspective, the internal search puts individuals more intimately in touch with the professional knowledge that is already at their disposal and with the belief systems that underpin their practice. In so doing, it inscribes the foundation of personal professional capacity.

External Search

Personal capacity consists not just in personal qualities and knowledge bases but also in the available sources of new information and knowledge. From this perspective, building personal capacity entails searching one's professional networks to identify the extent to which the educator is exposed to new and different ideas. Network theory has a long history in the social sciences but has only recently found its way into the educational literature. In that context, most of the work has either described the networks that teachers build (e.g., Aston & Hyle, 1997; Bakkenes, Brabander, & Imants, 1999; Smylie & Hart, 1999) or promoted more extended professional networks (e.g., Lieberman, 1990; Little & McLaughlin, 1993). We believe, however, that network theory can be more than an analytic lens for researchers and scholars. It also constitutes a practical analytic tool that educators can use, on their own, to assess the degree to which their contexts exert a conserving force or a growing force on their professional knowledge bases.

Network *theory* assumes that individuals' thoughts and behaviors are at least partly dependent on the ties they establish with other folk in their social or professional community (Smylie & Hart, 1999). The strength of the ties can be assessed in relation to time in contact, intensity of the relationship, intimacy between the actors, and the presence of reciprocal services; homogeneity of networks can be assessed in terms of demographics, proximity, and affiliation (Mitchell & Hyle, 1999). To put this in more concrete terms, strong ties are likely to be forged when individuals spend considerable time together, when they participate together in emotional or deeply engaging activities, when they share common knowledge, and when they receive mutual rewards. Weak ties, of course, emerge from the opposite conditions. Homogeneous networks are characterized by similar demographics (e.g., age, sex, family background, socioeconomic status, educational background), close proximity (e.g., the same school or district), and common affiliation (e.g., the same educational discipline or teaching assignment). Network theory assumes that strong ties and homogeneous networks limit the amount of new information or different ideas to which the members are exposed and consequently restrict their thoughts and actions to a small repertoire of options. This implies that the more homogeneous the network and the stronger the ties, the more likely the individuals will exhibit conserving trends in their thoughts and actions.

From an educational standpoint, strong ties are likely to develop between educators from similar demographic and educational backgrounds, of similar professional belief systems, with similar professional practices or teaching assignments, and in close proximity to one another. Such networks provide a stable foundation and encourage incremental change. That is, they provide a measure of safety, predictability, and stability – but they also generate a conserving trend in practice. Weak ties, by contrast, are likely to develop among educators from diverse educational backgrounds, of diverse professional belief systems, and with diverse professional practices or teaching assignments. Such networks provide a rich source of new ideas and new possibilities and a foundation for experiments in practice. While this condition may not feel particularly safe or predictable, it does encourage teachers to try out new strategies for dealing with the difficult problems or the deep mysteries of teaching and learning. This sort of experimentation holds the potential for profound improvement.

Network *analysis* is an exercise that deconstructs the characteristics of the networks in which educators participate and the ties that they have forged with others in the networks (Mitchell & Hyle, 1999). To begin the process, we ask educators to list the formal and informal professional associations to which they belong. This list should be as comprehensive as possible, including the informal social associations that they make within their own school. Next, the educators describe the characteristics of the associations in terms of demographics, proximity, and affiliation and the strength of the ties in terms of time, intensity, intimacy, and reciprocity. Third, we ask them to articulate as far as possible the dominant professional narratives of each association and to analyze the degree of coherence between those narratives and their own professional narrative. Finally, the educators map the relationships among the narratives in terms of similarity and difference. A map that shows a high degree of similarity is likely to promote conservatism and stability. A map that shows a wide range of variability is likely to promote new ideas and greater professional learning. This sort of map deconstructs the degree to which the educator's professional narrative has been subjected to challenges from external sources and it signals the extent to which the individual has access to new professional ideas and learning. This information can indicate whether or not there is a need for educators to begin connecting with other networks.

Diverse networks and weak ties can provide educators with new professional knowledge, without which stagnation can set in. Donna's story is a case in point. Donna worked in an experimental elementary school that had been instituted to design educational practices that followed the principles of Gardner's (1983) multiple intelligences theory. Donna arrived at the school in its first year and became deeply involved in designing a professional development program that would enable the teachers to plan and implement appropriate curriculum and instruction. In the early years, the educators were constantly learning new and interesting concepts and teaching strategies, and an aura of enthusiasm and excitement permeated the school. The teachers became good friends as well as professional colleagues, and a number of them socialized only or primarily with one another. Over the years, Donna noticed the excitement waning, as teaching became more routine and less novel. Upon the completion of a network analysis, she realized that no new networks had been forged for several years, and no new ideas had entered the discourse. Personal capacity had peaked at some point in the past, and little new learning was now going on. She said, 'We're all good teachers, and I guess we thought we didn't need to learn anything more, but we've gone stale. It was easier to just keep on doing what we knew how to do for a while but we need to start learning again. I guess that means we have to start connecting with people outside our school again.' Although Donna had been concerned about the apparent diminishing of personal capacity, she had no idea how to address it until she had analyzed her own professional networks.

Donna's story implies that an educator's professional knowledge is not an unbounded field. Instead, it is constrained in part by the professional affiliations that individual educators pursue, and personal capacity will reflect the same sorts of constraints. Admittedly, this adds yet another layer of complexity to the already overburdened notion of professional competence, but it is a layer that promises to address one of the fundamental problems of professional development. This problem, which has plagued both the cognitive and the organizational perspectives on educational reform (Firestone, 1996), is the lack of new professional knowledge for practicing teachers. This condition, according to Firestone, is implicit in most of the current research on teacher knowledge, but it has seldom been given sufficient, direct, or sustained attention. Until clear and careful attention is paid to ways in which educators might be exposed to new and revolutionary ideas, professional development is likely to consist of little more than tinkering at the margins of typical practices.

Our own analysis of the literature suggests that current research on professional development and educational reform focuses on intact groups and assumes ready access to new ideas. Network theory implies that these sorts of assumptions are misguided. Intact groups are not likely to overcome the tendency to conserve prevailing practices and belief systems, nor are they likely to provide access to revolutionary ideas that can engender profound improvement. Firestone (1996), for example, argues, 'There is considerable evidence that most teachers do not know how to teach in the way suggested by research on cognitive science and teacher thinking' (p. 223). This suggests that ready access to new ideas cannot be assumed. When network analysis reveals a high degree of similarity within professional affiliations and a high degree of stability in collective professional narratives, it should serve as a signal to educators that personal capacity may be languishing. In such cases, there will be a need for educators to break out of old habits, push past comfort zones, and carve out new affiliations – that is, to create weak ties. Although that may feel threatening in the extreme, and although there may be little organizational incentive for them to do so, it can ultimately be a most satisfying and edifying enterprise. It can open professional doors that may previously have been unimagined, and it can increase personal capacity for resolving the tough problems and confronting the deep mysteries of teaching and learning.

This does not imply that the only good ties are weak ones. To be sure, weak ties open people to new horizons and different frames of reference. But strong ties are essential for providing the safe ground upon which to experiment with the new ideas. Developing strong ties with colleagues provides support, stability, and trust, all of which are essential if educators are to break out of familiar, tried-and-true practices. From our perspective, a balance of strong and weak ties, which operate in harmony and synergy, is the most appropriate configuration of ties and networks in a learning community.

The Searches in Mutual Relationship

Taken together, the internal and external searches yield at least part of the content of a professional narrative. That is, reflective practice opens insights into the theory-in-use underneath professional actions and judgements, and network analysis indicates the nature of collective professional narratives and the degree of access to new professional possibilities. Such insights open doors for understanding why professional practice is enacted as it is, and they reveal, in part, the extent of one's personal capacity to handle unexpected or intransigent exigencies of teaching and learning. But inscribing the professional narrative is only the first step because the narrative can be expected to extend personal capacity in some ways but to limit it in others. The search for knowledge, then, also entails an honest examination of the ways in which theories-in-use and professional affiliations extend or limit personal capacity. This means searching the professional narrative for narrow versus broad interpretations, for limited versus variable repertoires, for restricted versus diverse affiliations, and for impoverished versus enriched knowledge bases. It means opening one's professional identity and expertise to the harsh glare of a reflective searchlight – and then making some indicated adjustments.

Adjustments can be made through a variety of strategies. Portraiture, for example, is a strategy that engages teachers in a dialogic relationship. One teacher (the portraitist) observes a colleague (the observed) and then draws a portrait of the perspectives, experiences, voice, and visions of the observed colleague (Lawrence-Lightfoot & Davis, 1997). The portrait is refined and re-drawn through subsequent dialogue between the portraitist and the observed. In this way, the portrait entails looking into the soul of the observed person and bringing to light many of the features that constitute the individual's professional narrative. Other strategies, some of which are quite familiar to most educators, are peer coaching relationships, professional portfolios, and personal professional growth plans. None of these strategies is expected to serve as a stand-alone practice but is to be embedded in a larger program of professional development that addresses all sorts of professional knowledge, including (but not limited to) propositional, procedural, and personal knowledge (Bredeson & Scribner, 2000). Adjustments occur when the scrutiny exposes gaps between one's existing professional narrative and the desired narrative.

A wholeness perspective assumes that the internal and external searches are in constant dialogue with each another. They do not work alone, and either one on its own will limit the kind of learning that can happen and the kind of transformation that can take place. One of our favorite examples of the synergy that develops from these two searches acting in concert is the story of Donald, the principal of a rural kindergarten-to-secondary school. The school had been in trouble for some time, and the principal, upon the advice of the director of education, finally enlisted the services of a cadre of reviewers from the university. During the interviews, which were conducted with the principal, all the professional staff, and selected students and parents, it became clear that, among other issues, there was a need for some major changes in the way that Donald was enacting the principal's role. The reviewers submitted the report to Donald, whose initial reaction was disbelief, anger, and hostility toward the report and the reviewers.

For a month, Donald kept the report to himself and pondered its meaning for him and for the school. At the end of that time, he called one of us and said, 'I didn't want to admit that I needed to make some changes in the way I was leading the school, but I know I do. I thought the school was better than this report makes it seem. I guess I was fooling myself. Actually, I've known all this for a long time but haven't wanted to face it. Now I guess I'm ready.' He admitted to going through several stages of reflection, from denial ('It's not as bad as all that.') to rationalization ('There's a good reason for things being the way they are.') to questioning ('If this is true, what does it mean?') to final acceptance and growth ('Let's fix this.'). His confrontation with his implicit knowledge added relevance and credibility to the information provided by the external reviewers. Once he brought the two sets of information into dialogue with one another, he was able to move past his initial defenses and to enlist the teachers in constructing a plan for school renewal. The dialogue between the internal and external searches represented a critical turning point in Donald's personal capacity and in the history of the school.

Donald's stages of reflection call attention to some of the challenges to growth identified by Senge et al. (1999). They argue that growth is checked by ten limiting processes: time, support, relevance, management consistency and clarity, fear and anxiety, assessment of progress, isolation and arrogance, governance structure, diffusion and transfer, and strategy and purpose. They say, 'If leaders do not understand the balancing processes and limits underlying each challenge, they do not understand what the system is *trying to conserve*' (p. 559, emphasis in the original). In Donald's case, the balancing processes and limits were related to longstanding patterns of accepted professional behaviors that had worked in the past, when there were more resources and a more homogeneous student body and teaching cadre. The principal and the staff were trying to hold on to those past practices. In so doing, they had allowed some serious dysfunction to creep into the school. Confronting these conserving tendencies opened the door to a more functional set of professional practices and belief systems. This is not to say that the subsequent change was trouble-free. It was anything but that. But this is to say that, without the dialogue between the internal and external searches in which Donald participated, the realization that the existing professional narratives no longer sufficed and that change was essential would probably have been a longer time in coming. In fact, it is likely that it would not have happened prior to Donald's retirement two years hence.

The Search for Personal Knowledge: A Synthesis

We see the relationship between the internal and external searches as being recursive in nature. That is, a growing trend in one search is likely to lead to a growing trend in the other and a conserving trend in one to a conserving trend in the other. Figure 2 presents an image of how the aspects of the internal and external searches might mutually interact to affect personal capacity. Growing trends in personal capacity emerge in response to participation in diverse networks, development of weak ties, and a well-articulated professional narrative with congruence between espoused theory and theory-in-use. These conditions enable the professional search by opening the discourse with oneself and with one's affiliates. By contrast, conserving trends in personal capacity emerge in response to participation in homogeneous networks, development of strong ties, and an implicit professional narrative with possible conflict between espoused theory and theory-in-use. These conditions limit the professional search by reducing access to new ideas and triggering internal defense mechanism. However, these conditions also provide safety and security for educators, and this kind of stability provides a firmer foundation for eventually moving forward. From this perspective, conserving trends should be seen not necessarily as negative forces but as opportunities for consolidation of prior learning and understandings. That is, they offer fallow ground and a period of rest and regeneration before, once again, cultivating the soil and planting the seeds for renewed growth.

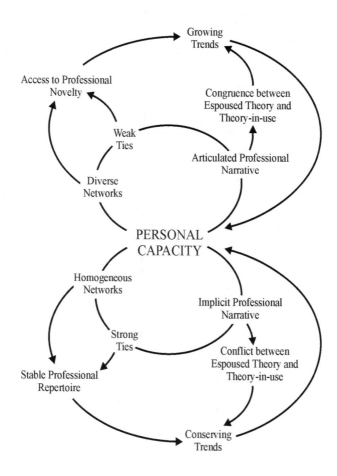

Figure 2.1. Elements of personal capacity.

There are a couple of signals that we use with educators (and with ourselves) to determine the extent to which the searches are leading to new insights and to possible transformations of the professional narrative. We call these signals the Aha/Oh Shit syndrome. To explain: when a learning opportunity causes an individual to say, 'Aha!'

this is an indication that the external search is working and the person has found some new and exciting piece of professional knowledge to add to the repertoire of professional competencies. When the opportunity causes an individual to say, 'Oh, shit!' then the internal search is working and the person has confronted an uncomfortable personal truth. But these two kinds of insights need to be in some sort of balance. Too many 'Ahas' can lead to information overload and unassimilated professional knowledge. Too many 'Oh, shits' can lead to psychological risk and a conflicted professional identity. We believe that a healthy blend of the two kinds of insight is essential for extending personal capacity in an environment of psychological safety.

3

Personal Capacity: The Construction of Knowledge

Extending personal capacity entails more than just a quiet (albeit critical) reflection in, on, and for practice. It also requires an active change in both cognition and practice. We acknowledge that this position has been somewhat of a controversy in academic literature, with some folks arguing that a change in cognition is sufficient and others arguing that a change in practice can be the first step on the road to changed cognition. We take some exception to both of these arguments. Our position in this debate is two-fold. First, we believe, along with Argyris (1993), that changes in cognition are meaningless in a professional context unless they lead to improvements in practice. That is, personal *professional* capacity is wrapped up in both the cognition *and* the actions of the practitioner. If cognitive change does not improve practice, then the sort of profound improvement that we associate with a learning community has not occurred. Our second point is that a change in cognition is the necessary first step in the process of building personal capacity. That is, unless the internal and external searches engender some shift in perception or belief system, then there is likely to be little real change in practice. The embedded theories-in-use will continue to exert unacknowledged but powerful pressure on what educators do in their work, and life in the school and the classroom will go on much the same as it always has. Our point here is that change in practice that is not associated with change in cognition merely tinkers at the edges of the familiar (*ergo* 'correct'). It does not engage the deep transformation of the professional narrative that leads to profound improvement.

What this means is that extending personal capacity requires the educator to move from reflection and analysis (deconstruction) into action (reconstruction). This sort of movement positions educators as active creators of knowledge, not simply as passive consumers of knowledge that has been created elsewhere. This is somewhat of a departure from the usual role of the teacher in the process of knowledge construction. Typically, the academic and professional literature has assumed a relatively passive role for teachers in educational improvement initiatives, and only in recent years has this position been opened to academic and professional critique. We could give pages of such criticism, but we will limit ourselves to observations from two renowned scholars of educational improvement. First, from Judith Warren Little (1993):

> Much staff development or in-service communicates a relatively impoverished view of teachers, teaching, and teacher development. Compared with the complexity, subtlety, and uncertainties of the classroom, professional development is often a remarkably low-intensity enterprise. It requires little in the way of intellectual struggle or emotional engagement and takes only superficial account of teachers' histories or circumstances. (p. 148)

Second, from John Goodlad (interviewed in Tell, 1999):

> Teachers are being pushed this way and that way – to phonics one day, to standards the next – and I think this destroys the profession. Teachers need freedom – freedom to make professional decisions. As long as we continue to force teachers to implement strategies from above, we will not get good future teachers entering the profession. (p. 19)

The kind of professional development against which these two people rail is the kind that takes school development and educational improvement out of the hands of the people who have the largest input into how education is enacted on a day-by-day basis. We too argue that this situation is seriously misguided. It leads to proposed improvements that may be completely incompatible with particular school contexts or completely incomprehensible to particular educators. We are not suggesting that ideas from the outside are not welcome in schools. To the contrary, our work with teachers' networks has clearly demonstrated the impoverishment of professional practice that ensues when external ideas are not included in professional discourse. What we are suggesting, however, is that these ideas cannot be implemented generically or generally. Instead, they must always be infused into the craft environment of particular schools and particular educators. In essence, the general surrenders to the particular, and the same idea is enacted differently in different contexts. Although the dominance of the particular has been cited as a fundamental problem in educational policy changes (e.g., McLaughlin, 1990), we do not see it as a flaw. We see it, instead, as a healthy and necessary outcome of extending personal professional capacity. Our primary argument is this: Knowledge creation is a process of disciplined inquiry that seeks answers to current or long-standing problems of practice or that addresses deep mysteries and emergent questions in education, and educators are central to this process. Because educators work in widely disparate communities and contexts, any one educational strategy will, *de facto*, be expressed in widely disparate ways. *Ergo*, the particular trumps the general.

   This position sees educators as both active creators of knowledge and facilitators of knowledge creation. That is, they ask questions of themselves, their colleagues, and their students; they seek out new networks, ideas, and practices; and they experiment with new professional strategies in their schools and classrooms. Through this process, they reconstruct their professional narrative. The creation of knowledge, the facilitation of knowledge creation, and the reconstruction of the professional narrative, working in concert with the internal and external searches, extend personal capacity. These are the concepts that constitute the core of this chapter.

Process of Knowledge Construction

How knowledge is constructed has occupied the minds of educational philosophers, researchers, theorists, and practitioners at least since the time of Plato. We cannot even begin to address all the various debates, principles, practices, and beliefs that have built up around the construct nor can we do justice to such a complicated and hotly contested notion. We acknowledge at the outset, then, that our representation of knowledge construction is partial and limited. Our intention in this book is not to enter into the philosophical debates surrounding knowledge construction but to advance specific principles and strategies that are in harmony with our understandings of a learning community and that we believe are essential for profound improvement in teaching and learning. We take as our point of departure Prawat's (1999) argument that people do learn, that their learning moves them to greater levels of knowledge and greater complexity of understanding, and that this sort of cognitive change relies on a constructivist view of learning. Prawat cites two central features of constructivist learning: '(a) Learning is a process of active construction, and (b) that process results in a qualitative change in understanding' (p. 48). These notions are at the heart of the kind of learning that should be expected to go on in a learning community.

What this signifies for us is that learning (both of educators and of students) is a process of knowledge construction, not merely a process of knowledge absorption, and that it is knowledge-dependent. That is, people use current knowledge to construct (or learn) new knowledge. People learn by actively 'weighing new information against previous learnings, thinking about and working through discrepancies (on their own or with others), and coming to new understanding' (Conley, 1993, p. 142). In this way, knowledge is situated in activity and used within specific contexts and cultures (Brown, Collins, & Duguid, 1989). Knowledge construction, then, is a product of both context and activity. Similarly, knowledge itself is not context-free and, in fact, has little meaning except within a given context and culture because of the central role played by pre-existing mental schema (Brooks & Brooks, 1999). In other words, an individual can only understand knowledge as it is constructed by the mind, and what is in the mind is a complex and curious amalgam of prior personal and collective history – the 'stuff' of context and culture. From this perspective, knowledge is 'a web of connections actively and continually reconstructed by the individual to form a fabric of internalized meaning' (Prestine & LeGrand, 1991, p. 67) that is shaped and constrained by the institutionalized meaning frameworks of the larger culture (Douglas, 1986). This approach to knowledge construction is fundamentally different from approaches rooted in an objectivist view of truth, which assumes that warranted knowledge yields universal truth and that truth can be considered apart from the context and culture in which it has been 'discovered.'

A constructivist approach implies that learning can occur in a host of ways, and the task of distinguishing among different levels of learning has interested scholars for some time. We are most familiar with the literature on organizational learning, which locates the learning of people in an organizational context and directs it toward organizational activity. One of the earliest frameworks for different levels of organizational learning comes from Argyris and Schon (1978), who contend that learning may be either single-loop or double-loop learning. *Single-loop learning* is concerned with stabilizing or maintaining the existing system. An example of a single-loop system is the thermostat in a home. *Double-loop learning* involves questioning the system itself. That is, it raises the question of whether the existing system is adequate to meet current needs and exigencies. From Argyris and Schon's perspective, both of these types of learning are necessary for effective organizational functioning and for deep organizational change. Single-loop learning allows for more responsive routine practices, and double-loop learning opens spaces for more transformative initiatives.

A framework that we have found to be useful is provided by Marquardt (1996), who identifies four different levels of learning: adaptive learning, anticipatory learning, deutero learning, and action learning. *Adaptive learning* occurs when an individual learns from experience and reflection, from doing something and then reflecting as to whether or not to continue doing the same thing. That is, the outcome is analyzed to determine if it is congruent with the goal, and a new action or modification of the previous action is initiated if the outcome was not what was intended. In this sort of learning, action precedes and follows reflection. *Anticipatory learning* occurs when an individual learns from anticipating the future. By envisioning the future and reflecting on what it means for a specific context, the individual can take action to deal with anticipated future events. In anticipatory learning, reflection is preceded by vision and followed by action. *Deutero learning* occurs when people learn from critically reflecting upon their taken-for-granted assumptions. In this form of learning, individuals try to understand what inhibits or impedes learning and then invent new strategies for taking action. *Action learning* involves working on real problems, focusing the learning acquired, and taking action on the solutions developed. Important in action learning is the skill of reframing, which allows the examination of taken-for-granted assumptions to move into an experimental action phase. In adaptive learning, the individual reacts to events, whereas in anticipatory, deutero, and action learning, there is a proactive stance. Although these levels may operate at different times in different circumstances, they are not necessarily exclusive. Instead, each type of learning depends on, builds from, and extends the others.

Our position here is that action learning, otherwise known as participatory action research or, more simply, action research (our preferred term), is a useful strategy for professional improvement because it holds the potential to blend all the other kinds of learning in pursuit of a new professional narrative. Action research captures the notion of disciplined inquiry (research) in the context of focused efforts to improve the quality of what occurs in the classroom, part of a school, or the school as a whole (action). It requires critical thinking and reflection, the collection of data, and the implementation of action plans, all of which are implicated in one way or another with the other three kinds of learning noted by Marquardt (1996) and with single- and double-loop learning noted by Argyris and Schon (1978). Furthermore, action research can be conducted in a variety of ways and by various actors. For example, one individual teacher might engage in research, collaborative research might be undertaken among educators or between educators and university faculty members, or a school-wide action research focus might be undertaken to deal with a school-wide problem. Each of these levels addresses different issues and problems. Together, they constitute a powerful program of disciplined inquiry that can lead to the resolution of difficult problems and the engagement with deep mysteries of teaching and learning.

Marquardt's (1996) types of learning correspond loosely with the plan-act-observe-reflect cycle of action research experimentation (Kemmis & McTaggart, 1988). Adaptive learning might take the form of a preliminary act-observe-act-observe cycle, deutero learning the form of an observe-reflect-observe-reflect cycle, anticipatory learning a plan-act-plan-act cycle, with action learning putting all the elements together into the familiar plan-act-observe-reflect-plan- cycle. This is a useful strategy for reconstructing professional narratives because it brings all the types of learning together in pursuit of more effective practice. The cycle might look something like this: When observation and critical reflection signal a need for some change in past practice, educators embark on an active search for underlying problematic assumptions and for new possibilities and practices (the planning or envisioning phase). They test the new ideas in their classroom or staff room (the action phase), track the outcomes of the experiment (observation and reflection phase), plan interventions to offset the negative outcomes and to bolster the positive ones (planning phase), and thereby embark again on the next round of plan-act-observe-reflect. This process entails an ongoing dialogue between practice and the effects of practice, whereby educators continually reframe their assumptions, belief systems, and actions as a consequence of deep critical reflection on the outcomes and warrants of directed experimentation, trial and error learning, and anticipatory envisioning.

When teachers and school administrators, as individuals, begin to reframe their belief systems and practices, it is exciting. But when this sort of reframing becomes a school-wide phenomenon, it is truly transformative. An example of this sort of transformation comes from an alternative secondary school that served high-risk students in an urban setting. For most of its existence as an alternative school, it had suffered from a poor reputation within the entire system. Many teachers regarded the school as an undesirable assignment and the students as unteachable. The usual practice of the board's supervisory council was to send in the newest administrators and teachers and to take a hands-off approach to the operations of the school. The poor reputation and the perceived lack of administrative concern had exacerbated the already difficult teaching and learning conditions within the school, and there was a deep sense of malaise and impotence among much of the teaching staff. Until Peggy arrived as a new principal, fresh from a 4-year stint as an assistant principal in a large secondary school in an affluent neighborhood – conditions unlike anything that she could expect in her new assignment.

Peggy had listened to the 'horror stories' told by current and former teachers of the alternative school and she had heard the rumors circulated by other teachers and administrators. After a few weeks in the school, she realized that the stories were much more horrific than the reality, that the school's bad reputation was not justified, and that the teachers needed some help in articulating a different story about the school. Peggy discovered that most of what was happening in the school was serving well many of the students who had been written off by other schools, but she also found some deep divisions and mixed understandings over the fundamental purposes and

operations of this kind of school. These problems, along with some ineffective procedures (most notably in the area of teaching assignments and behavior management),
had caused the staff to believe that they were doing less well than student outcomes
indicated they were. Peggy undertook to reframe some of the beliefs and attitudes
under which the teachers were laboring.

She spent the first few months in the school asking questions. She asked the
teachers how things were done, why they were done as they were, and how else they
could be done. She encouraged them to tell her about the successes that they and
their students had enjoyed, and she enlisted their participation in school-wide experiments with new practices. She found ways to bend rules and bypass procedures that
interfered with the success of specific students or teachers, and she encouraged
teachers to try out new rules or procedures, even if they looked suspicious or inefficient. These were small steps and in the early months were undertaken by only a few
of the teachers, but gradually the spirit of experimentation spread. By the end of the
first semester, the teachers were questioning some of the taken-for-granted practices
that had built up over time, and they told Peggy that they wanted some time to talk
about the purposes, programs, and philosophy for the school. They were ready for
action research.

To start the process, Peggy scheduled a retreat day for the teachers and enlisted
the services of a process facilitator who helped the staff to begin the discussion about
purposes and philosophy and to plan steps for writing new program requirements and
updated curricula. At the time of writing this book, Peggy and the staff were still in the
early stages of the action research project, but already the spirit in the school had
changed. As Peggy told us, 'There are some people on staff who have come alive. In
the last two weeks we have done more things with and for our kids than we did for
months. Doing all these things is only the half of it. We're doing them for all the right
reasons. We're trying things and actually saying out loud, "Well, if it doesn't work
we'll do it better next time."' No longer did the teachers apologize for being assigned
to this school, nor did they tell horror stories outside the school. They began to see
their school not as a dumping ground but as a lighthouse, and they started to exhibit
deep pride in the school, the students, and the new initiatives. They had reframed their
belief systems in relation to the school and the students, and a new energy swept
through the halls and classrooms.

In the case of this school, the teachers decided to undertake action research in
relation to programs and curriculum, but action research projects can entail any activity or project that is new for a particular individual or group. These new ideas can come
from many sources because there is a wealth of pedagogic knowledge available in the
educational domain if educators are able and willing to expand their networks into
unfamiliar educational territory. New ideas might include the implementation of new
instructional strategies, classroom configurations, playground activities, school-wide
activities or special events, parental visitations, materials and resources, curriculum
programs, instructional units, faculty professional development workshops, professional conversation topics or forums, or any other new or alternative engagement with
students, parents, and colleagues (Mitchell & Hyle, 1999). As these ideas are implemented, educators move through an iterative process of action and reflection, with
some knowledge gaps closing and others opening at each iteration of the cycle.

Capacity to promote student learning increases as teachers find alternative practices that are successful in improving student performance – and in improving the teacher's own professional performance.

The story of Peggy's school is instructive in another way. It demonstrates that action research (and school improvement) does not necessitate a complete break with the past. In our work with educators, we have been surprised to discover that, to many of them, calls for professional improvement automatically signify that they must sever their commitments to past practice. This is not our understanding, and we do not believe that such an outcome would be wise or helpful. Much of past practice is educationally sound and should not be discarded. Instead, it should be acknowledged, honored, and valued for its intrinsic efficacy. But it should also be examined critically and honestly in the light of desired educational goals and actual achieved outcomes. This sort of deep critique provides educators with a more solid foundation for claiming that they operate from 'warranted practice' (Richardson, 1990, p. 14). From this perspective, reconstructing professional narratives does not mean the end of all past practice. It means, instead, that educators engage in professional practice, past and new, from a thoughtful, critical, and empirically informed position.

Action research encourages and develops professionalism. It offers, on the one hand, a framework for recognizing ideals-in-action, and, on the other hand, 'a concrete procedure for translating evolving ideas into critically informed action and increasing harmony between educational ideas and educational action' (Kemmis & McTaggart, 1988, p. 7). The process allows teachers to experience problem solving and to model it for their students. Action research can revitalize the entire learning community – and it can aid educators in changing or reflecting on their classroom and staff room practices. It offers all participants in education a flexible approach to school development through critically informed action and reflection that is grounded in the real, complex, and often confusing circumstances and constraints of contemporary school life.

Facilitation of Knowledge Construction

The process of knowledge construction is, essentially, a process of learning. But that is only part of the equation. A second part, the process of teaching, is equally critical to the construction of knowledge. From a constructivist perspective, however, it is teaching with a difference. In the traditional view of learning, teaching is the process of transferring knowledge from one individual (the teacher) to another (the learner) or from the educational context (the school) to the practice context (the workplace). By contrast, the constructivist approach views teaching as an intervention in a continuous process of knowledge construction that is always contextually sensitive. Instructional practices from this perspective entail valuing and seeking the learner's point of view, structuring learning opportunities that will extend or challenge the learner's suppositions, offer curriculum and ideas that are relevant to the learners, and assess learning in the context of daily living. In other words, it is a process of facilitating the construction of knowledge rather than one of dispensing knowledge.

The traditional approach further assumes that knowledge, once acquired, is transportable and remains in immutable form across different contexts. What teachers have discovered, however, is that what works with one group of students or colleagues, or with one subject or topic of study, does not necessarily transfer directly to another group of students or colleagues or to another subject or topic. The constructivist approach recognizes the situated nature of learning, and it promotes a flexible instructional milieu that allows learning to emerge differently in different contexts and for different purposes. From this perspective, the transfer of learning is an organic process that emerges naturally from the sense-making activities of the individual learner.

For teachers in the classroom, the constructivist approach is relatively straightforward. It means that they provide opportunities for the students to explore phenomena, to speculate and predict, to share their thinking with others, and to revise their original thinking, *inter alia*. Constructivist classrooms are places where teachers do not depend upon the lecture approach as the dominant instructional strategy. Instead, it is a place where interactive strategies are prominent, where higher order thinking skills are evident, and where cooperative learning strategies are common. It is also a place where emphasis is upon authentic learning (Newmann & Wehlage, 1995). That is, it highlights knowledge and learning activities that address the real mysteries and challenges in the learner's world rather than esoteric knowledge or learning activities that have been designed elsewhere.

The matter is less straightforward for facilitating the construction of knowledge within a professional learning community. Although the strategies that might be used in the classroom can be instructive, the relationship between colleagues is fundamentally different from the relationship between teacher and student. Colleagues are peers. They are fellow professionals. They are not the primary responsibility of the instructor nor do they come to a learning episode *tabula rasa* (nor do students, by the way). Instead, they are autonomous adults who bring a wealth of knowledge and experience to the learning enterprise. They are not likely to take disingenuous suggestions or inappropriate instructions happily, nor are they likely to suffer inept facilitation gladly. This means that the facilitation process among peers is multi-layered, complex, and unpredictable.

The types of professional development to which educators have typically been subjected often fail to take any of these preconditions seriously. Instead, most professional development consists of one-shot workshops on programs and processes that have been developed outside the educators' context or of 'feel-good' talks by educational gurus who expound their ideas on the lecture circuit. These sorts of learning opportunities do not take into account the prior knowledge and experience of the audience, nor is the content necessarily positioned within a local context. Although the speakers may be enormously entertaining and the content terribly innovative and exciting, there is likely to be little professional learning taking place if there is a large disconnect between what is happening in the workshop or lecture and what happens in the daily lives of the educators. In such cases, considerable resources will have been expended on expensive speakers, with little return on the investment.

This sort of professional development fails to honor one piece of wisdom that has been generally accepted in relation to children. That is, that active engagement in learning usually leads to better retention, understanding, and active use of knowledge (Perkins, 1999). In order to transfer this wisdom to the realm of educators' learning, professional development must be contextually sensitive and it must engage the educators directly in some sort of active process. Even for ideas that are brought in from outside, there needs to be time built in for educators to think about the ideas in relation to their own contexts and to experiment with the ideas in relation to their own problems of practice or professional mysteries. Educators always construct their own knowledge, regardless of what sorts of learning opportunities are being offered. What we are advocating here is that facilitators who offer formal professional development should understand this point, honor the existing knowledge of the audience, and find ways to bring the educators' worlds into the discussion from the outset.

One of the finest examples of how this can take place occurred in relation to the infusion of a technology-based language arts and science curriculum in several elementary classrooms in Ontario. The curriculum had been developed in another country and was being brought to Ontario by the educational branch of a public television station. Costs for professional development were shared by the curriculum consortium and the television station. The learning opportunities consisted of 5 full-day workshops with all teachers, the school administrators, and the developers of the program, three days at the beginning of the year and two mid-way through the year. The facilitators began each of the workshops with a round-table discussion about the teachers' content knowledge and pedagogic understandings and assumptions. They then showed how this knowledge base articulated with the philosophy, pedagogy, and content of the curriculum. From that foundation, they began to engage the teachers in some of the actual activities that comprised the curriculum. Following the first three-day workshop, the facilitators kept in close touch with the teachers through fax, telephone, and e-mail connections and were readily available to answer questions or to offer suggestions. Furthermore, the teachers involved in the project were connected to one another through the same means, and many of them contacted one another frequently throughout the year to sort out issues or to share stories. At the mid-year workshop, the sessions began with the teachers' stories about their own experiments, their successes, and their failures. They shared examples of what had worked and what had not, they shared some innovative solutions that they had discovered, and they shared the ways in which the students were responding to the curriculum. The program developers then led them in another round of critical reflection and advance planning.

This was professional development at its finest. The content and activities were explicitly connected to the teachers' professional knowledge base and instructional repertoire, they were embedded in the daily activities of the classroom, and they pushed the teachers beyond 'past practice' to a reconsideration of what constituted good teaching and learning. Furthermore, the relationships that developed among the teachers and with the external facilitators encouraged the creation of a learning community within which the teachers had considerable support and encouragement to experiment. This kind of professional development moved far beyond the typical lecture or 'training-and-coaching' model (Little, 1993) into a mode of discourse that encouraged and advanced the analytic, critical, and reflective skills of the professional staff. It provided a mechanism by which these educators began to reconstruct their knowledge base. Nor should the long-term engagement be overlooked. The reconstructive elements came later in the year and only after intensive and critical reflections about the experience.

One important lesson is that this professional development enterprise was labor-, time-, and resource-intensive. These costs cannot be ignored when the advancement of professional knowledge is at stake. The sorts of discourse, collaborative learning, and reconstructed knowledge that grew out of this experience are not supported by 'P. D. days' that are planned in isolation from the educators' normal world of work or that are carried out after school or on Saturday. A serious commitment to professional learning means that it is not seen a 'sacrifice' or as an incidental part of professional activity. Rather, it is directly and explicitly linked to the daily work of educators and it is grounded in the contexts within which they conduct that work. Only when that kind of time, attention, and commitment is paid to the professional learning of educators is profound improvement likely to happen.

Formal, planned professional development, however, makes up only a part of the professional learning milieu. Unplanned, informal learning takes place on a day-to-day basis and is much more difficult to get a handle on than the planned aspects. Louis, Toole, and Hargreaves (1999), for example, contend that unplanned learning accounts for a large part of school development but that 'we know little about when or how unplanned but productive change occurs' (p. 258). This indicates a need for specific attention to be paid to this sort of ad hoc and in situ learning. That is, the facilitation of knowledge construction includes attention to the part of school development that is not subject to planned intervention. It pays attention to the changes that are initiated internally, from the desire of individuals and groups to make certain changes, to solve certain problems, or to address certain mysteries. Change happens organically, as the character and culture of the organization shift in response to unplanned, daily learning. From our perspective, this means that the facilitation of knowledge construction is an integral part of how work is done in a school and it is deeply embedded in the daily interactions of the professional staff.

This kind of embedded facilitation is found in Peggy's story, told earlier in this chapter. Peggy asked questions that pushed teachers to reconsider their professional narratives, but she did it in a way that acknowledged and honored their individual and collective histories and their professional knowledge bases. She never implied that she had better ideas or that she was there to teach them the 'right' way. Instead, she opened spaces for them to think deeply and critically about what they were doing, what the consequences were, and what else they might do. When they indicated a readiness for direct action, she freed up school time, brought in an expert process facilitator, and found money for additional resources. In this instance, Peggy's administrative practices gave the teachers freedom to identify problem areas and to come up with directions for future action. It empowered them to direct school improvement and to structure professional development in ways that made sense for themselves and their school. In this case, Peggy did not approach her facilitation tasks from a typical instructor's perspective. Instead, she facilitated the construction of professional knowledge by the conditions that she created in the school. This, of course, is a major leadership role, even though it has not enjoyed as prominent a position in leadership literature as have the more traditional approaches to leadership.

The sorts of unplanned learning that emerged in Peggy's school are only some of the forms that unplanned learning can take. It might, for example, be an individual teacher trying out some new instructional strategy or classroom management technique.

It might be groups of educators engaging in informal professional conversations in the staff room or visiting one another's classrooms. It might be administrators talking about perplexing conditions in their respective schools or bringing teachers together to think through the perplexities. It might take the form of mentoring or peer coaching or any other mechanism by which teachers share knowledge and ideas. Regardless of how and by whom unplanned learning is initiated or how it unfolds, it is a powerful mechanism for constructing professional knowledge. As with planned learning, conditions need to be in place that honor and extend existing professional knowledge, that provide opportunities for educators to deconstruct their narratives, and that situate new ideas in the local context. Together, unplanned learning, planned efforts, and unanticipated events (Louis et al., 1999) form a professional development milieu that can yield reconstructed professional narratives and lead to profound improvement in teaching and learning.

The process of knowledge construction entails a transition from familiar terrain to new territory. Managing transitions is a topic that is gaining some currency in management literature (e.g., Bridges, 1997) but that has typically been ignored in educational circles. The typical practice in education is to see innovations as the salvation of the school or the solution to all educational woes. Such views imply that everything that has been done in the past is now wrong. But the past has not been wrong. It has been useful in many ways and under many conditions. The trick is to celebrate the past and to manage the transition with dignity and respect for what has gone on before. Facilitation of knowledge construction means honoring past successes as much as it means infusing new ideas. It also means, however, that some past practices will need to be lost, and this is likely to usher in a period of grief. Facilitation of knowledge construction, then, also means acknowledging the losses openly and sympathetically. This implies a constant interplay and mutual influence between the familiar and the novel, as new information is assimilated and old information is transformed. Cognition is always situated in specific contexts and histories, and 'understanding is intertwined with specific physical and social situations' (Firestone, 1996, p. 212). From this perspective, innovations are better positioned as developments that build on the past and that help to realize the potential of former practices rather than as a complete break with the past.

Reconstruction of the Professional Narrative: A Synthesis

For quite some time now, educational scholars have noted the link between teacher learning and school improvement, and this has placed professional development at the top of the agenda of many educational reform initiatives (Scribner, 1999). But scholars have likewise noted that professional development opportunities do not automatically translate into improved professional practice or enhanced teacher learning. Scribner, for example, argues that work conditions and the work context deeply affect teachers' motivations for, perceptions of, and experiences with professional learning. Our own work has indicated that political and socio-cultural conditions in the school and in the larger educational community also affect professional learning (Mitchell, 1999a; Mitchell & Sackney, 1998). We have found that negotiating the reconstruction of a professional narrative can be personally disconcerting and psychologically threatening. We have also found, however, that those who have negotiated the process successfully can show clear evidence of the ways in which their own learning has enhanced the learning of their colleagues and of their students. They work from a thoughtful, critical, informed position of warranted practice, and they speak with a clearer voice and greater conviction about the efficacy of their practices. The stories of these teachers (and our own observations) have convinced us that time and resources devoted to professional learning are time and resources well spent.

The sorts of professional learning that lead to reconstructed professional narratives and profound improvement derive from a capacity-building model rather than a deficit model. According to Darling-Hammond and McLaughlin (1996), most professional development policies and practices assume that teachers are deficient in some way and that they need to be 'fixed' in the direction being promoted by some professional development program. When professional development emanates from this assumption, knowledge gaps are assumed to reflect a weakness or a flaw in the individual. This is a threatening and disrespectful assumption that discounts prior knowledge and devalues the person. Under such conditions, teachers are likely to resist the ideas or to defend themselves against disrespectful and unwarranted intrusions into their professional practice. Teachers are resourceful, and most of them welcome constructive help and suggestions for improvement, but if their voices are marginalized or ignored, then their worth is devalued, and resistance is likely (Gitlin & Margonis, 1995; Roemer, 1991). Wignall (1996) notes that teachers often feel overloaded not so much by the changes in their programs or by new ideas but by the introduction of pedagogical approaches and methods of evaluation that minimize the role of the teacher, that are implemented without adequate support or training, or that are inappropriate for a particular educational context. Wignall argues that, within such an environment, the work of the teacher enlarges and intensifies, but the job of the teacher becomes more routinized and deskilled. This is more likely to lead to disillusioned and unhappy teachers than to reconstructed professional narratives or profound improvement.

A capacity-building model operates from different assumptions and situates prior knowledge differently. In this model, educators are assumed to have a wealth of information and professional knowledge upon which to build. Further, they are assumed to have considerable expertise in their own area of practice, and new ideas are there to extend and enhance rather than 'fix' their practice (Darling-Hammond & McLaughlin, 1996). Knowledge gaps are assumed to be natural and desirable aspects of a living professional narrative – natural because they are always and already part of everyone's knowledge base, and desirable because they constitute areas for professional growth. These embedded assumptions respect the person and honor and value the professional expertise of the educators.

From such assumptions, a capacity-building model gives educators voice and visibility in the process. It affords spaces for them to take up the challenge 'not just to transform practice, but to restructure basic assumptions about learning and learners' (Conley, 1993, p. 150). From our perspective, this means that all the various elements of a professional narrative are up for grabs. Figure 3.1 presents a diagram of how the reconstruction of the professional narrative might unfold. The process of knowledge construction is situated within a particular context that, at some point in time, is expected to trigger a need or desire for critical reflection. The process of reflection leads to the identification of knowledge gaps that are addressed through action research. This action phase yields information on those aspects of the professional narrative that deserve to be retained and those that should be reframed. The process of active retaining and reframing increases the individual's personal professional capacity and yields a reconstructed professional narrative. This process flows through cycles and iterations of planned and unplanned learning, supported by embedded facilitation and respectful transition management. Through continuous dialogue between practice and the effects of practice, between prior knowledge and new learning, and between and among educators from many levels of the educational community, educators determine what elements of the deconstructed narrative deserve to be honored and what need to be changed. It is an ongoing process of continuous dialogue and continuous transformation and innovation.

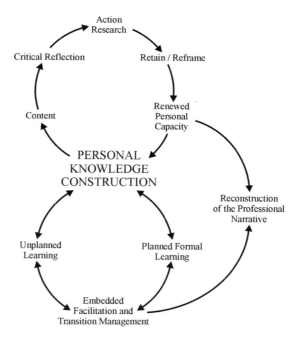

Figure 3.1. Reconstruction of personal professional knowledge.

This model should not be read as implying that there are no limits to personal professional capacity. There are, in fact, many things that each of us cannot do, or at least cannot do well or willingly. Coral, for example, cannot remove the mice and squirrels from her attic or basement. Larry cannot swim for any distance. These limits, of course, have little to do with teaching and learning, but they serve as warnings that there will always be certain limits to each individual's professional repertoire, and these limits will always place certain restrictions around professional learning. The model that we have provided should not be used to lay blame or to shame anyone into doing things that are completely alien to their learning styles or personal capacities.

Professional narratives frame the context of the learning and the knowledge base, and reconstructing the professional narrative enables educators to enhance teaching and learning – for themselves and for their students. Teaching and learning are closely interconnected, and we agree with Wineburg and Grossman (1998) that 'schools cannot become exciting places for children until they first become exciting places for adults' (p. 350). This excitement is what brings heart, passion, and emotion into schools and classrooms. People get passionate about their own ideas, about what they hold near and dear to themselves. The trick of reconstructing knowledge is to find areas of passion and then to move deeper into those areas. People get to areas of passion by deconstructing and reconstructing their professional knowledge. In this way, 'knowledge is not so much an external object for possession as it is a web of connections actively and continually reconstructed by the individual to form a fabric of internalized meaning' (Prestine & LeGrand, 1991, p. 67). From this perspective, knowledge construction happens when the passion kicks in. Without passion, life and learning are routine and sterile; with passion, they are exciting and meaningful, and knowledge is not simply accumulated but also transformed.

4

Interpersonal Capacity: Building the Learning Community Climate

The focus in this chapter shifts from the individual to the group. From this perspective, learning takes place in and through interactions with and between a number of people who operate as a community of learners. Learning, in this light, is a collective process (Swieringa & Wierdsma, 1992) that is influenced over time by the context within which people work. One of the contextual influences, for example, will be the sets of expectations that students, teachers, administrators, and parents have for professional practice and learning. What this signifies is that the construction of professional knowledge is no longer the solitary pursuit of one individual. Instead, it is a heavily contested process of negotiation among different people with different knowledge bases, different histories, different hopes and aspirations, different personal styles and emotions, and different desires and needs. Under these conditions, the climate within which people work becomes a concern of deep importance.

Over time, educators (and others) internalize the expectations that people have of them and the norms that have developed within the school. The process of internalization leads to routinized behaviors, as educators come to accept the familiar as the correct way of behaving. But as Albert Einstein once observed, 'No problem can be solved from the same consciousness that created it; we must learn to see the world anew.' That is, learning needs to be manifested through changed cognition as much as through changed behavior. Changing cognition and behavior in groups is similar to changing individual cognition and behavior: It is a dynamic process that moves in cycles with periods of activity followed by periods of inactivity. As with individuals, there may be times when no learning appears to be going on. These are times for consolidation and integration of the ideas that group members have been experimenting with in previous growth cycles.

The idea of collective learning has caused us some definitional angst. The term is a convenient shorthand form for describing the ways in which group dynamics influence human learning processes. But this is not to suggest that groups learn. They do not. People learn. Groups, however, shape the environment within which the people learn. That environment may facilitate learning or it may not. In either case, it certainly has a huge impact on how the people approach learning opportunities or how they engage in learning tasks. The group can support the learning, it can sustain the learning, it can engage the learning, but it cannot learn. The group provides some scaffolds (or shared understandings) for individual learning and directs it toward goals and purposes that are shared by the members of the group. And the creation of shared goals, purposes, and understandings can only happen through a group process. Collective learning, from our perspective, is a process of mutual influences and mutual learning that transpires in a group context and that is shaped by group norms, expectations, interactions, knowledge bases, communication patterns, and so on.

What we are talking about here is the climate within which learning (individual and collective) occurs. In a learning community, where individual and collective learning are deeply embedded in one another, contradictions and paradoxes (Swieringa & Wierdsma, 1992) are welcome. Conflict is seen as a challenge to be met rather than as a condition to be avoided. What is important is not so much the solution to any given problem, but consensus about how the problem should be solved. The learning arises from solving the problem, and different solutions to the same problem can be found in different contexts and with different group members. The process of learning also includes an element of unlearning. This too is a difficult process because so much emotional energy is tied up with what is known and valued. Emotions and heart come into play when people are in a position to learn something new. They may not be certain that they will be able to master the new way of doing something, nor may they be sure that the new approach is better. The contested nature of learning, then, implies that certain conditions need to be part of the school culture. This chapter explores two of these conditions: the affective climate and the cognitive climate.

Building the Affective Climate

Building an affective climate entails valuing the contributions of colleagues (affirmation) and inviting them to be participants (invitation). These are two of the elements of a growth-promoting affective climate. The first element, affirmation, does not imply agreement. People can disagree radically on a host of issues, but affirmation means that, even in the face of deep disagreement, they still acknowledge the values of others' opinions, ideas, or contributions. As one teacher told us, 'You need to know you can speak and will be heard. You need to feel that you are respected and that what you say is valued. The person does not have to agree with you. What is important is that they value what you have to say.' When teachers' ideas are given consideration, it affirms them as professionals. This kind of affirmation is an important contributor to their learning and to their participation in school life.

In our experience, when teachers' ideas are not affirmed, they tend not to be active participants in the life of the school. Jerry's case is an example of what happens when affirmation is missing from collective processes. Jerry taught Grades 7 to 9 students in a rural kindergarten-to-secondary school that appeared to be in somewhat of a holding pattern. It was not a 'moving' school nor could it be considered a 'stuck' school (Rosenholtz, 1989). Two female elementary teachers and three male secondary teachers wielded considerable influence over school directions and decisions, and these individuals controlled staff room conversations whenever they were present. As a consequence, the ultimate decisions always reflected the input and the wishes of this powerful cabal, and other teachers usually went along with what these people wanted. Other teachers did not challenge the status quo nor did they try to present alternative perspectives. Jerry was not part of the powerful group. In an interview with us, he said, 'Yes, I don't say much in our staff meetings. I've learned that others do not give my opinions credence. They either ignore my comments or cut me off when I speak. As a result, I've learned to keep quiet during our meetings.' Jerry did not feel valued or respected for his ideas. On the other hand, consider this response from Pat, who was an active participant in the same school: 'When you know your input matters, then it's worth spending the extra time – knowing that it's going to be appreciated in the end.' Pat felt affirmed by his participation; Jerry did not. Pat was actively engaged in school decision-making processes; Jerry was not. His case is not atypical. We have observed many schools where particular teachers are marginalized. We noticed that the devaluing process occurs in several ways. Their opinions are ignored, others interrupt them, and their suggestions are not given due consideration. Consequently, these teachers tend to speak less frequently and make fewer contributions.

Yet marginalization does not need to go unchecked. In one project on developing the school as a learning community, we spent considerable time discussing with staff members the sorts of conditions that they each needed in order to feel comfortable enough to take part in collective processes. These discussions often centered on ways in which they had been affirmed or not affirmed by their colleagues. Gradually, collective processes evolved in some interesting ways. We found that the discussions were causing people to think differently about their colleagues and to begin listening intently to what they had to say. In this way, the individuals who had originally been marginalized were accorded more input into school decision-making processes. This change took place after the more dominant educators began to realize that their own behaviors had limited the input of others. As one teacher commented, 'I began to notice that I talk a lot and do not listen well. I've learned to be a better listener so that I really understand what the other person is trying to say. I've also learned to include others in the discussion and to interrupt less often. I still catch myself on occasion, but I'm getting better at affirming others.'

This story demonstrates that professional affirmation does not happen by accident. Rather, educators need to encourage and affirm individuals who might be new to the school, who might be shy, or who tend to be intimidated by others. On every staff there will always be people whose sense of self-efficacy is not high. They are likely to need extraordinary or persistent affirmation. Even in cases where the sense of efficacy is initially high, however, affirmation or the lack thereof can seriously affect self-concept. This can be seen, for example, in the ways that senior teachers respond to beginning teachers. In Jerry's school, we met a new teacher who was trying to make a contribution in the school. He came with new and interesting ideas that he had learned in his teacher education courses and shared some of these ideas at one of his first staff meetings. A senior teacher told him, 'You haven't been in the school long enough to speak on school matters. Once you've been here for a few years, you will then be in a position to comment on issues.' Needless to say, he learned quickly not to speak in group meetings. Because he kept his ideas to himself, learning was stifled for himself and for all of his colleagues. This teacher's experience is reminiscent of Hargreaves' (1993) observation: 'If most teachers in a school prefer solitude, this is probably indicative of a problem with the system – of individualism representing a withdrawal from threatening, unpleasant, or unrewarding personal relationships' (p. 73). In this school, lack of engagement was directly connected to systemic conditions rather than to personal desires.

Affirmation is only one element of the affective climate. A second element is invitation, whereby individuals are explicitly asked to participate. Teachers, students, and parents will more readily join others when they are invited, when colleagues make sincere efforts to draw them into discussions or into collaborative practices. Some people may be reluctant to speak up because they think that the issue under discussion is really someone else's concern, and most people are reluctant to intrude into the domains of others. In such cases, they need to be specifically invited into the conversation. Over and over we have seen the value that comes from explicit invitations. As a teacher commented, 'If you're approached, then you feel valuable and consequently you feel empowered and what you're saying is worthwhile.' Similarly, another teacher told us, 'I've even had the principal call me a couple of times about issues, and that makes me feel good. It makes me feel good that he felt that I was a person that he could talk to and ask me about this.' In both cases, these individuals were quiet, relatively passive teachers who tended not to insert themselves into collective processes. Only when the principal or other key opinion leaders asked them to participate did they share their thoughts or ideas. Interestingly, they often presented an idea that was substantially different from the more typical ideas, and their participation was helpful in moving collective learning into unfamiliar terrain.

An affective climate does not discourage diversity. In our work with teachers, we found that as they began to value one another, so they began to contribute more fully to what took place in the school. For example, one of the teachers in our learning community project commented, 'You saw it was everybody's style and you didn't think, Oh gee, I'm not doing anything like that in my classroom. I'm not going to say what I'm doing.' Because the educators in this school recognized and valued diversity, this teacher felt comfortable sharing her ideas, some of which were quite different from what she had been hearing in group deliberations. She trusted her colleagues not to belittle or discount her contributions. Her story demonstrates the clear importance of establishing a trusting relationship because where trust is lacking, it is unlikely that people will share different ideas and consequently it is unlikely that learning will occur.

Obviously, then, trust is a necessary element for building a learning community. Walker, Shakotko, and Pullman (1998) have this to say about trust:

As . . . people work to sustain healthy practice and build new ways of learning and relating to one another, it does not take long for the subject of trust or trustworthiness to enter the conversation. At the very least, the importance and pervasiveness of trust (or its betrayal or absence) are implicit in our every effort to establish communities of learners and the generative setting for the expression of our shared educational ambitions. (p. 2)

According to these authors, trust is a required element for generating communities of learners. But trust is a tricky thing to define. In general, we say we trust people when they have our best interests at heart and we can depend on them to come through for us. Hoffman, Sabo, Bliss, and Hoy (1994) define trust as 'a general confidence and overall optimism in occurring events; it is believing in others in the absence of compelling reasons to disbelieve' (p. 486). Most definitions of trust seem to imply that people can be depended on to do what they say they will do. Walker et al. (1998), for example, contend that there are many dimensions to trust: integrity, honesty, truthfulness, competence, consistency, reliability, predictability, good judgment, loyalty, openness, sharing, and concern. According to them, definitions of trust can be distinguished between impersonal trust (contextual and other features) and interpersonal or human-to-human trust. From their perspective, trust has three dimensions: the trusting relationship between individuals, the trust between the individual and the organization, and the trust in events or processes.

In schools, teachers need to trust their colleagues and the principal. They need to feel that they can rely on other people for support and assistance when required. For example, in a study of a secondary school, Tartar, Sabo, and Hoy (1989) found that supportive principal leadership helped to create a culture of trust. However, it was the level of trust among colleagues that best determined the effectiveness of the school. What was most important if the school was to move forward was the advocacy of sound ideas in a climate of trust. These authors contend that 'the sources of the ideas is less important than their critical acceptance and trial by teachers in a supportive environment of openness and trust' (p. 299). What the research on trust seems to imply is that teachers need to be able to depend on their colleagues and principal in novel and difficult situations. In other words, trust is especially necessary when the risks are high.

This signifies that trust is a critical factor in bringing profound improvement to a school. Without trust, people divert their energy into self-protection and away from learning. Where trust is lacking, people will not take the risks necessary to move the school forward. Without trust, communication tends to be distorted, making it more difficult to solve problems or to confront deep mysteries. People are less likely to openly state how they feel about a particular situation, nor will they take the leadership necessary to address difficult conditions. When distrust pervades a school culture, it is unlikely that the school will be an energetic, motivating place. Instead, a culture of self-preservation and isolation is likely to pervade the school.

These conditions are just what we found in a study of school effectiveness. In that project, we found ourselves in a school that had a low level of trust among the staff and administration (Sackney, Walker, & Hajnal 1998). This school had been designated as an unsuccessful school according to a number of objective and self-report measures. We went to the school to conduct a series of in-depth interviews in order to get a better understanding of the environment in the school and to explore the reasons why the school would have received such a scathing evaluation from the professional staff. When we entered the school and walked by the staff lounge, we noticed a large sign on the staff room door. It read: 'No shop talk in the staff room.' Staff tended to work alone, the teachers covered the glass panels on the classroom door, and few teachers taught with the door open. Teachers and students alike noted that the teaching was not particularly exciting. In the first interview with a teacher, her opening question to us was, 'Why are you in this school? We know we're not an effective school. We do not work well together. We tend to keep to ourselves and do our own thing. This is not an exciting school.' Upon completion of the data collection, we found that over 75% of the staff did not trust their colleagues. That same attitude seemed to pervade the community and school board relations with the school. In fact, one teacher confided to us that the school staff did not trust the community, and the community did not trust the school staff. We found this school to be a depressing place. As we left the school, one of us said, 'Can you imagine working in this school? It must be difficult to get up each morning and go to work.' Needless to say, we did not find this school to be a model of learning (either for students or for educators).

In other schools, we have found trust to be displayed somewhat differently. In one school, for example, the teachers were divided along gender and grade level lines. The women, who taught at the elementary level, tended to meet in the school staff room while the men, who taught secondary, congregated in a small room near the principal's office or wandered into the office area. The principal (a man) tried to offset the gender differentiation by spending some of his free time in the women's room, but his efforts were not perceived by the women to be inclusive or equalizing. In our conversations with the professional staff, we noted a perceived lack of trust and care. The women felt that the men had greater access to the school resources and to decision-making processes. They attributed this to a perception that the principal paid greater attention to the secondary program than to the elementary. In essence, many of these women felt marginalized and disempowered. The staff did not display any of the characteristics of a professional community (Louis & Kruse, 1995). On the other hand, we have also experienced schools where the trust level was high. In these schools, teachers enjoyed each other's company and supported one another. We have seen people who had fun with one another, who enjoyed working together, and who shared a sense of purpose. In these schools, we sensed a feeling of pride, enthusiasm, and accomplishment.

Trust, however, is fragile. It is like any other moral resource in that it can be enhanced or diminished. It is difficult, for example, to respond in a fashion that will make everyone happy, and educators can easily misinterpret a colleague's good intentions. Furthermore, leadership often entails making choices in response to multiple and sometimes conflicting demands, and teachers may lose trust in the principal when the dominant demand does not address their current needs. Without trust, a true sense of community cannot be developed, nor can a collaborative culture exist. Under such conditions, people will cooperate only under a system of formal rules and regulations. In essence, the lack of trust is likely to yield a more bureaucratic school where administrators rely on rules and standard procedures for compliance and cooperation. The less trust, the less likely that learning will occur because community building is difficult, if not impossible, in a bureaucratized environment. People in such environments tend to do the minimum necessary to comply with the institutional demands. Schools just do not function well in this kind of climate.

It takes time and effort to develop trust, but it is not an impossible task. It requires, *inter alia*, honesty and competence (Kouzes & Posner, 1995). Principals, if they are to gain the trust of the people with whom they work, need to know the hopes, aspirations, and desires of individual staff members. And they need to share openly their own desires for the school. This positions them well to gain the confidence of colleagues, students, and parents. That is, principals need to 'walk the talk' rather than 'talk the talk' if they are to sustain and enhance the trust level in their school. Principals can further enhance the trust level by trusting others, by establishing good relationships with all staff members, by working towards a shared sense of vision and mission, and by showing that they care and support the staff. This is not to imply, however, that the responsibility for creating an environment of trust lies exclusively with the school administrators. The same attributes and conditions apply to teacher relationships with colleagues, students, and parents. Establishing trust is the responsibility of everyone in the school community.

Smylie and Hart (1999, p. 423) position trust as an element of social capital. From their perspective, trust creates a context for predictability, stability, assurance, and safety. These conditions can either support reflective conversation and professional learning or they can inhibit innovative action by keeping individuals satisfied with the status quo. This means that trust might not lead to professional learning and improved professional practice. While we acknowledge this possibility, we view trust as a necessary element in taking the risks that lead to innovation and change. That is, trust is a key ingredient to developing a learning community. Only with trust do people allow others into their minds and hearts. Only with trust do people have a reason to engage in learning with another person or group of persons. This is as true for teachers as it is for students. Louis and Kruse (1995), for example, found that professional communities were characterized by high levels of trust among stakeholder groups and by high levels of innovation and support for learning and personal growth. From our perspective, this implies that trusting relationships lie at the heart of a learning community; learning communities cannot exist without commitment, collaboration, and collegiality, all of which are supported by trust among the members.

The affective climate is also influenced by the degree of caring among individuals. Schools are places where there is persistent and pervasive human interaction, and a sense of caring can sustain individual and group efforts. Noddings (1992), for example, contends that schools should be defined as centers of care and that caring themes should permeate every aspect of school life from relationships and organization to curriculum and instruction. Beck (1994) has similarly argued that caring promotes human development and responds to human needs. From our perspective, caring carries with it a sense of openness, honesty, and flexibility. It means giving people voice and inviting them into caring relationships. A sense of community emerges when individuals care about what happens to one another (Whitney, 1995, p. 201). Our position is that no one will perform well in a school where a caring environment is lacking. This was evident in Jerry's school and in the school where the men and women were deeply divided. In these schools, the teachers worked alone and cooperated only to the extent necessary to keep school operations in motion. But a healthy environment for learning did not exist, and student achievement was diminished.

The affective climate deals specifically with the development of human relationships, for it is in community that people feel connected, value others, and are valued by others. It is community that provides the connections, affections, and obligations that bind individuals together. To be a learning community means to be a community of relationships, for it is through relationships and connections that people learn. As educators learn to work with one another, so they become more confident in expressing their ideas. As trust levels increase, participation in collective processes also increases. Where trust levels are not high, sensitive issues and conflict are avoided. But in a healthy affective climate, people understand that conflict is inevitable, that it is an essential and necessary process towards growth and understanding. Affirmation, invitation, trust, caring, and relationships: these are the elements that contribute to the affective climate for a learning community.

Building the Cognitive Climate

Once the affective conditions are in place, educators can turn their attention to the cognitive elements of a learning community. But just as one cannot assume the existence of a healthy affective climate, one also cannot assume the existence of a healthy cognitive climate. Rather, explicit attention needs to be paid to the conditions and processes that engage individual and collective cognition. The collective nature of a learning community signifies to us that the cognitive climate is deeply influenced by social constructivism, an outgrowth of constructivist notions of learning.

Constructivism positions learning not as a process of knowledge absorption but as a process of knowledge construction. *Social* constructivism positions learning as a process of negotiation among the individuals in a learning community (a school, a staff, or any other group of people who engage together in a learning enterprise). What this means is that individual learning is rooted in the society and culture within which the individual learns. In other words, learning is deeply influenced by the dominant metaphors and implicit understandings that are shared by members of the community. This is an inside-out view of human growth and development because concepts, rather than being external facts waiting to be discovered, are embedded in the implicit assumptions and belief systems of the culture. Prawat and Peterson (1999), for example, argue that 'facts do not force themselves upon us but are constructed in the process of developing and testing out concepts and ideas' (p. 204). They contend that concepts and ideas must pass both an individual and a social test.

In a learning community, social constructivism implies that everyone has the opportunity to verify, modify, or discard ideas but that the community ultimately decides which ideas are worth keeping and which ought to be discarded. In Prawat and Peterson's (1999) view, communities may resist new ideas, preferring instead to rely on familiar (*ergo* correct) understandings. By contrast, 'a vibrant learning community is hungry for new ideas; it eagerly embraces them and quickly seeks to determine how deeply and widely they illuminate things about which the community cares' (p. 219). They see the community doing this in two ways: through apprenticeship learning and through idea-based knowledge construction. In apprenticeship learning, novices work closely with expert mentors and learn new concepts and skills in a real-world setting. In idea-based knowledge construction, community members (novice and expert alike) test out ideas in the community and hammer out a set of shared anticipations and understandings. From our perspective, both of these strategies are useful for under-standing how knowledge is constructed in a school. This is as true for educators' learning as it is for students' learning.

What this means for educators is that ideas about learning, teaching, students, curriculum, and assessment have to be negotiated with other members of the community – with colleagues, administrators, students, parents, and other interested parties. It is naïve to think that an educator can or should implement initiatives that are not supported by the community or that have not been negotiated with community members. Ben, a principal in an urban elementary school, demonstrated just such naivete, with some rather troubling consequences. Ben had decided to implement an integrated teaching method that combined out-of-school experience, collaborative learning, blocked time-tabling, and project-based classroom activities. However, he did not test his ideas with parents and other community members before putting them into action. He truly believed that his approach was in the best interests of the students and that parents and other teachers would 'see the light' once they began to see the effects on student learning. But parents did not see the light. They were angry that they had not been consulted and that their children were, from their perspective, being used as 'guinea pigs' for a new and virtually untested program. They threatened to remove their children from the school, and the story hit the local media. In the face of extreme controversy, Ben still did not engage the parents in authentic dialogue. Instead, he continued to insist that the new program was worth pursuing, and at the time of writing this book, he remained under fire from parent groups and the media. In this case, the process of idea verification (Prawat & Peterson, 1999, p. 222) did not take place, and an idea that may have benefited student learning was in jeopardy.

In a learning community, the social construction of knowledge is expected to emphasize authentic learning. Newmann and Wehlage (1995) identify authentic learning as that which is intimately and directly connected to the real lives of students and educators that occur outside the school walls and that validates and enables the unique learning styles of individual learners. From the perspective of professional learning, this means that educators will be most engaged by learning opportunities and collegial interactions that address the real problems and mysteries that they regularly face in their classrooms and/or staff rooms. Authentic learning also implies a collaborative base because people do not live alone in the world. Because individuals are always and already in relationships, authentic learning acknowledges and honors the character of the relationships, and it positions learning within a relational milieu. As Prawat and Peterson (1999) argue, 'novices often learn as much from one another as they do from the master craftsman. Collaborative learning is the norm rather than the exception' (p. 206). What this implies is that discourse and dialogue promote concept development and professional learning as much as (and perhaps more than) direct instruction does.

Education is an ill-structured domain, where students vary in their capacity to learn, where teachers vary in their capacity to engage student learning, and where administrators vary in their capacity to facilitate teaching and learning. It is ill-structured in relation to educational goals, pedagogic understandings, and educational knowledge bases (Shulman, 1987). What is needed, therefore, is a context-sensitive and situation-sensitive schema that allows knowledge to be used in different ways for different situations. This is the type of condition that aligns with postmodern understandings. For example, Starratt (1996) argues that postmodernity implies multiple understandings because of the centrality of the individual. He contends that the practice of teaching should be involved in the creation of spaces for the development of understanding rather than the transmission of the 'best' understanding:

> Within the postmodern mood we discover a series of insights concerning the nature of knowledge as a social and cultural construct, the understanding of learning as involving the learner in knowledge production, the understanding of learning as inescapably involving the self's own narrative, the relation of learning to self-realization and self-creation, the relationship of learning to communities of language and communities of memory, and hence to the meta-narratives of communities. (p. 53)

This rather eloquent statement confirms the importance of context and the social nature of learning. It signals that situated knowledge will be recast 'in a new, more densely textured form' (Brown et al., 1989, p. 33) than knowledge that is divorced from a real-world context. From this perspective, one of the desirable characteristics of socially constructed knowledge is that there is a full range of learning opportunities and a diverse set of learning outcomes.

Even though responsibility for learning is shared by all members of a community, the school administrator plays a key role in the process, at least insofar as most schools are currently constructed. For these individuals, social constructivist theory means 'encouraging members of the organization to learn and develop, realizing that that goal is apt to be met when members of the organization work together to make it happen' (Prawat & Peterson, 1999, p. 223). In particular, administrators are in a position to nurture the school arrangements that enable learning to occur. Administrators, who are often structurally separated from the classroom context, need to keep in mind that the practice of education is about learning, about knowledge, and about finding oneself in community, but mostly it is about how children make sense of the world (p. 224). Our position is that the administrators should be actively engaged in creating social arrangements that enable the creation, use, and evaluation of knowledge for students and for teachers.

Social constructivism is the premise that underlies several strategies that foster and enhance collective learning. One strategy that we have discussed earlier in this book is that of reflective practice, but that discussion was primarily concerned with individual reflection. From a social constructivist perspective, reflective practice moves beyond the individual to the group. From this perspective, collective reflection and professional conversation is necessary if teachers are to challenge their own practices, habits, beliefs, and assumptions. That is, it is only as teachers engage in critical discourse with colleagues that they begin to confront and to challenge their assumptions and beliefs, to understand how and what they learn, and to apply their knowledge in novel ways and in novel situations.

Learning communities exist where educators think together about professional practice. It is a mindful consideration of professional actions, a focused and critical assessment of professional behavior, and a means of developing professional crafts-manship. And all of this is done in and through relationships. That is, educators ask themselves and one another such questions as, What are we doing and why? What effect are we having? What have we learned from this experience? How might we do this differently? What are we trying to accomplish in this school, and are we achiev-ing that goal? These questions, along with others, position the educators to reflect deeply about how individual and collective practices and school goals might be im-proved. Furthermore, as with individual reflection, collective reflection is expected to embed the three common types of reflective thinking: reflection in action, reflection on action, and reflection for action. This pattern of reflective practice encompasses a close examination of skills and techniques, underlying assumptions and beliefs, and moral and ethical underpinnings of professional practice. That is, educators reflect on the cognitive, critical, and narrative aspects of educational life, thereby gaining insights into possibilities for profound improvement in professional practice.

In a project designed to foster organizational learning in an elementary school, the teachers took many opportunities to reflect on their professional practice, alone and together. As they did so, we observed a change in their personal understandings about teaching and learning. As one teacher in the project commented, 'As I've learned to reflect, I've become more perceptive about myself. I've learned things about myself that I perhaps did not want to know. And that has made a difference.' Teachers in this school also noted that as others reflected on their learning, so they collectively learned. Another teacher stated, 'As we reflect about teaching and learning, I've learned things from my colleagues. They've helped me to clarify much of my thinking about what we are trying to accomplish in this school. I've also felt more comfortable in approaching my colleagues about teaching issues. It has become evident to me that we're better at learning together now.'

Collective reflection, however, is not easy. Teachers find it difficult to reflect on their work and how they accomplish it, nor do they often find the time to come together to reflect. In many schools we have found that collaborative processes are neglected, group work is poorly structured and ineffective, and teaching (and professional reflec-tion or learning) is still an isolated activity. This suggests to us that the reflective process (collective and individual) has to be built into the school structure and that it has to be carefully facilitated. We take up this issue in Chapter 8. Here we want simply to point out the need for careful attention to the conditions under which teachers typically work and the conditions that can facilitate their endeavors to think together about professional practice.

Along with collective reflection, the cognitive climate is constructed through pro-fessional conversation, which entails in-depth discussions among educators about specific professional issues, problems, concerns, perplexities, and mysteries. (This differs somewhat from collective reflection, which can be about anything and which often deals with tacit understandings, beliefs, or assumptions.) Professional conver-sations help educators, students, and parents to develop common understandings and to clarify the vision and goals for the school. They provide an opportunity for people to explore others' 'mental models' (Senge, 1990) in order to find out what different individuals value about teaching and learning. Only when mental models are brought into the open can people negotiate the grounds upon which they might establish common understandings and shared purposes. From the foundation of common knowledge, professional conversations provide a forum for raising and re-solving issues. That is, if there are places where individuals do not share similar views, then conversation provides the opportunity to understand alternative perspectives and to reconstruct the collective narrative in a way that honors diverse values and yet brings a sense of cohesion out of diversity.

From our perspective, dialogue is the preferred style for professional conversa-tions. Senge (1990) was one of the first people to distinguish between dialogue and other forms of conversation, such as discussion or debate. He positions dialogue as a deep engagement with the thoughts and feelings of one's conversational partners. This sort of conversation requires intense listening and attentive inquiry in order to plumb the depths of the others' minds. Isaacs (1999) outlines four skills of dialogue: listening, respecting, suspending, and voicing. *Listening* entails deep attention to others' points of view and deep attention to one's own personal thought patterns, reactions, and assumptions. *Respecting* means honoring others, legitimizing their rights and value, and being alert to what they can teach. *Suspending* causes an individual to step back to see things with new eyes and to suspend judgements, beliefs, assump-tions, decisions, preferences, opinions, and so on. *Voicing* is the process of self-disclosure, where individuals open their hidden theories to others and expose the thoughts that they might be inclined to keep private. These four skills, although not particularly familiar to most people or characteristics of most conversations, are the ones that provide the necessary safety for the deep disclosure that can lead to pro-found understanding – and to profound improvement.

What this implies, of course, is that professional conversations need to be con-ducted in an environment of respect and trust. Learning best occurs in an environment where people can openly express their opinions and test their ideas and not feel that it is inappropriate to do so. In our work in schools, several people have spoken about the connection between professional conversations and learning. This from one teacher: 'The important decisions you want people to talk about, to toss it around, and to come to some form of consensus. These discussions need to be done in an environ-ment of mutual respect.' From another teacher: 'If it makes more sense than what I think, then I would change my mind. That is the value of professional conversation.' And a third: 'As long as we can come to some consensus on a philosophical basis as to why we're doing it, that's the most important thing. If you can't agree on why you're doing it, then you don't have a chance.' In this school, professional conversa-tion was useful for developing a sense of the team among educators. As the profes-sional staff talked to one another, they came to know each other better and they came to appreciate the strengths that each member brought to the team. Professional con-versation was grounded in trusting, respectful relationships, and it also served to expand the level of trust and caring that the staff exhibited toward each other.

Building the Learning Community Climate: A Synthesis

Together, affective and cognitive conditions generate an interpersonal environment that either supports or limits professional learning. Our argument is that the affective processes of invitation and affirmation establish a climate within which the cognitive processes of reflection and professional conversation can occur (Mitchell & Sackney, 1998). That is, the affective processes are the 'heart' of the learning community, and the cognitive processes are the 'mind.' Figure 4.1 presents an image of how these elements conjoin. Affirmation affords to individuals a sense of trust, and invitation brings them into a caring professional relationship. These provide the foundation upon which the cognitive climate rests. The cognitive climate relies on collective reflection and professional conversation to develop shared understandings and values. Working in concert with one another, invitation, affirmation, collective reflection, and professional conversation advance professional discourse. In this way, enhanced interpersonal capacity emerges through the development of both the affective and the cognitive climate.

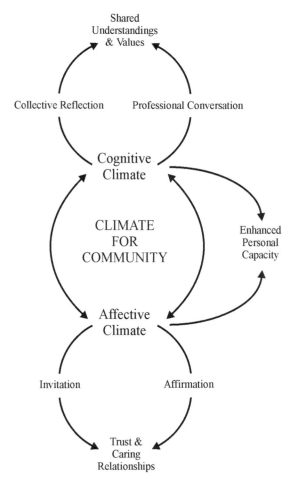

Figure 4.1 Elements of interpersonal capacity.

The importance of interpersonal capacity locates in its effects on the ways in which educators and students develop individual and common understandings of their practices and the effects of their practices. It offers a ground upon which to develop alternative solutions to intransigent issues or deep mysteries, and it provides a foundation for reconstructing 'basic assumptions about learning and learners' (Conley, 1993, p. 150). This kind of climate helps school people to develop a 'capacity for openness' (Senge et al., 1999, p. 244), and it enables the sorts of collegial transformations that Leithwood, Jantzi, and Steinbach (1999) have discovered in some of their interviews with teacher leaders. They have found, for example, that 'teacher leaders provided their colleagues with "intellectual stimulation", "modelled best practices", and helped "develop structures to foster participation in school decisions"' (p. 128).

Interpersonal capacity affords people a network of relationships within which they can see themselves and their world differently. As Mahatma Gandhi has stated, 'You must be the change you wish to see in the world.' This statement implies that, as people begin to see more of the good in their colleagues, they also see the change that they wish to become. From this perspective, building interpersonal capacity is fundamentally about empowerment and self-change. In environments with enhanced interpersonal capacity and with empowered individuals who engage in deep self-change, learning communities can be expected to emerge and profound improvement in teaching and learning can be expected to flourish.

5

Interpersonal Capacity: Building the Team

Interpersonal capacity in a learning community implies the presence of a well functioning team of people who work and learn together. The development of a collaborative
team is supported by a particular kind of communication that blends advocacy and
inquiry. We see both distinctions and overlaps between advocacy (the advancement
of one's opinion or belief) and inquiry (the exploration of a colleague's opinion or
belief). Those distinctions and overlaps form a pattern of communication that is characterized by questions as often as by statements. It is a pattern that allows individuals
to contribute freely without fear of recrimination or reprisal and that opens spaces for
consideration of sensitive issues, problems of purpose, and unarticulated dreams or
dreads. This kind of communication allows individuals to engage in collective inquiry
and to develop shared understandings about purposes, values, and commitments.
Within the discourse, people talk together effectively about the important aspects of
their collective enterprise, they come to grips with some tricky problems of practice,
and they work out guiding principles and useful strategies for their work.

This communication pattern is the foundation for building a cohesive and effective
team in a school. In recent years, the notion of teamwork has enjoyed considerable
play in educational and management literature, and it is now vogue to connect organizational development with team building. It seems that teams have an almost seductive
quality to them, perhaps grounded on an assumption that 'great' teams can solve
tough problems that individuals (or poor teams) cannot crack (Haskins, Liedtka, &
Rosenblum, 1998). A great group, according to Haskins et al., 'creates true colleagues
fueled by investments of spirit and heart, thus producing energy and enthusiasm' (p.
35). Senge (1990), in fact, shone a spotlight on the notion of great teams through his
inclusion of team learning as one of the five disciplines of a learning organization. This
suggests that, in any consideration of a learning community, it is a good idea to pay
attention to the kind of team operating (or not) in a school. Consequently, in this
chapter we explore some of the foundational concepts of teams and teamwork, some
characteristics of effective and ineffective teams, and some strategies for developing
a collaborative culture and a 'great' team. Our position is that interpersonal capacity

can lead to profound improvement in teaching and learning when educators work together within an ethic of collaboration (Haskins et al.).

Teams and Teamwork

The word *team* implies a group of people acting together. The most typical under-standing of teams is that of the transactional team, which is formed to accomplish a task (Haskins et al., 1998, p. 35), and this sort of teamwork is becoming as common in schools as it is in the business sector. But for teams and teamwork to be cornerstones of the learning community, they need to move beyond transactional status and be conceived and perceived as true collaborative cultures. That is, they should be configured as autonomous or semi-autonomous, self-managing, and self-leading work units (Gronn, 1998). Fullan and Hargreaves (1996) use the terms *collaborative culture* and the *collaborative school* when speaking about school teams, which again foregrounds collaboration as the basis of any team efforts. Haskins et al. extend the notion of collaboration by suggesting that it consists in 'an *ethic* – a system of moral principles and values grounded in a sense of calling and stewardship' (p. 34, emphasis in the original). This implies that team members (which, according to Haskins et al., include all members of the community) are charged with a moral purpose and with clear and present responsibility for the growth and development of one another and of the school.

The basic assumption underlying teams is that they provide a flexible form of work organization. In a school, for example, groups can vary from two individuals working together to the whole school staff collaborating on specific projects. Furthermore, one individual can be a member of a variety of different groups or teams, and the same individual can serve different roles on different teams, depending on contextual condi-tions and functional exigencies. Groups of people come together to serve various functions in a school, including (but not limited to) curriculum and instruction devel-opment, pedagogic exploration, goal setting, strategic planning, and professional learn-ing. What this implies is that different roles and purposes are likely to define different groups quite differently. That is, no one particular pattern of grouping or of role func-tioning will serve equally well in all settings. Instead, collaborative units need the autonomy to self-organize, self-manage, and self-regulate in response to specific tasks (Gronn, 1998). If those conditions exist, then teams can be expected to make better decisions than individuals do, and their decisions are likely to be better supported and implemented. This argument is essentially one of empowerment. When people have control over their work, they are more likely to support and fulfill the institutional obligations to which they are committed.

Teams and teamwork represent one expression of the recent interest in collabora-tive modes of performance improvement. This assumes that collective learning cannot occur unless groups of individuals collaborate. The collaborative process enables the development of socially distributed knowledge, whereby individual knowledge bases become part of the collective discourse and expand the professional capacity of the entire team. This is the phenomenon at the heart of Senge's (1990) concept of team learning. From his perspective, team learning aligns individual activity and creates a synergy among individual efforts. Members of the team provide cognitive scaffolds upon which others can stand as they reach for new insights. Team members test their theories and assumptions about teaching and learning with one another, and the public testing helps educators to confirm, to discard, or to reframe their original thoughts. In these ways, the discourse that goes on in a team improves individual and collective cognition and learning.

The Collaborative Ethic

Linking teams with a collaborative culture has enjoyed a long history in educational literature. Smith and Scott (1990), for example, define the collaborative school as one that 'provides a climate and structure that encourages teachers and professionals to work together and with the principal and administrators toward school improvement and professional growth' (p. 3). Rosenholtz (1989), similarly, views collaboration as the 'extent to which teachers engage in help-related exchange' (p. 53). In both of these definitions, a collaborative culture is presented as an environment within which educators are empowered to engage with colleagues and other community partners in collective reflective practices and collective learning to solve the teaching and learning problems and deep mysteries of their school.

For some time now, educational scholars have argued that collaboration is important for continuous learning. As early as 1982, for example, Little argued that professional learning is enhanced when teachers engage in concrete talk about teaching with one another, observe and provide feedback about their teaching, help each other in planning for instruction, and teach each other the practice of teaching. Her position is that the collaborative effort depends on certain social relations such as reciprocity, interdependence, mutual trust, and a common focus on teaching. When these conditions are in place, collaborative practices unfold in a space of safety and mutual support, and colleagues are then more willing to open their professional practice to one another. By 1990, Little had identified different forms of collaboration. She viewed scanning and storytelling, help and assistance, and sharing as common but relatively weak forms of collaboration. Her research indicated that *joint work* was the strongest form of collaboration and included aspects such as team teaching, collaborative planning, peer observation, action research, sustained peer coaching, and mentoring. She concluded that joint work led to the most sustained changes in teaching and learning practices in schools.

Although collaboration embodies joint work, this is rare in many schools for at least two reasons. First, they are structured in ways that keep educators and students separated from one another and, second, a culture of isolation, with its claims to privacy and individualism, is typical of most schools. For these (and other) reasons, meaningful collaboration among teachers appears to be rare. What is more typical is what Bakkens, deBrabander, and Imants (1999) call 'serendipitous collaboration,' which consists of collaboration about relatively inconsequential matters (such as deciding when and what the Christmas concert will be), sharing stories and trading secrets, or simply discussing the latest community goings on. This sort of collaboration is not likely to deepen professional learning, to enhance the craft environment, or to encourage teachers to disclose the private aspects of their professional practice.

Our position is that the world within which teachers work is far too complex for any one teacher to manage successfully all the problems that students bring to school. This means that individual teachers should no longer bear the sole responsibility for the success of the students in their classrooms. Instead, teachers need to share tasks and responsibilities with colleagues, administrators, parents, and community members. And this implies a need for teachers to be open with other individuals about how they conduct their practice on a daily basis. This kind of intense collaboration goes far beyond simple collegiality or congeniality.

In much of our work with educators, we have found that they sincerely desire increased opportunities for collaboration but rarely find the time to meet and, even when they do so, rarely manage to move beyond surface level discussions. We believe that this is partly due to teachers not knowing how to go about engaging in collaborative work and partly due to the multiple, varied, and layered nature of schools. What we mean by this is that teachers teach different content, grades, and subjects, and they tend to see collaboration only in relation to their own context. They do not necessarily see the merits of talking to someone at a different grade level whose work is different from their own. Thus they are likely to speak more often and more intimately with educators who share similar teaching assignments or similar teaching patterns, which severely limits the opportunities for teachers to come into contact with unfamiliar practices. Furthermore, collaboration is somewhat uncomfortable to most educators because it requires that they open up their work to scrutiny. This can be extremely threatening to people who are accustomed to working alone behind closed doors away from the prying eyes of other professionals. Both of these conditions keep educators away from collaborative ventures and limit the extent to which they can develop skills for effective collaboration.

A further complication is that, in many schools, and especially larger secondary schools, adult subcultures can exist. Louis, Kruse, and Marks (1996), for example, found that secondary school teachers rarely agreed on basic educational goals, and they attributed this condition to the departmental structure. Within such a structure, teachers spend considerably more time talking to members of their own departments than to other teachers in the school. As a result, they know a great deal about their own unit but much less about what is happening elsewhere. Furthermore, the departmental subculture is exacerbated because of the disciplinary basis of teachers' work. That is, teachers at the secondary level tend to have networks that are subject-specialized, and there is little cross-departmental work in secondary schools. Thus, familiarity with team members and lack of familiarity with others creates a set of isolated subcultures, with the potential for miscommunication, misunderstandings, and cross-purposes that typically follow such divisions. Yet the more that teachers engage in work-related activities, the less isolated and the more responsive and creative they become. Even in secondary schools, then, there is a need for persistent collaboration among cross-disciplinary and cross-departmental teams.

This implies the need for teams and networks to be established outside as well as inside the department. We have seen these sorts of networks achieved through the use of school-wide teams made up of teachers from different departments. One example of such a structural arrangement comes from a large secondary school where the staff had been working for several years on a comprehensive school improvement initiative. In the early years, school improvement committees had been struck to address issues related to curriculum, school management, and instruction, but the committees worked in relative isolation from one another. As time went on, the professional staff realized that these arrangements were causing their efforts to be fragmented and to lack direction. To counter these effects, they restructured to form a steering committee with members from all departments, all instructional areas, and all smaller committees. This steering committee coordinated all school improvement activities and facilitated communication among the multiple layers and levels of school operations. This structural arrangement enabled teachers from various departments to work together and led to the establishment of teaching teams, discipline teams, student assessment teams, and other forms of collaboration.

These teams became a key mechanism for professional learning as colleagues sorted out various issues, problems, and mysteries in the teams on which they worked. The information and understandings from individual teams became widely distributed through the steering committee. This was accomplished through the representatives to the larger committee. The team representatives were responsibile for sharing the activities and discussions taking place in their team and for reporting back the information they had garnered from representatives of the other teams. This kind of intensive and extensive communication not only kept everyone 'in the know' but it also eliminated hoarding or brokering of information.

This school demonstrates the power of a collaborative work culture to advance professional learning. As the staff engaged in the work of the committees, they learned to share, to trust, and to support one another. So too they learned to work with one another and to learn from one another. As the school staff dealt with increasingly complex problems, they realized that they needed to become skilled in team learning. We have found this story to be repeated in every school where there has been careful and skillful attention paid to the creation of collaborative teams. Even though working in teams is not an easy task, it is one of the best ways that we have found to engage educators in learning how to create, think, and learn together. Sharing among educators can progress from swapping of war stories and complaints to sharing ideas, joint work, collaborative problem-solving, and shared responsibility for the work and well-being of the school (Firestone & Louis, 1999; Little, 1990; Louis & Kruse, 1995; Rosenholtz, 1989). In other words, collaboration and teamwork join to create a culture that sustains professional learning and supports school renewal.

This means that, just as collaboration is at the heart of teamwork, so too is it at the heart of a learning community. That is, collective professional learning is best promoted when mutual support, respect for others' ideas, and risk taking dominate the norms of collegial relations. Receiving open, honest, and candid feedback from colleagues can encourage individual teachers to embark on a process of professional learning and growth. This is likely to translate into improved professional practice; there is some empirical evidence to suggest that when teachers make a commitment to collective learning, they also place greater emphasis on the needs of all students (Leithwood & Louis, 1998). For example, Louis et al. (1996), in their study of professional school cultures, concluded that as collaboration increased, teachers' collective sense of responsibility for student achievement and common understandings of collective instruction also increased. This finding links collective professional learning with student learning, as is expected to be the case in a learning community.

The Effective Team

Much has been written about teams, some of it advocating teams and some of it raising issues about the kinds of problems that teams create. What this signifies to us is that teams can be either effective or ineffective. Over the years we have spent some time teasing out the elements that distinguish these two sorts of teams. One strategy we have used is, in team-building workshops, to ask teachers, non-instructional staff, administrators, parents, and other educational partners to describe their experiences with teamwork. We have asked them to describe a particularly effective team and a particularly ineffective team of which they have been a member. We have asked them to describe an effective team leader and an ineffective team leader with whom they have worked. We have asked them to describe the ways in which team work has been effective and ineffective. The data from these descriptions (and the attendant discussions) have been juxtaposed with that garnered from numerous research projects and observations that we have conducted of teams at work in school contexts. From these data, we have learned much about effective and ineffective teams.

Our participants have taught us, for example, that, in effective teams, the atmosphere tends to be informal, comfortable, relaxed, and tension-free. People appear to be involved and interested, and they show few signs of boredom. In fact, we have often observed a sense of enthusiasm for the work when people are part of an effective team. The discussion tends to be lively and inclusive, with virtually everyone involved in the discourse. We have noted a tendency for the discussion to be on topic, and when it strays, someone usually brings it back to order. We have also observed attempts being made to involve others in the dialogue. The debate that ensues takes place in an atmosphere of trust and respect. People are respected for their contributions, and all ideas are given due consideration. Risk taking is encouraged, and individuals are not afraid to express ideas that may be perceived as being 'far out.'

When teams are initially formed, effective teams provide time for members to understand their task and to get to know one another. Furthermore, when new members join the team, an orientation takes place, whereby veteran members make an effort to facilitate the learning of new members. What this means is that all teams go through a process of 'naming and framing' (Mitchell & Sackney, 1998), that is, of generating some common knowledge and shared understandings about the team and the task before getting on with the work. This phase is common to all effective teams, including those of which we have personally been members on various university committees.

When there is disagreement in the group, the members do not avoid conflict. Instead, they carefully analyze the nature of the disagreement and attempt to resolve the problem. In a later part of this chapter, we outline a process for decision making called *dynamic harmonization* (Hudson, 1997), which can be used for achieving group consensus. Here we want simply to say that effective teams work to resolve their problems and try to reach consensus. It should be noted that consensus does not mean that everyone is happy with the final outcome, but it does mean that each individual can live with the group decision. Furthermore, criticism is frank, open, and honest, but it is not associated with personal attacks. Instead, criticism is viewed as constructive and is designed to help the group reach good decisions. Members have a high degree of trust in each other, and they feel confident in expressing their feelings openly and honestly. These are the sorts of conditions that lead to a capacity for openness (Senge et al., 1999). With this kind of foundation upon which to rest the discourse, information is not withheld from group members, and there is high motivation on the part of each individual to communicate fully and frankly so that all information and issues are on the table.

Effective teams are clear about their task and know what is expected of them. Furthermore, they are task-oriented and do not waste a lot of time. Problems are resolved and conclusions are reached after careful analysis. The group does not let issues remain unresolved but instead focuses on addressing sensitive issues and completing the task. Effective teams assess their performance on a regular basis in order to enhance group performance and decision making. This sort of ongoing review ensures that the mechanisms and procedures are in agreement with the wishes of the members and with the goals of the group.

We have often observed a sense of community among the members of an effective team. They feel as if they are part of a family where each member is equally important. There is genuine caring for the members of the team, and they enjoy each other's company. This translates into a feeling of *gemeinschaft* or an emphasis on the *we* (Sergiovanni, 1996). Under such conditions, the team leader does not dominate the team nor do group members defer unduly to the designated leader. We have noticed that various individuals may take on a leadership role, depending on the task to be accomplished or the issue to be resolved. Power does not seem to be an issue with effective teams, and there is no attempt by any one person to control the work of the group. Instead, group members help others to develop their potential by engaging in persistent dialogue, questioning, and reflection and by teaching members the processes of shared decision making.

The Ineffective Team

Much of what has been written and that we have seen in relation to ineffective teams is the opposite of what makes an effective team. The atmosphere is likely to be one of indifference, boredom, or tension. Individuals are often engaged in side conversations, some are not involved at all, and others seem to do something else during the meeting. Team members often do not come to meetings on time, and when they arrive, their first question is usually, 'How long will the meeting last? I have to be somewhere else.' People do not appear to listen to each other, and suggestions made by a team member are often ignored or not given credence by members of the group. Usually a few people dominate the discussion, which often swerves off topic, and little is done to bring it back on track. Personal feelings are seldom expressed. Instead, people hide their true feelings and are extremely careful about what they say. This is perhaps because there is a lack of trust on the team and there is considerable risk in disclosing anything personal to the group.

In many instances, the team appears not to be clear about its task. Much time is spent on deciding what is to be accomplished, and one often hears individual agendas being forced on the group. These agendas are likely to be in conflict with the group and with the task to be accomplished. Problems are usually inadequately aired, and decisions are made on the basis of simple majority or the dominance of a small number of powerful individuals. After a decision has been reached, non-included individuals (or the minority) remain resentful and uncommitted to the decision. Moreover, a final decision does not mean that any real outcome will be achieved because there is seldom a clear direction for the course of action to be followed. When individuals are handed a task, they may fail to complete their assignment on time, and a multitude of excuses might be offered as to why the assignment could not be completed. As a result, the implementation of assignments is uneven, and team results are subsequently subject to complaints and grumbling.

Conflict is poorly handled in ineffective teams. The group rarely, if ever, deals with disagreements, and sensitive issues are usually suppressed altogether. In some cases, there may be a 'tyranny of the minority,' in which an individual or subgroup may attempt to usurp the agenda. In order to preserve peace and harmony, the group may accede to the individual or subgroup's demands, but they are not likely to work at bringing the demands to fruition. Ineffective or weak teams seldom review their per-formance, even though there is likely to be considerable discussion outside the meet-ing about what is wrong and why. But because these issues are seldom, if ever, brought to the meeting, there is no forum for resolving them or for moving the team in a more positive direction.

We have witnessed little, if any, sense of community among team members be-cause ineffective teams do not invest energy in developing their relationships or their task environment. In general, there is a focus on *gesellschaft* or the *I* (Sergiovanni, 1996). There is no synergy of efforts such as is evident with the effective team. In-stead, individuals appear to be out to promote personal benefit or to advance a par-ticular perspective that may not coincide with the task at hand. Leadership tends to remain in the hands of the chairperson, who often attempts to control the group, and power is seen to be vested in the role. In some cases where the chairperson is weak, other members may attempt to usurp the leadership role. Leadership is generally not shared in ineffective teams, and criticism of the designated leader or of team action is discouraged. On occasions where criticism is presented, it is usually done in a nega-tive and derogatory fashion. This results in individuals not being willing to 'stick out their necks.' All of this conspires to make decision making uneven at best and down-right disastrous at times.

Developing the Team

The existence of ineffective teams has convinced us that team development is essen-tial; the existence of effective teams has shown us that it is possible. But teamwork is not easy, nor is it particularly familiar to most people. Furthermore, when individuals come together, they bring with them tacit, unexpressed differences in perspective. In other words, teams do not happen automatically just because a group of people has come together. Rather, there needs to be intense and ongoing investment in team development by ensuring that team members understand how teams operate and by providing opportunities for individuals to develop the capacity to work well in an interpersonal milieu. People need to understand that there will always be differences of opinion, differences of style, differences of personality, and differences of purposes. Team development means looking intently at these differences, both the articulated and the unarticulated ones, in order to develop knowledge about and understanding of others in the group. To begin the process of such intense exploration, teams need to establish some ground rules for the team discourse and some expectations for dealing with violations of the ground rules. If no one in the group has had experience in such processes, it may be useful to hire an outside facilitator who is trained in the techniques of building effective discourse.

Certain conditions are necessary for building and maintaining effective teams. We see the following ten points as some of the essential conditions. This list is an amalgam of ideas that we have used in our own team building workshops and that we have gleaned from Parker's (1994) work on effective teams. First, *positive team norms* are necessary for teams to work well. These norms are such that team members disclose their ideas and feelings, encourage colleagues to disclose their ideas and feelings, validate the ideas and feelings of colleagues, experiment with unfamiliar practices, care about the well-being of colleagues, listen carefully, and commit themselves readily to the work of the team. Second, there is a *clear sense of purpose*. Team members need to know why the team exists and what they should be doing. They need to know and to share the vision of the school. Third, the team atmosphere is *relaxed, informal, and comfortable*. Team members enjoy each other's company, and they conduct their work in a spirit of camaraderie and congeniality. Fourth, *participation is inclusive*. Everyone participates freely, and members strive to invite others into the discussion and to ensure that individual voices are heard. Fifth, team members practice *active listening*. Active listeners nod their head, prompt the speaker, paraphrase what they have heard, ask questions, or otherwise acknowledge that they care about what their colleague is communicating. Sixth, team discourse is characterized by *civilized disagreement*. When conflict inevitably arises, it is handled constructively, with disagreements focusing on an idea rather than on a person. Team members do not attack colleagues, and they are able to dissociate their emotions from the ideas being debated. Seventh, *consensus* is the preferred method for making important decisions. Consensus requires unity but not concurrence or unanimity. Eighth, *trust* is an avenue to open communication. Over time, trust increases with a corresponding increase in openness, and each individual (and especially the designated leader) shares the responsibility for creating trust and open communication. Ninth, *leadership is shared*. Leadership shifts from time to time, depending on the issue or problem to be addressed, and leadership skills are developed among all team members. Finally, members conduct *continual maintenance*. Ongoing effectiveness cannot be taken for granted, and team building needs to happen at all stages of team development.

These ten conditions signal that team development takes time and effort. Initially, people 'feel their way around' to find out where different individuals stand on a given issue, and it seems that little gets accomplished. This seemingly unproductive phase affords individuals the time and space to define the context and the working parameters. Isaacs (cited in Senge et al., 1999, p. 362) calls this the 'crisis of collective suspension,' and we have labeled it 'naming and framing' (Mitchell & Sackney, 1998). It is at this phase that members begin to listen and to ask, 'What is the meaning of this?' Incidentally, people need to listen not only to others but also to themselves. It is as important for individuals to confront their own thoughts as to discover the thoughts of others. Once a group safely negotiates the crisis of collective suspension, they enter what Isaacs calls the 'crisis of collective pain' (p. 363), which we have labeled 'analyzing and integrating.' During this phase, individuals begin to loosen up, to trust others, to confront old habits, and to engage in genuine dialogue. In the final phase, individuals begin to take up the notion of group meaning and to see themselves as part of a collective whole. We have called this phase 'experimenting and applying' because it is here that members begin to be creative and to find appropriate solutions to the problems and mysteries that they face. Over the years, we have worked with various groups (educational administrators, students, teachers, parents, university professors, and nurses), and the team development process tends to follow these phases. (We provide a more detailed treatment of the phases in Chapter 8.)

During all phases of team development, attention needs to be paid to the nature of the discourse among team members. Typical or familiar communication patterns do not appear to serve team functions well. For example, people have a natural tendency to defend their own position strenuously, and this sort of strident communication often serves to stifle the discourse. To offset such tendencies, teamwork requires the use of more complex and sophisticated communication skills. These skills should enable team members to balance advocacy with inquiry and to become aware of the assumptions and beliefs that guide the work of team members. According to Senge et al. (1994), team learning emerges from two conversational skills: dialogue and skillful discussion (p. 353). These authors define dialogue as 'sustained collective inquiry into . . . what we take for granted' (p. 353). For them, the goal of dialogue is

> to open new spaces between the words, not only the words; the timing of action, not only the result; the timbre and tone of a voice, not only what is said. We listen for the meaning of the field of inquiry, not only its discrete elements. In short, dialogue creates conditions in which people experience the primacy of the whole. (p. 353)

Team learning transforms dialogue and skillful discussion into capabilities as 'they become collective vehicles for building shared understanding' (Senge et al., p. 354). The distinction between these two skills is one of orchestration rather than lyrics. As Senge et al. point out, 'In skillful discussion you make a choice; in a dialogue, you discover the nature of choice. Dialogue is like jazz; skillful discussion is like chamber music' (p. 354).

When teams use dialogue, they learn how to think together. Where this sense of sharing exists, effective teams have a collective sensibility such that the thoughts, emotions, and hopes belong not to one person but to all of them. Isaacs points out that 'It is a specific way of talking, in which people learn not just to speak, but to listen, not just to one another's words, but to all facets of their presence' (cited in Senge et al., 1999, p. 375). In other words, dialogue requires the open and creative exploration of issues, intense listening to one another, and the suspension of one's own views. When these facets are in place, genuine learning can happen.

To provide some of our own understandings, discussion is where people talk at one another to present their own point of view, skillful discussion is where people talk to one another to address a particular issue, and dialogue is where people talk with one another to develop deep understandings. Discussion, on its own, has been seen to promote incoherence, fragmentation, and disintegration (Senge, 1990, pp. 240-248). *Skillful* discussion, however, is positioned somewhat differently in the discourse. In skillful discussion, people use 'a repertoire of techniques (encompassing collabora-tive reflection and inquiry skills) for seeing how the components of their situation fit together, and they develop a more penetrating understanding of the forces at play among the team members themselves' (Senge et al., 1994, pp. 353-354). Although skillful discussion does not typically lead to the intense collective sensibility that is evident in dialogue, it does provide a mechanism by which group members can work collaboratively to resolve the problems before them in a creative and consensual fashion. Together, dialogue and skillful discussion generate a discursive climate that can support the development of strong, effective teams.

The nexus between communication patterns and team development was particu-larly notable in our study of two schools (one elementary and one secondary) from a school division that was engaged in a system-wide school improvement initiative. The director of education in the school division had decreed that all schools should inves-tigate the possibility of implementing the school effectiveness model that was cur-rently being promoted in the province. In the secondary school, the principal was not enthusiastic about the initiative, but a group of teachers and the vice-principal were anxious to try it out. They tried to build support for the program, but their efforts were undermined by the principal's open disdain for the initiative. Consequently, when the decision was first put to the test, the staff turned down the proposal. At the end of the year, the principal retired, and the vice-principal succeeded him. The following year, he and his cadre of key staff members worked diligently to inform the rest of the staff about the challenges and the opportunities of the program. In this regard, they initi-ated some intensive dialogue and discussion with the entire school staff about school development. When the proposal was put to the test at the end of the year, 80% of the staff voted in favor of implementing the program in the school.

The staff established a school effectiveness steering committee, with one of the initial proponents of the model as the chair. Three action committees were established, with each teacher enlisted on one of the teams. Because some teachers in the school did not support the initiative and were not anxious to see it succeed, the steering committee asked one of the major detractors to serve as chair of an action committee. Through some intensive team building and some critical early successes, this indi-vidual was quickly co-opted and became the program's strongest proponent. The school principal played an interesting leadership role. He did not place himself in control of the process, but he became an ex-officio on the various committees. He chose to facilitate, encourage, and support the work of committees and to recognize and reward the teachers' efforts. This school succeeded in many of its improvement initiatives. Over the years, the original model has been modified, and the program is now deeply embedded in the school culture. In part, the school was effective because the team processes and the dialogue and discourse that ensued in team meetings supported the work of improvement.

The elementary school down the road was not as successful in its attempts to implement a similar program. In this situation, the principal was a strong proponent, but the vice-principal was not. Although the principal was able to obtain the support of staff to try the program, the efforts were not sustained for the long term. In the early days of implementation, the vice-principal enlisted a cohort of teachers in sabotaging and undermining the efforts of the principal and the other staff members. Through these actions, they were able to subvert the plan. The teachers never took the initiative seriously nor did they adopt any authentic measures for improving the school. Instead, they simply went through the motions, and eventually the program was dropped. In this case, the teams were never fully functional, and the processes of discourse and dialogue did not take hold. The school effectiveness program could not be implemented because there was insufficient support for it to succeed. In effect, the capacity for establishing a learning community was not in place.

Developing the Collaborative Culture

The stories of these two schools confirm that team development depends on the existence of a collaborative culture in the school. But the development of a collaborative culture is as deliberate and as extensive an enterprise as is the development of a team. Perhaps the opening play in developing a collaborative culture is for school administrators and key opinion leaders on staff to signal the value of collaborative work. This can be done through formal pronouncements that collaboration is encouraged and supported. Reference to collaborative work can also be part of the metaphors heard around the school. This is evident when words such as *we, team, pull together, joint, community, connection, association, meet,* and *share* (to name but a few) are common in the lexicon of the school. Development of a collaborative culture is enhanced when opportunities for collaboration are built into the formal structure of the school and when attention is devoted to the training and maintenance of teams. It is further enhanced when principals foster collaboration by including it as a factor in teacher performance feedback and when it emerges in the shared vision for the school. The principal also needs to recognize and reward team effort and personally to model collaborative work. These strategies allow teachers to see collaboration in action.

Collaboration is best fostered when there are deliberate structures built into school operations that require educators to work together on a joint task. One strategy for building these sorts of structures is to ask educators to engage in data collection, analysis, and interpretation around common issues or operations. For example, a school system may ask teachers to collect intensive data in relation to student performance. The data might include student test scores, achievement records, attendance records, perception surveys, or any other sorts of information that can be collected to inform teachers about how and what specific students are doing in their educational experiences. The staff comes together to discuss patterns evident in the data, to identify issues or concerns that might be reflected in the data, and to consider action plans for addressing the concerns or for renewing the educational experience. Although we have presented student data as an example, we do not want to leave the impression that this is the only sort of data that should or could be collected. We think that educators need to collect data on their own performance as well as on the performance of the students. The database approach to collaboration is one of the best strategies that we have found to help educators depersonalize sensitive issues, to move past implicit assumptions and attributions, and to address effectively deep mysteries or recurring problems. Rich data give educators sufficient substance to inform their collaborative deliberations.

Yet another way of developing a collaborative culture is for the educators to extend their networks outside the school walls. In recent years, schools have begun to connect with partners from the business sector. Such connections can provide additional resources for the school through such arrangements as work experiences sites, computer acquisition opportunities, and mentorships. More important, however, the connections open new learning horizons for educators by exposing them to unfamiliar contexts and concepts. By going beyond the school boundaries, educators can enhance their capacity for creating new structures and new learning opportunities. For example, when teachers work with parents and the community, they learn more about their students. These relationships are likely to result in some serious questions (from students, parents, community partners, and educators themselves) about the school's culture, its values, and its structure. In these ways, the new networks encourage the school staff to recreate the school culture so as to facilitate persistent and extensive collaboration.

The benefits of a collaborative culture are not the exclusive privilege of the adults in an educational community. Students also stand to gain considerably. Rosenholtz (1989), for example, noted that when collaboration was supported and encouraged by the school culture, teachers were more energized and student achievement rose. We want to emphasize that when we talk about collaboration, we expect it to include students and parents on various teaching and learning issues. For example, in most school effectiveness reviews, students and parents contribute to the feedback process and to the development of the vision and mission for the school. Teachers report stronger support for school activities when students and parents have had input into those decisions. In all of our work with educators, we have noted that they prefer to work in collaborative environments, but they also feel that it is not actively encouraged, nor is collaborative work given adequate time. This suggests to us that collaboration will only flourish when it is deeply and authentically embedded in the school's culture.

Dynamic Harmonization

Throughout this chapter we have emphasized that building the team and encouraging collaborative work depends to a large extent on consensus and shared decision-making. Dynamic harmonization, designed by Hudson (1997), offers an approach for achieving these conditions. The model, based on a modification of the approach used by the

Society of Friends (Quakers), attempts to arrive at consensus through what Hudson calls *coming to the sense of the meeting*. Premised upon Habermas' 'ideal speech situation,' consensus involves both an intellectual and an emotional response to the issue under discussion. Habermas (1984, p. 98) says that consensus is the ultimate agreement or final opinion. He further adds, 'consensus not only implies the dissolution of contradictions, but also the extinguishing of the individuality of those who are able to contradict each other – their disappearance within a collective group' (p. 110). From Habermas' perspective, consensus means that the collective *voice* trumps the individual voice even though the individual *person* remains intact. Through the process of discourse, individual perspectives blend and merge until all can live with the ultimate decision. In this regard, consensual decision making is a team *thinking* process where individuals meet, think, and work together in a highly organized and systematic manner to review information, generate ideas, and make decisions in order to change some present situation to some desired situation (Hudson, 1997, p. 29). It is through the deep, mutual understanding that people come to the sense of the meeting.

Hudson (1997) views shared decision making as providing the synergy necessary to make effective decisions. The components of shared decision making are collaboration, empowerment, and leadership dispersal. The expectation is that individuals will participate willingly but will not be forced into participating in any of the three components. If, however, individuals have any concerns, they are expected to voice those concerns openly to the rest of the group. In this way, the three components of collaboration, empowerment, and leadership dispersal form the interaction patterns that enable team members to move past individual differences or power imbalances and to harmonize diverse ideas and understandings about the issue under discussion. This sort of harmonization is a dynamic process that is enacted through three cognitive patterns: release, long focus, and transition to light. *Release* involves allowing the participants to 'clear the air.' This clearing of the air is done in an atmosphere of acceptance and trust (p. 50). A *long focus* to the problem or situation enables people to see more of the situation over a longer time frame. *Transition to light* involves turning inward to transcend differences and to shift toward the achievement of harmony. This inward turn is a time to reflect on what has been said to this point and to consider where the solution might locate. A method used to facilitate the inward turn is to permeate the meeting with silent periods. These quiet times are important for reflection and inward listening. Hudson labels this whole process *dynamic harmonization*.

Using the concepts derived from Friends, Hudson (1997) notes that there are three ways to disagree. For the least serious disagreements, a person may say, 'I disagree but do not wish to stand in the way,' or the more common way is to say, 'I can live with the decision.' In this case, the decision goes as stated. The second way to disagree is to say, 'Please minute me as opposed'; this represents a middle ground. The decision may or may not go forward depending on the comments of others. The last way to disagree is to say, 'I am unable to unite with the proposal.' In this case, the decision is dropped or readdressed at some future date (pp. 49-50). These sorts of disagreements are the mechanisms for overcoming the differences that typically stand in the way of decision making. In effect, dynamic harmonization does not use formal voting, and the decision leader's role is to facilitate the discourse. The decision leader has no more power or rank compared to any of the other participants. The leader steers the meeting but does not dominate or impose his or her will on the group

In the school where Hudson (1997) taught dynamic harmonization, teachers became more adept at reaching consensus, especially around issues where emotions were high. Furthermore, Hudson found that participants believed the decisions to be of higher quality than previous ones had been, and they gave more support for the implementation of those decisions. One drawback Hudson noted was that consensus took more time compared to the typical voting procedures used in many schools. However, the staff was ultimately happier with the end goals.

Futures Search

Another way of achieving consensus, particularly with respect to mission and vision, is to engage in a futures search. Generally, a futures search is conducted by all interested parties, including teachers, administrators, non-instructional staff, students, parents, and community members. Groups can be as small as a dozen people or as large as 100 participants or more. A futures search proceeds through a number of stages, and the groups work toward consensus at each stage of the process.

Stage 1 deals with *mission clarification*. The first task is to enunciate the beliefs or assumptions that guide the work of the school and that form the philosophy of the system. The second task involves identifying alternative futures. In this task, participants envisage the kind of school they would like to teach and learn in. The third task is to identify the mission for the school or system. The mission statement 'names the game' that the school or system will play. The mission statement should be no longer than one or two sentences and should convey succinctly what the school or system is attempting to achieve. The final vision statement should be empowering but realistic.

Stage 2 entails doing a *SWOTs analysis*, which is an outline of the current strengths, weaknesses, opportunities, and threats of the school. In Stage 3, participants use the information from the previous two stages to determine the *critical issues* that the school needs to address if it is to achieve its desired future. This stage entails determining the gaps that exist between the present state and the desired state. The critical issues are categorized into short and longer-term operational goals. In Stage 4, *action plans* are developed for the various operational goals. The action plans should fully elaborate how the critical issues will be addressed to achieve the desired future. Stage 5 requires a *financial assessment* of the various action plans developed. As a rule, most initiatives require little, if any, monetary commitment. In most cases, what is required is a new way of accomplishing the existing tasks. Stage 6, the final stage, requires that a *results management plan* be devised. This stage answers the question of whether the desired results have been achieved. In most cases, ongoing assessment needs to occur as the plans are being implemented. Generally, formative assessment is preferred over summative assessment. The first three stages constitute the *strategic thinking* phase. It is at these stages that the people in the school community determine the desired future for the school. The final three stages constitute the *tactical planning* phase. It is here that the steps are put in place to achieve the dreams that emerge from strategic thinking.

The futures search committee and the school staff should approve all plans, and all stakeholder groups should receive regular feedback about the progress of the plans. Our experience has been that the more people that are involved in the process, the easier it is to get support for the plans. In particular, we find it useful to have all school staff members involved in the search process. It is also important that the plans be implemented in ways that do not overtax the staff. In most schools that we have worked with, school staff members are divided into action plan teams, each of which is ultimately responsible for elaborating and implementing the plans that were developed. Finally, it is important to keep the larger community informed of the progress being made on the action plans. Continual feedback through newsletters, memos, celebrations, and rewards are suitable strategies for informing those who need to know.

The futures search model allows all stakeholders to have input into the vision for the school, and it also builds teamwork among school staff members. This model provides a structure and process for fostering teaming, learning, and community building. It should be noted, however, that as strategic learning takes place, strategic readiness must also exist (Redding & Catalanello, 1994). In effect, in a learning community, planning is a continuous, evolving process, 'with plans being questioned, refined, and modified based upon the most current information about environments as well as through insights gained from the implementation efforts' (p. 24). Deep reflection becomes a regular and embedded part of the way things are done, and people are ready to move should the circumstances change. In this way, strategic readiness shines the spotlight on the cyclical, non-linear nature of school development and educational renewal.

Building the Team: A Synthesis

In this chapter we have presented a case for developing interpersonal capacity by building effective teams and creating collaborative cultures. It is our contention that, if a learning community is to develop, collaborative action is required; collaborative action is best supported by the presence of a strong, effective team. Our model proposes that team building is enhanced when certain conditions are in place, when certain processes occur, and when certain phases are allowed. The interactions among these elements are depicted in Figure 5.1.

Our experience with school people suggests that the conditions are foundational; if they are not in place, the processes are less likely to be successful. The conditions consequently gain ascendance when there is a need for group maintenance. The processes gain ascendance when team members focus on a task. The phases gain ascendance when issues of sustainability emerge. In effect, the recognition that team processes (as well as team development and team learning) will move cyclically through these phases lessens the likelihood that people will become discouraged when, for example, they discover a need to return to the naming and framing phase. This model implies that even well-functioning teams need continual maintenance and occasional refocusing.

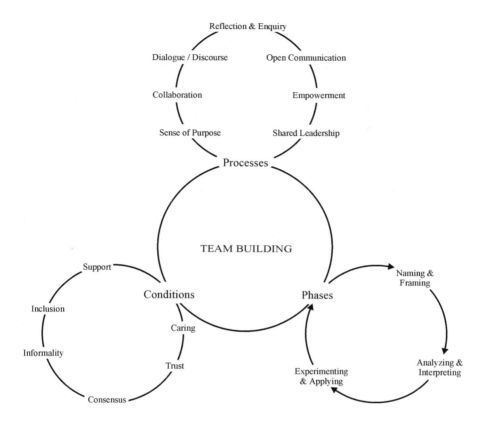

Figure 5.1 Interpersonal capacity for teambuilding.

Our co-authoring venture with this book represents a rather personal mini-case of team building and collaborative processes in action and of the learning power embedded therein. Even though our shared history dates back more than a decade and even though we have worked together on many projects, we are two very different people. We have different family configurations, different academic histories, different belief systems, different thought patterns, different writing styles, and different working patterns. We have read different academic literature and developed different academic networks. Taken together, these differences could easily have torpedoed our desire to co-author a book. But over the years we have developed a deep respect for one another, a mutual regard for the other's knowledge base and cognitive schema, and a trust in the other's integrity and commitment to education.

The relationship that we have forged over the years has been put to the test many times during the writing of this book. At times we have worked on separate writing tasks, only to discover that we have covered the same terrain differently or have left out the same important chunks. This has launched us into a round of intense debate and dialogue as we have tried to sort out the differences and to come to some common understandings. At times, we have had to reconstruct entire sections and even entire chapters in order to arrive at a set of understandings with which we are both comfortable. At times the ideas and understandings have been hotly contested. We have each had to let go of some ideas that we believed to be essential but that have compromised the spirit of the book. At times we have discovered that what we believed to be crystal clear looked more like mud to the other person. We have found ourselves constantly moving back and forth between advocacy and inquiry as we balanced the promotion of our own positions with the search for the other's thoughts and perspectives.

Throughout the process, we have continually learned new concepts and have seen old concepts in a new light. This particular collaborative process has stretched each of us in ways that we never anticipated when we first set out on the journey. This book, as it stands, would not have been possible if either of us had tried to write it alone because, alone, we did not have all the knowledge or the insights found between the covers of the book. Such is the learning power that has come from our capacity to work together on this particular venture. We believe that a similar kind of learning, empowerment, and expanded capacity awaits those people who venture into collaborative processes with the intent to improve teaching and learning. The payoffs for students and for educators can be profound (Rosenholtz, 1989).

6

Organizational Capacity: Opening Doors and Breaking Down Walls

Structural arrangements can open doors for teachers and break down walls between them – or they can slam doors shut and keep people away from one another. This means that personal and interpersonal capacity will be shaped and constrained by the kinds of organizations within which the individuals work. From an educational perspective, the capacity of the organization to support teaching and learning is every bit as important as the personal capacity of the educators and the interpersonal capacity of the groups. Organizational capacity begins with the awareness that a learning community requires a different kind of organizational structure than has been the case in most schools. Traditional structures have typically been characterized by separation of individual administrators, teachers, and students; by uniform standards, procedures, and expectations; by control of the students' work by teachers and of the teachers' work by administrators; and by dominance of decision-making by a few elite individuals. These conditions have served to isolate teachers and students, to minimize contact among educators, and to engender defensiveness and resistance among the professional staff. Such conditions are not conducive to the creation of a learning community, nor are they likely to generate profound improvement in teaching and learning.

Organizational structures have, in recent years, taken some hard knocks from people interested in organizational development. For example, systemic issues are implicated in at least seven of the ten challenges to growth identified by Senge et al. (1999): time, support, management consistency and clarity, assessment of progress, isolation, governance structure, and strategy and purpose. The other three limits – fear and anxiety, relevance, and diffusion and transfer– might also have systemic origins or implications. Of course, Senge et al.'s empirical work has largely been conducted in the business world, but systemic barriers to professional growth have also been identified in studies of schools. By far the most common barriers noted are the inherent isolation of the professional staff and the lack of time for professional discourse among teachers (Lieberman & Miller, 1990). Other scholars, such as Wirth (1989) and Gitlin and Margonis (1995), have noted that the lack of voice for teachers within the educational decision-making hierarchy often leads to resistance to change and reluctance to participate on the part of the teaching staff. From their perspective, resistance and reluctance might be signaling a flaw in the system rather than a weakness in the individual.

We too have found these sorts of barriers in our own work with educators. In one study of an elementary school, for example, we found that collective learning processes were hampered by marginalization of certain staff members, dominance by powerful individuals, conversations about trivial issues, over-extended workload, event-driven priorities, and frequent staff turnovers (Mitchell, 1999a). Reluctance to participate in collective activities was accompanied by a feeling of being excluded from the dominant group, unheard in group deliberations, or unappreciated by the dominant teachers and by the administrative cadre. Although the teachers were able to overcome some of the barriers and to navigate around others, and although they worked hard to create a professional learning community, systemic limits continued to haunt their efforts. After two years, most of the participants had departed for other schools, where there were no concerted efforts to develop a professional community or to create a culture of inquiry among the staff. When we visited the teachers in their new settings, we could find few traces of the collective learning processes with which they had been experimenting in the original school. They still valued the experience and still spoke fondly of what they had gained, but they had no systemic supports or structural arrangements for re-creating the conditions elsewhere.

To be sure, structural conditions are not the only limits to the creation of a learning community. Some individuals do not want to share professional activity or learning with colleagues (Hargreaves, 1993), some prefer to protect classroom and student time as much as possible (Lieberman & Miller, 1990), and some have different opinions about what sorts of things deserve or demand collaboration (Bakkenes, de Brabander, & Imants, 1999). In other words, different individual characteristics are likely to generate different responses to the same organizational conditions. Within the discourse on the learning community, then, there needs to be an appreciation of individual differences, individual needs, and individual learning and teaching styles. Furthermore, we acknowledge Firestone's (1996) observation that 'changing organizational arrangements without helping teachers to become more knowledgeable is not likely to lead to great change' (p. 226). But none of that excuses the organization nor does it imply that any organizational structure will work. Given the desire of individual educators to work together in the creation of a learning community, and given the capacity of people to participate in individual and collective professional and school development, schools should be structured so as to enable rather than to disable the discourse. And that means creating a structure that is strikingly different from what is found in most schools.

Organizational capacity for a learning community implies that schools are structured to support connection rather than separation, diversity rather than uniformity, empowerment rather than control, and inclusion rather than dominance. It implies that individuals feel confident in their own capacity, in the capacity of their colleagues, and in the capacity of the school to support professional development and educational improvement. Building organizational capacity, then, means paying attention to the socio-cultural conditions, the structural arrangements, and the collaborative processes in the school. These are the topics that we explore in this chapter.

Socio-Cultural Conditions

Perhaps the first walls to be breached are those that exist in the minds of people. Schools are not typically places where the educators collaborate easily or often with one another. Instead, schools are characterized by 'strong norms of privacy and equality among teachers. To offer advice is often viewed as putting oneself above others, whereas asking for advice is seen as a sign of weakness' (Firestone, 1996, p. 222). These norms constrain professional discourse and keep the conversations firmly on inconsequential topics that have nothing to do with teaching and learning. We have spent many hours observing in staff rooms, and seldom have we heard informal conversations that dealt deeply or consistently with professional topics. Instead, educators talk about the latest party, the latest movie, the latest recipe, or the new pavement on Main Street. These sorts of conversations honor the norms of privacy and individualism, but they do not advance professional learning nor do they promote profound improvement.

Furthermore, negative socio-cultural conditions *do* exist in some schools, and they are likely to exacerbate the inherent isolation of teachers. Deal and Peterson's (1998) work on toxic cultures offers a strategy for dealing with problematic conditions. In one particularly negative school, 'The key ingredients of transformation were bringing toxicity to the surface, giving people a chance to vent, providing a chance to believe things could be better, and, finally, offering a more positive path and a large dose of hope' (p. 127). In that case, external researchers served as catalysts for the school people to recognize the interaction patterns and embedded practices that had harmed their relationships and undermined their ability to work together (and probably alone, as well). Once the negative conditions had been confronted, the staff was able to break through the negativity and to construct a more positive school culture.

We encountered a similar situation in one elementary school where a handful of individuals made a unilateral decision about an issue in which all the staff felt an investment. This incident violated a longstanding norm of collaborative decision-making and threatened to throw the whole school into turmoil. The principal raised the issue in a staff meeting and asked the offending teachers to indicate their intentions and the offended teachers to indicate their feelings. Once the underlying intentions and feelings had been aired, the individuals in each of the camps were better able to see the issue through the eyes of their colleagues in the other camp. They began to see how their own actions and reactions had led to misunderstandings, negativity, and hurt feelings. As one teacher remarked, 'I had no idea how my behavior was affecting the other teachers. If I'd had any idea how hurt and left out they were feeling, I never would have done it.' Opening their eyes to the intentions and the consequences of colleagues' actions helped the teachers to ultimately negotiate a solution that satisfied all parties.

Tackling conflicts head on does not imply that conditions will always be harmonious and inclusive, nor does it imply that individualism and privacy will disappear. It does imply, however, that when professional learning or collegial processes are in jeopardy, the socio-cultural conditions need to be confronted directly. The people in the school need to put the conditions at the top of the agenda for a staff meeting and talk about what is happening and envision other ways of interacting. This is not an easy task, especially in the face of deep divisions, longstanding conflict, or entrenched isolation. But it does absolutely no good to allow negative undercurrents to drag down an entire staff. Leaving problematic norms or toxic cultures to ripple underground reduces personal and interpersonal capacity to improve teaching and learning. Bringing them to the surface at least provides a platform for negotiating a more positive set of norms.

Of course, even when healthy socio-cultural conditions exist, some educators will still prefer solitude and silence to collaboration and conversation. We agree with Hargreaves (1993) that individualism and isolation are not necessarily psychological defects but, instead, often serve useful educational purposes and lead to worthwhile consequences. A learning community should not violate individual rights nor should it impose rigid standards on everyone. Instead, there should be room for all individuals to participate as and if they wish. As Hargreaves (1993) points out, 'A system that cannot tolerate interesting and enthusiastic eccentrics, that cannot accommodate strong and imaginative teachers who work better alone than together, and that calls individualists prima donnas and turns creative virtue into nonconformist vice is a system devoid of flexibility and wanting in spirit' (p. 73). Our vision of a learning community does not include groupthink or blind adherence to collectively developed norms and teaching methods. A standardized environment does not work any better for teachers than it does for students.

Having said that, however, we argue that isolation and individualism become problems when they lead to stagnation, disharmony, divided purposes, or miscommunication. In such instances, even the reclusive teachers will need to work with colleagues long enough to develop common understandings and common purposes. Although breaking down the walls between teachers should not stamp out individualism, it should accommodate a shift from individualistic practices to a collegial culture that supports professional learning. The culture in a school should open spaces for people to talk deeply and personally about the professional affairs that matter to them. Different people are likely to engage in collegial interactions differently, but the socio-cultural conditions should serve to support both personal and collective learning. If they do not, then there will be a serious need for school personnel to change the culture of their school in some rather dramatic ways.

The dangers of isolation and individualism became apparent in one kindergarten-to-secondary school that we investigated. The school had been unable to retain a principal for longer than one school term. In the school, a cabal of three teachers ran the entire operation, and all other teachers retreated to their classrooms. Each new principal who tried to introduce any new ideas or more extended collaboration was quickly overpowered by the triumvirate. After three years and three different principals, the director of education moved two of the three teachers to other schools, thereby eliminating their power base. The new principal quickly instituted a number of collaborative structures, and the rest of the teachers slowly emerged from their classrooms. The removal of the powerful cabal, the influence of a collaborative principal, and the response of formerly isolated teachers served to bring about a more inclusive and democratic school culture.

This story should *not* be read as an implication that a learning community demands the development of teachers who are always loyal, cooperative, and satisfied with the status quo. As Firestone (1996) argues, 'Those characteristics make teachers more compliant and easier to work with but not necessarily more professional (because part of professionalism includes independence) or effective instructors' (p. 215). Building the professional capacity of individual teachers and of whole school staffs is likely to generate some iconoclasm, and sacred traditions will come under fire if they turn out not to enhance teaching and learning. This is an uncomfortable situation, especially for educators who have invested their professional identities in those traditions. When traditions have caused strong walls to be built up around particular embedded practices, it will be necessary to break through the walls, if only to see how they have served to shape and to limit the professional narrative.

Another wall to be broken is the one built by an implicit belief that the need for ongoing learning is a sign of incompetence (Osterman, 1990). This belief is evident in almost all school jurisdictions where teachers are expected to teach, not to learn, and where insufficient time, attention, and resources plague most professional development initiatives. For the most part, teachers have not been particularly supported or encouraged in their attempts to learn or to experiment with new professional practices. In one system-wide curriculum change initiative, for example, principals and system administrators undertook formal summative evaluation of teachers' performance with the new curriculum during the first year of the project. This kind of surveillance did not encourage the teachers to take any risks, and most of them continued to operate in ways that had served them well in the past. Only the very brave teachers went out onto any kind of limb. Our conversations with a number of teachers indicated that they were reluctant to seek help, advice, or training because they did not want to appear incompetent and risk a poor performance appraisal. Our conversations with the administrators indicated that they expected teachers to be able to 'do' the new curriculum well, with little training and no institutional support, because, as one administrator said, 'After all, they are teachers, aren't they? They know how to teach, don't they?' Of course, the upshot was an inappropriately delivered curriculum, distressed teachers, frustrated administrators, and precious little professional learning.

In a learning community, this kind of narrative would not be tolerated. In a learning community, both teachers and administrators value ongoing professional learning and see it as adding value to the educational enterprise, not as signaling incompetence. From a capacity-building perspective, knowledge gaps are desired because they indicate spaces for renewal, and continuous learning is expected of all educators – teachers, administrators, and non-instructional staff alike. That is, the socio-cultural conditions support the notion of teachers who constantly engage in critical inquiry, alone and together. One of the ways to elicit that kind of culture is for educators to ask professional questions of one another. Whether or not they already know the answers, or whether they *think* they know, asking professional questions signals a readiness to learn something new and affirms the professional capacity of the respondent. The questions might include the likes of: 'What do we expect the students to know? How do we know if or what the students are learning? In what other ways could we enhance student learning? Do we have any idea about what goes on inside the minds of the students? Do we know how they learn best? Do we care?' When all educators in a building continue to ask these sorts of questions of one another, then all are affirmed 'as intelligent, inquiring, perceptive, and informed professionals' (Phelan,

1996, p. 337). And ongoing learning becomes part of the natural daily discourse rather than an afterthought or add-on.

All of this implies that structures need to be in place for the people in a school to forge sustainable group dynamics and to share professional ideas. Creating a new culture is, first and always, the task of the individuals who share a common space. As Deal and Peterson (1998) say, 'The process [of cultural transformation] occurs inside a school, sometimes assisted by outsiders, but is always led by those who have a vested interest in a new beginning' (p. 128). But they can only do so when the structural arrangements open doors for them to talk with one another about professional matters.

Structural Arrangements

The question of school restructuring is a tricky one that has been approached from any number of directions. Some, such as Elmore (1992), Schlechty (1991), and Barth (1990) have argued that fundamental changes need to be made to the current practice of grouping students by age- and grade-level, dividing learning into discrete subjects and topics, and assessing student learning in relation to pre-determined expectations. Although this is an appealing notion, any decision to restructure according to the 'needs' of students is fraught with troubling social, ideological, and power dynamics, especially if it ensues from an assumption that certain students are 'deficient' in some way (Lipman, 1997). Furthermore, as Firestone points out, 'when one moves away from the conventional structure, it is not clear what range of options exists, and whether some more effectively promote active learning and flexible teaching for higher-order thinking than others' (p. 227). (And those of us who have been around schools for some time are pessimistic about the possibility of changing the existing organizational arrangements for students, especially in high schools.) Because we have had little personal experience with alternative grouping structures, we cannot contribute to this debate. (That is, we both have taught in schools where students have been grouped in multi-age and multi-grade configurations, but still these schools have been structured around grade levels, age groups, and disciplinary subjects.) We mention it here to point out the complexity of structural arrangements. Although restructuring the educational world experienced by students is one more idea on the structural horizon that might deserve some attention and that might be included in action research projects in particular schools, it is not one for which we have any suggestions.

The complexity of structural arrangements is further evident in Lipman's (1997) note:

> Restructuring may include re-organization into schools-within-schools, charter schools, and teacher teams; school-based management and shared governance; school-community collaborations; and reconstruction of curriculum and instruction. Teachers may have new opportunities for leadership (through steering committees and task forces, governance councils, district bodies); greater initiative to design curricula, pedagogy, and assessment; and new responsibilities as student mentors and liaisons with youth-serving agencies. (pp. 33-34)

Furthermore, each strategy on this rather daunting list entails political and technical considerations as much as it does structural ones. For example, Guskey and Peterson (1996) point out that site-based management (or school-based decision making) has been plagued with power, implementation, mission, time, expertise, culture, avoidance, and motivation problems. Their analysis of research on this particular restructuring option indicates that it has seldom led to the deep improvements in teaching and learning that its advocates proffer. Our own experience with site-based management has also demonstrated that it has very little to do with daily classroom operations or with teaching and learning even in a broad sense (Sackney & Dibski, 1994). Instead, we have found it to be fundamentally concerned with who holds the levers of power in a school and whose ideas will be placed at the top of the school agenda.

In spite of the complexities and perplexities surrounding the notion of restructuring, there appears to be a clear link between professional learning and structural arrangements. As Firestone (1996) points out,

> It is fairly clear that attending to the knowledge base of teachers without considering organizational arrangements is likely to lead to a situation where new ideas are adopted by a minority of practitioners and are weakly institutionalized. However, changing organizational arrangements without a clear sense of what teaching and learning should be like can lead to goal displacement, where these arrangements become ends in themselves and do not contribute to the educational outcomes they are expected to produce. (p. 231)

In this book we cannot even begin to touch on all of the proposed configurations of restructuring. What we have had experience with, and what we will limit our discussion to, are structural arrangements that promote and extend professional discourse and professional learning. However, we do not want to suggest that the ideas we present in this chapter are the only ones that can or will lead to the development of a learning community; a wholeness perspective does not lend itself to one particular form or one regular structure. Instead, we anticipate that multiple forms and diverse structures will grow out of exigencies and circumstances in particular schools. We expect that structural arrangements will be situated in a specific context and will serve specific purposes. If educators are self-regulating, it makes sense that the structures will shift and change as circumstances shift and change. This condition signals that the structures are in the service of the work rather than the work being in the service of the structures (Schlechty, 1991).

A structure of first importance is that of heavy and persistent investment in professional development. Too often we have heard educators and parents say that classroom time cannot be 'sacrificed' for professional development. Too often we have seen dollars for professional development slashed from educational budgets to 'balance the books.' Too often educators have refused to participate in professional development opportunities because they didn't want to 'waste the time.' To our way of thinking, such sentiments and practices are clearly misguided. Time spent in professional learning is not wasted, and professional learning is not a disposable frill. The time spent on professional learning can (and ought to) enhance the time spent in the

classroom. It is not a sacrifice of instructional time for the students but is an investment in more effective classroom time. (Of course, we recognize that some 'PD days'
are a complete waste of time because they have little, if any, relevance or meaning for
the teachers. Our previous arguments hold only when professional development is
directly and explicitly linked to classroom practices and school life, even when the
topic is theoretical or philosophical in nature.)

One compelling case of insufficient attention to professional learning is what is
happening in school systems around the world in relation to the infusion of technology. In most of these initiatives, large chunks of money are being spent on state-of-
the-art hardware equipment and software applications, but there has been almost no
investment in teaching the teachers to use the systems. Consequently, expensive
equipment sits idle at the back of the classroom or in a computer lab, or it is used
inappropriately and seldom to advance student learning in any real sense. What this
demonstrates is that the failure to invest in professional development of teachers is
likely to result in unsustainable innovations. In our work with school systems, we
have often proposed a 60-40 rule, with 60% of the available funds being devoted to
technology and 40% to professional development. We know of no organization other
than school systems that would fail to invest in the professional education and training of the people who will need to implement an initiative. To us, this simply must
change.

The investment in professional development needs to be made not just by school-
based educators but also by all stakeholder groups, including teacher unions (Bredeson
& Scribner, 2000) and central office administrators (Firestone, 1996). Firestone, for
example, argues that system administrators ought to give a clear signal that professional learning is important. He suggests three means: 'through (a) their own involvement in professional development activities (as both participants and facilitator); (b)
the allocation of resources to the task; and (c) the creation of opportunities for teachers to discuss what they are learning and to act and reflect on their efforts' (p. 227). Our
point here is that if professional learning is seen as a frill or a waste of time, then
perhaps the wrong sorts of learning opportunities are going on. If professional learning truly gets at the tough problems and deep mysteries of teaching and learning, then
it is as essential to life in the classroom as chalk and books. Administrators and
teachers need to protect professional learning time as vigilantly as they now protect
instructional time.

If a learning community means (as we believe it does) that educators engage in
professional conversations and build a culture of inquiry, then it stands to reason that
they need structural mechanisms to enable this kind of discourse. This is not to say
that the mechanisms can be unilaterally imposed or that they can be rigid, static structures. Too often we have witnessed the demise of well-intentioned collaborative ventures because there was insufficient preparation, flexibility, or connectivity. When
collaboration is mandated, when teachers are forced to attend formal meetings, and
when meeting topics are disconnected from classroom life, the collaborative efforts
are not authentic and teachers are likely to resist. In fact, many educational researchers have found this sort of reaction. Bakkenes et al. (1999), for example, noted that
even teachers who had built strong collaborative alliances showed an aversion for

formal meetings, and Hargreaves (1991) has documented numerous cases of what he calls 'contrived collegiality'. What this implies to us is that, in the case of structures for professional exchange, form must follow function rather than the other way around (Sergiovanni, 2000, p. 6). While there needs to be time built into the school day for teachers to meet and to talk, the actual arrangements for structuring the meetings will shift and change depending on the circumstances of the day and the frames of reference of the teachers.

The use of time and how it is structured in schools has captured the attention of a number of people. Fullan (1997), for example, cites it as one of the fundamental problems and critical resources for educational improvement. Most scholars (e.g., Louis, 1994) argue that teachers' time needs a complete overhaul in order to free up time for collaborative processes and professional learning. While we sympathize with this argument, we also believe that the problem is not that there is no non-instructional time available in schools. The real problem, in our point of view, is that this sort of time has seldom been devoted to the kind of learning that is necessary in a learning community. We have noted that teachers would rather be in their classrooms teaching or preparing for upcoming lessons, but we have also noted that, in many cases, collaborative work has been poorly organized and unrelated to the perplexities of teaching. Structuring more time for teams to meet, under these conditions, will not lead to the depth of learning and the quality of discourse that characterizes a learning community.

Having said that, we agree that the dearth of discretionary time for professional collaboration is one of the major structural flaws in the system. It is a shame that, as Bredeson and Scribner (2000) point out, 'sometimes the only way teachers and principals can find the time to work together is to leave their schools' (p. 11). This implies that time for teachers to meet must be included in a school's timetable. A number of means can be used to free up this sort of time. We have witnessed collaborative time being found in preparation periods, staff meetings, noon meetings, professional development or planning days, and special student groupings. Each particular school staff will need to find where discretionary time resides (or where it can be arranged) and devise plans that put it to use for discourse and dialogue and for the attainment of shared meanings and shared purposes. In fact, there may need to be times when the students are dismissed from class in order to free up time for teachers to meet. We repeat: If the collaborative time is spent in dealing with the complexities and perplexities of teaching and learning, then it is an investment in, not a sacrifice of, instructional time.

A useful structure that we have observed for keeping the collaborative time focused on professional learning has been the creation of learning teams in the school. These teams, which should be comprised of both within-discipline and cross-discipline groupings, have been responsible for facilitating conversations about the tough problems and deep mysteries of teaching and learning. The enabling structures have taken the form of collective reflection meetings, problem-solving think tanks, formal opportunities for collaboration, connections to educational research and development, and networking. In previous pages of this book, these structures and strategies have been at least implicit in the school stories that we've shared, and we have found them to be structured quite differently in different contexts. What has been common to all of them is that they have served to take educators outside their own cognitive cases and to usher in new understandings.

From our experience, learning teams have worked well in elementary schools but have foundered in secondary schools because of the rigid structures therein. Hannay and Ross (1997), however, offer some successful examples from secondary schools. The common element in the successful cases is that the team leaders provide systemic ways for the professional staff to connect with colleagues, to discuss local educational issues, and to share new ideas. Of course, not all of the examples we have witnessed or read about have led to the development of a learning community or to the sorts of profound improvement that we envision. The less successful experiments have usually been characterized by 'the absence of reflective conversation about beliefs and practices or school policies' (Lipman, 1997, p. 30) and by resistance or neglect from the administrative cadre (Hannay & Ross, p. 586). Regardless of the outcomes, the creation of learning teams is a structural arrangement that gives teachers control over professional learning. This is a key element in the creation of a professional learning community because if a principal or supervisory officer controls the process, the content, and the outcomes, then the learning will stop the minute the pressure is off. By contrast, learning teams build organizational capacity that, when conjoined with deep commitments to building personal and interpersonal capacity, can lead to profound improvement in teaching and learning.

One of the most critical elements in this regard is for learning teams to institute a database approach to professional discourse (Hannay & Ross, 1997). In this approach, the teams collect extensive and intensive data on a multitude of indicators, not the least of which are student retention, student achievement, student interest, and student perception measures. Such data are often collected in formal student assessment measures, in student satisfaction surveys, or in class clinics where educators talk about some of the issues that come up on a day-to-day basis or with individual students. But these are only the more typical sources and measures. Data also can be collected from colleagues, parents, community members, other educators, or anyone else who might have a stake in a particular educational experience; data can be collected in relation to educational, social, financial, and political conditions. Our belief is that whatever an individual educator or a group of educators are involved with, all sorts of data should be collected on that element. The data provide a solid foundation for engaging in critical reflection and deep analysis of the relationship between practice and the effects of practice. Without sufficient data, there is a danger of relying on past practices and past assumptions that are separated from actual outcomes and that are unsupported by factual evidence.

A school effectiveness review can serve as a starting point for developing a database of school operations. In our experience with such reviews, we have served as outside consultants for staffs that want a disinterested party to study the performance of their school. The request for the review usually comes from the school administrator or a supervisory officer. We first work with representatives from all stakeholder groups (including parents, students, and community members) to develop the sorts of data that will be collected for a specific school. Once the data points have been established, we conduct individual interviews with all teachers and school administrators and focus-group interviews with representatives from the students, parents, and community members. We also provide survey questionnaires to everyone in the school and to all parents. Data might be gathered in relation to school climate, facilities and resources, parental involvement, instructional expectations, academic emphases, school vision and purpose, student involvement, school leadership, professional community, or any other categories of information that the participants believe to be important. We compile the data with both statistical and qualitative analyses and present a written report that includes strengths of the school and areas requiring improvement, along with a set of recommendations. We present this information to participants and discuss it thoroughly with them. They then have sufficient data from which to build on strengths and to develop plans for renewal. This is one of the most data-intensive structures that we have ever experienced in educational circles.

Other structural arrangements that have been suggested for supporting and promoting professional learning are career ladders and formal mentor-teacher programs (Firestone, 1996, pp. 220-221). In both of these arrangements, novice or early-career educators work with senior or mentor educators to learn the tricks of the trade. Although the mentors are expected to have the lion's share of expert craft knowledge (and are expected to pass that knowledge on to the new recruits), our experience with such programs is that the new educators, as well, have considerable professional knowledge to pass on. For example, they might have come from a professional training program or from university courses where they have been exposed to the latest developments from educational research or from their disciplinary fields. They also are unlikely to have been socialized into 'correct' ways of thinking about teaching and learning or about staff and students. Together, these conditions make new recruits a good source of new ideas, new assumptions, and new beliefs. What this means is that professional mentor relationships are most successful when both parties come to them with a desire to learn. They also are most successful when the individuals have had some say in whom they join with. From our experience, formal mentor programs have been a dismal failure when individuals are forced into them, when professional learning is paid 'lip service,' when mentors fail to respect the professional ideas that new recruits offer, or when new recruits are made to feel inferior or deficient. Although we think such professional relationships hold promise for individual and collective learning, we also think that they are loaded with social, political, and cultural baggage. Unless these relationships are carefully tended and are persistently focused on professional development, they are unlikely to deliver on that promise.

Probably the most important structural arrangement has to do with power relationships in the educational hierarchy. Typically, administrators have operated from control functions and teachers from service functions. In that arrangement, administrators have made decisions and teachers have implemented them. Furthermore, administrators have been responsible for evaluating teachers' classroom performance and have often written performance appraisals on the basis of very limited information. These conditions have served to disconnect teachers from many of the decisions that have profound implications for classroom practice and to disconnect administrators from the daily world of classroom practice. This is more likely to lead to defensiveness and self-protection than to experimentation with practice or to administrative support for new and unusual pedagogic ideas. Instead, a learning community is better served by

horizontal stratification than by vertical. In other words, hierarchical levels are re-
duced and power is dispersed throughout the school. In that kind of arrangement,
administrators serve facilitative functions rather than control functions, and performance appraisal ensues from a developmental perspective rather than an evaluative
one. This keeps administrators in touch with daily classroom circumstances and practices, and it keeps teachers in touch with the decisions that affect the ways in which
they work with their students. And when power is ubiquitous, it can be used to
facilitate the work rather than to control the people.

In all of the structural arrangements, there needs to be direct and explicit attention
paid to opening the lines of communication for all parties. In most schools that we
have observed, we have seen the need for improving the flow of information. Too
often we have witnessed hoarding or brokering of information. Too often we have
seen only certain people being privy to critical pieces of information. Too often staff
members have found out too late about specific learning opportunities, crucial lines of
supply, or key meetings. Too often certain individuals have been shut out of collective
processes. Such communication patterns serve to take power away from individuals
and to keep them in defensive positions (Kanter, 1978). Instead, schools need to be
characterized by ubiquitous communication, where information flows freely in all directions, from and to all individuals. There need to be places where everyone can (and
is expected to) write or share information and where everyone is encouraged to contribute to ongoing discourse. Some examples are regular newsletters or news bulletins,
daily log-in information binders, occasional memos, or photocopied circulars, to name
but a few.

Although in most schools communication has typically taken paper form, an electronic listserve or bulletin board can also serve this purpose. In the past, electronic
communication has primarily been the administrators' territory but it is rapidly becoming an access strategy for all people in the school. People log on throughout the day
to read what has already been posted and to post their own items. In fact, we have
found electronic communication to be one way of getting the interest and input of
individuals who might be a bit reclusive or inaccessible. And it has freed staff meetings for talk about the perplexities of teaching and learning rather than the one-way
delivery of information that could easily be sent around in a memo. In schools where
all individuals have access to electronic mail, ubiquitous communication appears to be
taking root. Whether or not that sort of access leads to improved teaching and learning depends on what purposes the communication serves and on the nature of the
collaborative processes in the school.

Collaborative Processes

Although we have dealt with the nature of collaborative processes in earlier chapters,
it bears some additional attention here because we believe that the nature of discourse
in a school is often shaped by systemic influences that are out of conscious awareness. From that perspective, attention to the structures of discourse is as important as
attention to the structures of organization. Our argument here is that, in a learning
community, the discourse needs to be structured around the perplexities of teaching

and learning rather than around mundane events or institutional information. This is the kind of discourse that goes to the heart of the educational enterprise and that is likely to hold the interest of the professional staff. Bakkenes et al. (1999), for example, found that teacher motivation to participate in collaborative work declined as the work became more distant from work with students, and Gitlin and Margonis (1995) found a similar disinterest among teachers who were asked to participate in school-based decision making. In both cases, when the decisions and issues were directly related to their work with students, the teachers were more willing to put in the time and effort that collaborative processes entailed. When the decisions or issues appeared to be politically motivated or organizationally inclined, the teachers resisted collaboration. If issues related to teaching and learning are relegated to the bottom of the agenda and are dealt with only after the institutional items have been taken care of, that is a clear signal that teaching and learning are relatively insignificant in the work of the school. However, if they are placed at the top of the agenda and are given dominance in the discourse, then they receive the time, attention, and status that they deserve, and the discourse can increase organizational capacity to improve teaching and learning.

In order to do so, the discourse needs to allow room for conceptualization of instruction and curriculum. Phelan (1996), for example, argues for a 'pedagogy of conversation' (p. 343) that positions teachers as knowing professionals who answer the problems and address the mysteries of teaching and learning from a reflective, analytic, discursive approach, in collaboration with others and responsible to others. Educators enter into a dialogue with colleagues, with practice, and with curriculum and instruction. The discourse positions practice as text, with which the educators sort out the meanings that inhere in particular expressions and outcomes of curricular and instructional practices. Through the discourse, teaching competence becomes 'a normative rather than merely descriptive notion' (Phelan, 1996, p. 343). Such a critical discourse embedded in professional practice reduces the tendency of teachers to blame the students when educational problems persist (Lipman, 1997). A pedagogy of conversation assumes that there is always a need to examine teaching practices, even (and especially) when dealing with troubled or poorly functioning students.

Of course, if the conversation only happens between the individual and his or her own practice, then there has been no transfer of learning from the individual to the group, and there is no learning community. This means that the discourse must be structured so that individual meaning becomes accessible to others in the school or the system. Dixon (1997) uses the metaphor of the hallway to indicate the organizational spaces and processes by which collective meaning is constructed. She notes, 'Hallways are places where *collective meaning* is made – in other words, meaning is not just exchanged, it is *constructed* in the dialogue between organizational members' (p. 25, emphasis in the original). (We are sure that each of our readers will be able to remember, as we have, specific hallway conversations where their minds were changed about some hot topic of discussion.) Dixon goes on to say that 'It is this joint construction of meaning that is organizational learning' (p. 25). She points to seven elements of hallway learning: '(1) reliance on discussion, not speeches; (2) egalitarian participation; (3) encouragement of multiple perspectives; (4) nonexpert-based dialogue; (5) use of a participant-generated database; (6) the creating of a shared experience; and (7) the creation of unpredictable outcomes' (p. 28). These elements correspond neatly with the discourse expected in a learning community. In other words, if the discourse fits Dixon's hallway metaphor, then the discourse is likely to lead to a 'sense of knowing more about the whole and how the parts relate and therefore being able to act in concert with that shared understanding' (p. 33). Through this kind of discourse, educators sort out relationships between individual and collective meaning and construct common understandings 'in the hallway.'

The hallway metaphor assumes, of course, that there is room for dissenting voices and alternative perspectives. Usually, these voices are pointing to deep, substantive issues that are uncomfortable for those in the dominant group to face but that desperately need to be aired (Gitlin & Margonis, 1995; Lipman, 1997). The deep issues can be many things: racism (and other isms), power imbalances, hollow process, co-optation, or manipulation, to name but a few. Usually the sensitive issues coalesce around systemic assumptions or practices that serve to advantage those who are in positions of relatively greater power and to limit the efficacy of those who are not. The dissenting voices are the most uncomfortable ones, but they are also the ones that could just be putting the spotlight on an issue that has typically been covered up or discounted. Unless the sensitive issues are sorted out, the outcomes of the collaborative process are not likely to yield real improvement in the educational experience of particular groups of students or teachers. Instead, they are likely to perpetuate existing practices that sort children and teachers into 'good' and 'bad' categories.

What all of this means is that the collaborative processes need to help educators sort out what different events, phenomena, or circumstances mean. As Weick (1995) points out, what *has* happened is not as important as what people *have construed* about an event. That is, what is important is how people make sense of different events or circumstances or conditions and what they mean to individuals and to the group. This is the foundation of the social construction of knowledge (Berger & Luckman, 1966), and it is the mechanism that lies at the heart of a learning community. It is the mechanism by which people engage in deep consideration of the mission and vision for their school, and it is mission and vision that align activities and directions. In this way, mission, vision, and meaning are as much a set of structures as are the more typical structural arrangements. In a learning community, people construct meanings and structures that extend personal, interpersonal, and organizational capacity in support of profound improvement in teaching and learning.

Organizational Structures: A Synthesis

Our position in this chapter is that organizational capacity to support improved teaching and learning is enhanced when structures open the doors and break down the walls that have typically separated people in schools. The structures that we have addressed in the previous pages are socio-cultural conditions, structural arrangements, and collaborative processes within and through which school people do their work (see Figure 6.1). Our argument is that these things have to be in place if a true learning community is to develop. Without these sorts of structures, people will remain isolated, and learning will remain fragmented.

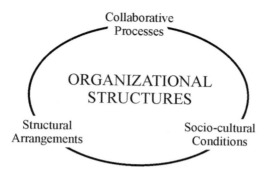

Figure 6.1 Structural capacity for the learning community.

Structures, as we have configured them in this chapter, go far beyond the typical understandings of time, location, space, and proximity. They also inhere in assumptions, values, belief systems, vision, purpose, relationships, culture, and process. They are, in effect, both visible and invisible. These sorts of implicit and explicit structures provide the mechanisms by which cultural scripts are developed and enacted. The more direct attention that is paid to the structures, the more likely it is that the scripts will be available for critique and, if necessary, for change. As Winston Churchill is purported to have said, 'First we shape our buildings; thereafter our buildings shape us.' This is as true for structures as it is for buildings, and many people can share stories of how the structural arrangements in different work places have caused them to react and respond differently from context to context. From our perspective, the structures in a learning community allow for coherence and congruency (Haskins et al., 1998) to develop in the school and they locate the people more closely in relationship with one another.

7

Organizational Capacity: Sharing Leadership and Sharing Power

In an educational community, leadership is all about making teaching and learning happen. It provides a sense of direction, energy, coherence, and coordination to the actions and activities going on in the school. That is, it is through leadership that the power to accomplish the work of the school is enacted. None of this, of course, is new. What is perhaps new is that, in a learning community, individuals feel a deep sense of empowerment and autonomy and a deep personal commitment to the work of the school. This implies that the people in the school form not just a community of learners but also a community of leaders. The concept of a community of leaders has been fundamental to many of the principles and practices that we have presented in previous chapters. This does not mean that leadership is necessarily shared by all or that there is no place for the school principal. Instead, it means that leadership is enacted throughout the school by a variety of individuals and in a variety of ways. Consequently, when we talk about leaders and leadership in this chapter, we are not always or specifically talking about the people who have formal leadership roles (such as the principal, the department head, the supervisory officer, and so on) nor are we always or exclusively talking about the functions and tasks that have typically been part of the administrative role set (such as decision making, problem solving, control, supervision, and so on). What we are talking about is the whole set of people, roles, tasks, and functions that push forward the process of teaching and learning.

Having said that, we want also to acknowledge that there will be times when we *do* want to speak specifically about the formal leaders and about the typical tasks. They are every bit as much a part of the leadership matrix as are the community of leaders and the facilitative tasks. To ignore them is, in our mind, both foolish and naïve, for what the principal values gives a clear signal to other people (such as students, teachers, non-instructional staff, and parents) about what is important and desirable for the school. Principals and other administrators play a key role in enacting power dynamics and power relations in a school, and their role is crucial to the development of a community where power dynamics are directed toward teaching and learning and where power relations are mutual, interdependent, and responsive. That

94 C. Mitchell & L. Sackney

is, the school administrators play a pivotal role in the operations of any school, including (and especially) one that is being constructed as a learning community. This is true even when a school is characterized by shared leadership and shared power.

What this signifies is that the idea of leadership capacity for a learning community is a curious and complex dance between those who hold formal leadership positions and those who take up leadership tasks on an informal or ad hoc basis. Our discussions in this chapter engage this dance. At times the principal and other administrators will lead the dance and at times the collective leadership cadre will take up those sorts of roles. In this chapter, when we refer to *administrators*, we mean anyone who has a position of supervisory responsibility, including the principal, vice-principal, supervisory officers, and department heads. When we want to specify the school principal, we use that term. In all cases where we use the term *leaders*, we are referring to the larger set of individuals who take on leadership roles and functions for specific times, purposes, or situations. Under some circumstances, this may include all individuals in a school. It is not that we lack clarity in our understanding and use of terms. It is that the leadership dance in schools that are moving toward shared leadership and shared power moves back and forth among all these different configurations of leadership and leaders. It is important that this dynamic set of leadership relations be acknowledged in any consideration of a learning community.

This chapter is fundamentally concerned with issues of followership and leadership. We see these two processes as the yin and the yang of school action, with each one moving seamlessly around the another in reciprocal reinforcement and mutual arrangements. Both serve essential roles in the school, with leadership opening spaces for action and followership getting things done. For although Captain Picard of the starship *Enterprise* can say, 'Make it so,' only the helmsman can put the ship into orbit. Leaders and followers together create a place where there is a collective sense of belonging, and particular individuals will be both leaders and followers at different times and for different purposes. That is, leadership and followership flow through all aspects of school life in complex and dynamic ways. In this chapter, we concentrate on the flow of leadership, but we assume that followership is always a crucial part of the process.

Leadership as a Systemic Condition

A first assumption for building leadership capacity for a learning community is that leadership operates in and through the entire system. Systemic leadership signifies that all individuals hold certain levers of power and that different sorts of power are vested in different roles. What we mean by this is that, for example, knowledge power locates in those who hold particular knowledge bases (the chemistry teacher knows about chemistry, the English teacher about English, the vice-principal about scheduling, the students about . . .). Information power locates in those who are privy to specific facts. Power of personality locates in those to whom other individuals are drawn. Political power locates in those who have access to key resources and key lines of supply (Kanter, 1979). Position power locates in the administrative officers (the principal, vice-principal, department head, union leader, teacher, and so on). All of these power bases are essential in enacting the tasks of the school when power is defined as the ability to move from point A to point B.

Power, in and of itself, is a positive and necessary part of school life. Unfortunately, negative connotations have accreted onto the term because of the ways in which power levers have been wielded in abusive or disrespectful ways. Furthermore, principals are often loath to share power in many schools, and the hoarding of power can strain or break relations among colleagues. For example, in a study of site-based management schools in England, many head teachers were found to consolidate power in their office (Sackney & Dibski, 1994). This caused a fundamental shift in their role, from that of lead teacher to that of resource manager, thereby changing the nature of their relationship with the professional staff from one of equals to one of superior/subordinate. This caused teachers to be suspicious and resentful when power was wielded by the head teachers. In some North American schools, principals have been reluctant to share power because they perceive themselves to be accountable at the end of the day. Still other principals have told us that they are not prepared to share power because 'I've worked damned hard to achieve this position and be darned if I'm going to share power now.' When the administrators take these sorts of positions, power is not likely to be seen in a positive light by other members of the school community nor is it likely to be dispersed appropriately across the membership.

One of the unfortunate consequences of this sort of power relations is that people at different levels of the hierarchy perceive one another differently and receive different kinds of treatment. Over and over again, we have observed (and have fallen victim to) an intense and unarticulated deference toward authority figures. We have seen it when teachers defer to the school or system administrators, when students defer to teachers, and when our graduate students defer to us. We too have been guilty of deferring to our deans and university administrators. In all cases where we have witnessed this phenomenon, the deference has been given to the occupier of an office that is perceived to be elevated above the deferring individual's place in the system. This is in part because we have all been socialized to respect office holders and the power that resides in their office. It is also in part because the office imbues the holders with certain powers to reward or punish us. (Have you ever failed to stop when a police officer raised a hand in front of you?)

We have observed that, when people defer to authority figures, they often fail to take ownership for the direction of the school or to take responsibility for improving school conditions. They are much more likely to divest themselves of all joint ownership and to place responsibility squarely on the shoulders of the administrators (Hajnal et al., 1998). Consequently, attempts to bring about school development tend to be less effective and less compelling. Over a period of time, unless there is constant pressure from 'the top,' the changes simply disappear. This might be expected (and even acceptable) in a bureaucratic organization, but it certainly is not in the spirit or the interests of a learning community.

An interesting example of deference to authority happened in a graduate course being taught by a new faculty member and being taken by a senior faculty member. In one of the activities, class members were asked to give a dollar to a small group of classmates who had been designated by the instructor as decision-makers. The decision-making cadre was given the task of deciding what should happen with the money, with the majority of the class having no input into the decision. During the exercise, a host of problematic (albeit typical) power dynamics emerged, but no one (not even the senior faculty member) broke the rules of the exercise or questioned the instructor's right to designate the power players. During a discussion of the exercise, the class members who had not been part of the decision-making process, including the senior faculty member, complained loudly and bitterly. When asked why they had not stepped outside the rules, they indicated that it had never occurred to them as a possibility. In their minds, the instructor had absolute control over what transpired in the exercise, and their only option was to defer to the instructor's authority. The truly remarkable aspect of this case was that a senior faculty member deferred to a junior colleague simply because of the respective positions that they held in this one particular instance.

What this signifies to us is that deference to authority is deeply ingrained in the power dynamics that have built up in a society that is fundamentally hierarchical. The hierarchy, in other words, is enacted not just in organizational structures but also in assumptions and cognitive schema and in the relationships among the people. For this reason, we believe that the people who hold positions higher up in a hierarchy need to reach out to those who sit at the lower levels. What this means in schools is that, if genuine power sharing is to occur, school administrators have the first responsibility for creating the conditions under which power flows through all levels of the system. It is their responsibility to break through the hierarchical mindsets that 'keep people in their places.' Furthermore, they need to engage first in power sharing because that provides a model for others to follow. It does not suffice for principals to advocate power sharing but not to practice it. This is an inauthentic position and will cause teachers and others in the school to view the principal as not being credible. Power sharing requires principals and other administrators to sublimate their egos to the collective potentialities of the school staff. Although this is not an easy task, and principals are likely to face considerable role strain when they attempt to make these sorts of changes (Bredeson (1993), the ultimate goal is for an appropriate and ubiquitous flow of power in support of teaching and learning. From our perspective, that goal is worth the effort.

Systemic leadership and shared power have relevance for establishing and maintaining collaboration in schools (Crow, 1999). Individuals in different roles bring different perspectives on issues and provide different functions. In schools, for example, the director, board members, curriculum consultant, school administrator, classroom teacher, special education teacher, and students not only see their roles differently, but the expertise they bring to any issue varies considerably. When the school is characterized by systemic leadership and shared power, then there will probably be structural opportunities for at least some of these individuals to come together at particular times to address particular concerns. Expanding these collaborative networks enables individuals to take leadership positions and functions that are appropriate for their particular power bases. In this way, novel ideas and solutions can be applied to problems or issues, and learning can be furthered.

Leadership as a Cultural Condition

Shared leadership and shared power do not happen by accident nor are they typical of most schools. If they are to emerge in a school, there needs to be a particular culture in place that can support and sustain these sorts of assumptions and practices. By culture, we mean 'how the work of the school gets done,' or 'what keeps the herd moving roughly in a western direction.' Culture is the narrative glue that holds the participants together. Based on the norms, values, beliefs, assumptions, and guiding principles that undergird the work of the school, culture steers people in a common direction. It provides the norms that shape the way individuals behave and interact with each other. For example, an operating norm might be that teachers are expected to be in school early. When a teacher does not abide by this norm, someone reminds the individual that s/he is transgressing the norm by saying something like, 'Did the alarm clock not go off this morning?'

Some of the basic elements of a culture that supports shared leadership and shared power are trust, caring, commitment, common knowledge, equity, and democracy. It is a culture where leaders create spaces for more leaders, where each person who holds a lever of power wields it in ways that allow other leaders to emerge. That is, it is a culture that yields what Sergiovanni (2000) calls 'leadership density' (p. 134) and what we have called a community of leaders. In this kind of culture, the norms nudge people to listen intently to one another, to accept the contributions and divergent views of others as honest attempts to help, to treat each person with respect, and to share information so that every member is aware of the salient issues and facts. These conditions afford people the opportunity to develop more of a system-sensitive perspective of their educational community, thereby overcoming teacher isolation, one of the common systemic barriers to ubiquitous leadership.

The elements that can support and sustain shared leadership and shared power need to be explicitly embedded in the school culture, and leaders (both formal and informal) play a vital role in bringing to life such a culture. Leaders shape the culture by what they give attention to, what they talk about and support, and what they reward. Sustained attention to important school matters reinforces attitudes and behaviors (Deal & Peterson, 1994). Leaders can create a leader-rich culture by confronting resistance; by recognizing and celebrating accomplishments at individual, group, and community levels; by fostering collegiality; by emphasizing inquiry and reflection; and by promoting teacher development and continuous improvement (Fullan, 1992). A leader-rich culture changes the typical pattern of relationships. When people share information and decision making, engage in discourse and dialogue, and work in teams, they are interacting in ways that are not typical of most schools. And as teachers, students, and parents accept these new arrangements, administrators can expect to have considerable trouble controlling the people (or the arrangements, for that matter). There is an expression that if you teach a group of people to cook, don't be surprised if they challenge the layout of the kitchen. Administrators, then, will need to be prepared to change the layout if that is what ultimately is deemed to be necessary.

Creating a leader-rich culture is only the first step, however. There is also a need to manage and to maintain the culture once it has been established. One approach to managing the culture is to focus on symbolic leadership (Deal & Peterson, 1994). In this case, the principal, in particular, pays attention to the symbolism in the school by making sure that the rituals and ceremonies reinforce the notions of shared power and ubiquitous leadership. Administrators promote positive values oriented to distributed leadership and appropriate use of power. Particularly important in this regard are the metaphors and narratives that depict the culture of the school. That is, language and stories that focus on collaborative decision-making and power sharing are important determinants of maintaining and sustaining the culture.

Shared leadership and shared power are likely to be associated with increased incidents of conflict and disagreement. This happens for at least two reasons. First, people spend more time together, and, second, the nature of their relationship changes. In particular, they are positioned as equals, regardless of the position they hold within the hierarchy. Conflict can be expected to emerge when people who are in intense, interdependent work contexts differ in what they think, believe, or value. This means that, in a leader-rich culture, people must be able to deal with and to resolve conflict in a constructive manner. Conflict should be viewed as a learning opportunity rather than as a personal threat or attack; it is a natural and desirable aspect of community life that reveals and clarifies understandings and purposes. It is beyond the scope of this book to deal substantively with the huge topic of conflict resolution, but a number of strategies that we have mentioned in previous sections and chapters of the book can be used to move effectively through conflictual situations. Some of these strategies include dynamic harmonization, professional conversations, dialogue, testing assumptions and attributions, team building, power sharing, and skillful communication. Other strategies for and approaches to conflict resolution can be found in any number of books written about the topic. But regardless of the approach or the strategy being used, conflict resolution needs to take place in an environment of trust, openness, and mutual respect. If these conditions are not in place, then administrators are expected to find ways to bring them to life.

One of the potential problems of a leader-rich culture is too many Don Quixotes galloping off in too many directions. There must be ways to bring all these leaders into at least some sort of alignment. One of the ways to do so is to create a sense of shared vision and purpose. This builds commitment among various individuals 'by developing shared images of the future we seek to create, and the principles and guiding practices we hope to get there' (Speck, 1999, p. 65). Hammering out the shared vision and purpose is a collective task, even though the administrators are the ones who usually provide the opportunities for this to occur. This can be accomplished through a futures search, through focused professional conversations or reflection meetings, through think tank meetings, or through any other structural arrangement that brings together the people who are concerned about the direction of the school. Together they consider past practices and future alternatives, they share their dreams, and they come to consensus about what it is that would make their school a better place. This is always a lengthy and often a contested process, but it is the most effective method of bringing coherence to the different desires and directions that different leaders bring to the table.

Leadership as a Political Condition

Just as shared leadership and shared power rely on a particular cultural condition, so too do they rely on a particular political milieu. Politics and political games are manifested in all situations where two or more people come together for a specific purpose. This is an unavoidable part of the human condition. Our contention is that certain sorts of politics will promote ubiquitous leadership, and certain sorts will restrict leadership potential. For the most part, we are talking here about micro-politics (that which happens in the local setting) rather than about macro-politics (that which happens in the larger system or beyond). That is, we are interested in the ways in which people navigate political tensions within the school itself and between the school and parent groups (Murphy & Louis, 1999, p. xxvi).

In a leader-rich environment, micro-politics can be expected to emerge often and everywhere. This is at least partly because when people are in more intensive and persistent interaction, there are more opportunities for misunderstandings, miscommunication, and cross-purposes. If these differences are not discussed openly and honestly, they are likely to result in micro-political gamesmanship. This might be evidenced in building coalitions, hoarding resources, brokering information, appealing to emotions, and promoting hostility, to name but a few. We have so many stories of micro-political games that our problem is one of selection rather than description. Games take place over resource allocation, teaching assignments, workload, parking privileges, office or classroom assignment, supervision assignment, or any other operational configuration that appears to pit one colleague against another in the lineup for institutional goods. In any school (in any institution), this kind of gameplaying is a naturally occurring event, but it always reduces the sense of safety and trust among colleagues.

These conditions are not sustainable, nor do they promote any kind of sharing, especially power sharing. The games that we have outlined suggest that micro-political games not only emerge from but also contribute to communication dysfunction. Our experience tells us that, when schools are not working well, people usually complain first and loudest about the communication patterns. Where poor communication exists, in all likelihood the nature of communication is fragmented and isolated, and there are few conversations about the processes of teaching and learning. But effective communication patterns can be developed, and it is the responsibility of all members to heal the communication problems in their school. However, this is also a process that school principals can facilitate. For example, if the principal schedules time and opportunities for staff members to learn salient details and to discuss critical issues openly and honestly, this is likely to circumvent some of the more troublesome micro-political games that develop in many schools.

From an ideological perspective, shared leadership and shared power are rooted in communitarian values and democratic ideals. This is a fundamental shift in the philosophic orientation of most schools, which have typically followed individualistic values and bureaucratic ideals. A shift like this implies a different orientation to and an expanded understanding of leadership. That is, leadership is not simply about getting a job done, but it is also about critiquing existing conditions. This is the dominant function of critical leadership, a notion that is found in the work of Leithwood and Duke (1999), who build on the work of Foster (1989). According to Leithwood and Duke, 'Critical leadership assumes that because existing conditions of social life have been constructed by people. . ., they can be reconstructed to be more equitable, democratic, and just if they are found wanting in these respects' (pp. 63-64). To initiate the process of reconstruction, leaders need 'to engage colleagues in self-reflection on and analyses of existing social and organizational conditions, along with the social cultures of both the school and the local community' (p. 64). This implies that critical leadership is fundamentally concerned with the moral, ethical, and social conditions in a school. From our perspective, shared leadership is more likely than unilateral leadership to sharpen the critical edge and to bring forward problematic conditions for reconstruction.

Our experience with school effectiveness reviews demonstrates how quickly inequity and disempowerment become obvious when all individuals are invited into the halls of power. In many of the schools, we have found marginalized groups and individuals who have seldom been asked for their opinions or their dreams but who have been eager to share their stories with us. In our interviews, they have commented on feeling shut out of school processes and deprived of institutional benefits. This problem seems to be most acute in schools that house elementary and secondary students in the same building. In most cases, the elementary staff members feel that they do not get their fair share of the school resources. A further complication is that, at the elementary level, most teachers are women, and they perceive gender differences in how the decisions are made in the school, with the men at the secondary level having more input into the process. Critical leadership brings these sorts of discrepancies (both perceived and real) into the open. Critical discussion about the conditions (informed by rich data in relation to the conditions) can illuminate which are real and which are merely perceptions. This kind of information positions the staff to readjust imbalances. Through these sorts of interactions, critical leadership pays attention to issues of justice and fairness and promotes the ideals of equity and democracy.

The ideals of equity and democracy assume that the power base extends to all participants in the school. Of course, this does not mean that all individuals enjoy the same sorts of power nor does it mean that all individuals want the same amount of power. We have had several teachers, for example, tell us that they do not want to be bothered with wielding power in the hallways and staff room of the school. But this should be the decision of the individual rather than the dictate of embedded power dynamics. In a leader-rich school, the power base is consensual and facilitative in nature. That is, interested or affected people come to consensus about decisions, directions, and dreams, and power is expressed through people rather than over people.

In recent years, transformational leadership has been the prime candidate for leadership in a learning community. Leithwood and Jantzi (1990), for example, contend that transformational leadership encourages collaboration and gives to school staff an active role in the decision-making processes of the school. From this perspective, school principals involve the professional staff in goal setting, joint planning, power sharing, problem solving, decision making, and school renewal (Leithwood, Jantzi & Fernandez, 1994). It is assumed that this form of leadership raises the level of commitment to mutual purposes and to school development. This may be true, but it does not necessarily lead to a leader-rich school. Our problem with transformational leadership is that it still positions the administrators differently in school actions and assumes that they wield more powerful levers than the informal leaders or the followers (e.g., Leithwood, 1992). If this is the case, then leadership and power are not really shared nor are they really equitable.

We certainly recognize that the school principal is one of only a few individuals in the school who has access to the more formal levers of power and who sees the whole picture. This places principals in a unique position, but it should not place them in a superior position. Shared leadership and shared power means that, at times and as appropriate, other members of the school will involve the professional staff, encourage collaboration, and raise the level of commitment. Our point here is that power is not a commodity that the principal has the right to give or to withhold nor is empowerment the prerogative of the principal. Power is always and already dispersed throughout the system, and individuals empower themselves by wielding those levers that apply to their particular skill sets, task milieus, and personal desires. What this signifies, in part, is that the use of power is a moral activity, and leaders (formal and informal) need to use it to fulfill moral purposes. (We assume, of course, that the questions of moral codes and moral purposes are as open to collective critique and negotiation as are the questions of educational actions and purposes that we have been dicussing throughout this book.)

Leadership as Influence

A common assumption about leadership is that it involves a relationship of influence between leader and follower. From a traditional perspective, the leader is charged with the task of influencing the follower in the direction of institutional goals or norms, and the follower either accepts, subverts, or returns the influence. In schools, influence is pervasive as students try to influence teachers, teachers try to influence principals, and principals try to influence everyone, including teachers, students, parents, central office administrators, and community members. In a leader-rich school, the direction of influence among these stakeholder groups is a complex and fascinating matter. It represents a dynamic relationship where leader and follower roles are interchanged on given issues and contexts and with various power levers and where the flow of influence is multidirectional. Rost (1991), for example, contends that leaders and followers exert reciprocal influence through expertise, position, reasoned arguments, reputation, status, personality, and interpersonal and group skills. These power resources can appear at various times and places and are wielded by various people. Teachers, for example, can lead by influencing other teachers and the school principal on specific school issues. At the same time, the principal and other teachers can attempt to influence colleagues towards a certain mission or vision of the school.

Leaders exert a crucial influence by modeling what is expected in the school. Followers tend to pay attention to what leaders say and do because this gives them some important clues as to what will be valued and rewarded. And when people see that what is desired is actually being modeled, they are more likely to abide by the demonstrated norms. For example, when leaders model critical, self-reflective learning, then that sort of learning becomes embedded in the norms and expectations of school life. When the actions of the leaders (their theory-in-use) are consistent with their stated desires (their espoused theory), they are providing authentic examples for followers, and their credibility is enhanced. But leaders can also model and reward other not so desirable behaviors. This was the case in one rural kindergarten-to-secondary school that we observed.

In this school, leadership resided in a cabal of five secondary teachers known as 'The Party Animals.' These teachers (three men and two women) dominated discussions in the staff room and in most staff meetings, and they decided who would be invited and who excluded when they led the pack to the bar after work. They were capable teachers, and most students enjoyed being in their classes, but they all taught from a discipline-based perspective, and over the years, a number of students had failed their classes. When the school division instituted a new process-based curriculum, these five teachers were openly hostile to the change. They saw it as an attack on their professional expertise because it placed disciplinary knowledge (their strength) at the service of mastery learning (not their strength). They subverted the implementation process by refusing to make any changes in their own practices and by excluding from staff discussions and from social occasions any teachers who chose to participate in the new initiatives. Their position as key opinion leaders and key social leaders in the school gave them considerable power over others, and they wielded their power unabashedly to maintain the status quo.

This story raises the question of the purpose or the anticipated outcome of any attempt to exert influence. Of course, the hope is that all influence is in the direction of improved teaching and learning, but this is a somewhat naïve position. In addition to the school described above, we have witnessed several examples of teachers using the power of their personality, history, networks, or knowledge to undermine attempts to move a school away from familiar practices. A common strategy is the post-staff-meeting conversation in the hallway or parking lot, where teachers buttonhole colleagues and present arguments or issues that were never raised in the public meeting. This has been especially evident in areas where new curricula or different instructional strategies were being implemented or proposed. Our experience indicates that teachers are particularly resistant to influences that threaten to alter their professional practice or their professional identity and, under these circumstances, they will exert counter-influence to delay or subvert the initiative.

But we have also witnessed many positive examples of influence that has been successful in enlisting staff members in school renewal exercises. In one school, for example, a group of teachers saw the need for some major revisions to the existing discipline policy. They investigated other discipline plans and lobbied other teachers and the principal to undertake a review of their policy. In time, their efforts to influence their colleagues were rewarded with a new discipline policy. Similarly, Pounder, Ogawa, and Adams (1995) found that influence exerted by both principal and teacher groups can have a strong effect on the perceived ability of the school to change. That is, the greater the influence being exerted in the direction of the proposed change, the greater the perception that the change would succeed. This research also revealed that the principal had a profound influence on teachers' collective sense of efficacy, which indirectly resulted in improved student achievement, enhanced job satisfaction, and increased goal attainment. Similar positive outcomes have been evident in much of our own work with educators, as we have witnessed teachers and principals using their influence to focus collective discussions on issues and decisions directly related to teaching and learning.

Leadership as Direction

The constructivist view of life implies that school people construct a particular reality and create particular shared understandings about the work in their school. This view accepts that schools are constructed realities as opposed to structural arrangements that operate independent of the individuals in the school. As part of the constructed reality, teaching and learning locate within a rich social context, and the direction of the school is hammered out through embedded relationships and discursive patterns. According to this perspective, leaders help administrators, teachers, students, parents, and other community members to create meaning, purpose, and direction. The dominant language and metaphors communicate the essence of the school, and leaders take a large share of the responsibility for shaping and sharing appropriate metaphors that reflect and promote the agreed upon direction or purpose.

In a learning community, purpose and direction are linked to increased capacity for teaching and learning. In this case, leadership entails articulating the values and norms that advance the learning of all members of the community. These norms might include, *inter alia*, careful reflection and analysis of the environment for learning; reflection on the purposes of education; and ongoing professional discourse among educators, students, parents, and community members. Although the development of shared norms is the purview of all people in the school, principals play a pivotal role in fostering productive norms and social relations. They create trust and commitment to learning by modeling consistency, commitment, and contribution to the school community. They create an environment for experimentation and risk taking by rewarding novel practices (both those that succeed and those that do not). In other words, because of their position in the educational hierarchy, principals are well positioned to support the normative activities that promote professional and student learning.

Principals also play a vital role in establishing channels for new information. They can create such channels by facilitating professional development opportunities and by establishing linkages to external resources. Because they have access to institutional resources and lines of supply, they are able to promote interaction by generating structures and occasions for teachers to interact and to work together. And they can help to establish teacher networks to share with one another successful practices both internally and externally. All of these endeavors serve to direct school work toward the advancement of teaching and learning. It is through such purposes and directions that a learning community can develop and flourish.

Leadership is essential for generating school processes that direct action toward enhanced teaching and learning. In particular, the processes of dialogue and discourse can focus supportive, critical, and evaluative discussions on issues related to curriculum, instruction, and student learning. These sorts of discussion might focus on how students learn, what materials can be used or produced, or what teaching strategies might be effective. Dialogue and discourse on practice can direct teachers' actions toward team teaching, serving as a critical friend, jointly studying and trying new practices and ideas, and solving school problems. Without pervasive and persistent leadership, all of these efforts are likely to remain partial, fragmented, and disconnected. By contrast, directed leadership can align efforts and generate synergy from the power of coherent action.

What this signifies to us is that leadership as direction is concerned with issues of autonomy and self-regulation. That is, in a learning community, it is not appropriate for administrators to dictate or regulate professional practice. This sort of surveillance increases institutional threat and prohibits creativity, risk taking, and experimentation – all of the things that should be happening in the search for improved teaching and learning. But some sort of regulation is absolutely essential because it provides a mechanism for sustaining and expanding professional competence. Education is inherently an ambiguous, uncertain, and poorly defined domain, and educators need to bring some sort of coherence and balance to this domain. Direction, especially that which has been hammered out in and by the community (for example, via a futures search), provides a lightning rod for attention, coherence, and purpose and brings a measure of manageability to what could easily be unmanageable.

This begs the question of what we mean by self-regulation or how we think it might be configured in a learning community. To us, self-regulation is the set of processes and dynamics through which people define and monitor professional competence. This might include the actions, practices, assumptions, beliefs, and values that are seen as desirable elements of the professional narrative and it might include the mechanisms and responsibilities for assessing competence, for identifying and addressing competence concerns, and for maintaining competence. In a learning community, these tasks are the responsibility of all members of the community, and the leaders facilitate but do not dominate the regulatory processes. Of course, self-regulation only works if the people feel a sense of commitment toward the purposes and the health of the school. If not, then self-regulation breaks down and there is a need for administrative supervision. Our contention, however, is that if the commitment is not in place and if administrative supervision takes over, then there is little likelihood that the school is operating as a learning community.

Leadership as Change

The metaphor of the learning community is deeply connected with metaphors of change and renewal, but these are two of the most hotly contested and difficult concepts in the educational arena. Change is never easy, and it gets much harder before it gets easier. This is as true in a learning community as it is in any other kind of community. And productive change can take a decidedly long time. In our work with schools, we have spent long hours, days, months, and years working on school visions and plans for improvement, only to be frustrated with how long it took some schools to get moving. But those schools that were first off the mark were not necessarily more successful in the end. These experiences have taught us that school renewal is not a linear concept. For some schools, improvement just takes longer to take hold, but once it does, the change can be more enduring.

These issues suggest that leadership is deeply concerned with the provision of support mechanisms that encourage learning and growth. Leaders play a crucial role, especially in the early stages, in creating an environment that either encourages or discourages change. If improvement efforts are to be successful, leaders need to offer technical, financial, and emotional support. Emotional support, for example, can ensue from caring relationships between leaders and followers because individuals work best when they know people care about them. A sense of caring sustains individual and group efforts and reinforces people's sense of commitment to the work of the school. In a recent school system review that we conducted, the issue of caring was mentioned on numerous occasions as a prime reason for seeing the school system as being highly effective. Teachers and non-instructional staff members consistently commented on how enjoyable it was to work in this school district because the director, central office administrators, and board members genuinely cared about the entire staff. These individuals felt recognized and rewarded for their efforts to improve teaching and learning, and we observed many teachers expending extraordinary efforts in their professional practice and in professional development. As one teacher told us, 'I've worked harder in this school division than I've ever worked anywhere else before, but I've enjoyed it more.'

Leadership differs depending upon the order of change undertaken. First order change is less threatening than second order change (Cuban, 1988). First order change is linear and does not result in a disjunctive change. First order change is usually seen as trying to do better whatever is already taking place. Second order change, on the other hand, results in disjunctive change. It entails doing something that has not been done before. Individuals find it much easier to engage in first order change than in second order change. Less of their emotion is wrapped up in first order change because it does not threaten familiar patterns of thought or behavior. Second order change, on the other hand, means approaching the problem from a novel perspective that may require a change in behavior or cognition. Consequently, the need for intensive leadership support increases with second order change in order to create a culture of continuous improvement.

Unfortunately, in many of our school effectiveness reviews, we have found that a culture of continuous improvement does not necessarily exist. Instead, in many schools the people are continuing to do what they have been doing. The difficulty with this orientation is that they keep on getting what they've been getting. The embedded practices have worked against school improvement, and leadership actions have not addressed or challenged these embedded practices. A similar condition is described in the latest work of Senge et al. (1999). These authors contend that 'most serious change initiatives eventually come up against issues embedded in our prevailing system of management' (p. 1). Such embedded practices in schools might include the leader's tendency to commitment to the change as long as it does not affect him/her;

the tendency to ensure that risky topics are not discussed; and the habit of attacking symptoms rather than the root causes of the problem. According to Senge et al., team members are limited in their capacity to deal with problematic embedded practices because of inadequate collective learning capabilities. The difficulty is that most leaders, even those who desire or advocate improvement, seldom recognize the importance of learning capabilities. For example, a teacher who forces a child to read without understanding the reasons why the child cannot read is not likely to be helpful to that child. Similarly, a leader who forces a particular initiative without realizing why people are not responding well to it is not likely to help people implement the initiative effectively or to realize the anticipated benefits.

The point is that while some improvement efforts may be successful, they will always be associated with 'limits to growth' (Senge et al., 1999). That is, there is likely to be an initial spurt of energy followed by a discomfiting slowdown. These limiting processes have to do with leaders, followers, the situation, and emotions. Limits, therefore, locate in people as much in processes. Unfortunately, in most cases, the limiting processes are given little if any attention. Instead, the focus is kept on the change process itself. According to Senge, until direct and explicit attention is given to the limiting factors, learning may be retarded or not occur at all. But although it is a critical leadership task to understand that people's emotion, self-efficacy, and learning capabilities can be limiting factors, this is not the sole responsibility of the administrators. A fundamental learning dysfunction is the assumption that limiting processes are only the concern of the administrators or that only the administrators can fix the situation (Senge et al. 1999). What is required, instead, is for leaders from all corners of the school to recognize when the limits to growth are actually pointing out some sources of creative tension and then to develop the capacity for using the embedded tension to create synergy that can ensue from a sense of shared purpose.

Furthermore, where persistent and effective learning is evident in schools, leaders have generated creative tension and the expectation that things will be different. (One case in point is Peggy's story, which was told in Chapter 3.) Because creative tension exists throughout the school community, leadership and power need to be shared on all levels of the school. People at all levels have the capacity to create tension when they serve as communities of leaders rather than simply relying on the school principal to identify the areas where leverage for improvement is high. Shared commitment to improvement develops along with shared aspirations, which arise through critical reflection and inquiry into the current reality. As people begin to identify gaps between what they see and what they want, they begin also to see interconnections among issues and possibilities for improved teaching and learning.

The interconnections are what increase relevance for educators, and relevance is one of the major challenges to initiating school improvement. Leaders need to help teachers see the connections between their world of work and any particular improvement that is being proposed. They also need to help the staff understand how new initiatives fit in with, contribute to, and benefit their professional practice. If teachers cannot see these connections, a commitment gap will develop and they are not likely to participate fully. Some individuals will go through the motions to get the administrators off their back, but as soon as the pressure is eased, the participants will back off and return to doing what they had previously been doing. This is so because the initiative has not been ingrained in their psyche. Ultimately, improvement will take hold if the individuals can see how new approaches can help them to perform their jobs more easily, efficiently, or effectively.

For this reason, relevance is one of the mechanisms that might be helpful for engaging people who will neither lead, follow, nor get out of the way. These people have often been a burden on the backs of those who are interested in moving forward, and they have exerted a heavy toll on many school development projects. If they can be shown how their own work can be helped, they are more likely to increase their commitment to the work of the school. Of course, there is no assurance that this outcome will be realized, and people have struggled with this issue for a long time. We do not want to enter this debate here because it is not the purpose of the book. We simply point out that relevance has, in our experience, been at least partly successful in engaging these sorts of people in school-wide improvement activities. For example, in the school whose story we told earlier in this section, the director of education and the administrative cadre not only cared about the staff but they also were diligent in pointing out how different instructional and curricular initiatives could have direct and practical payoffs for students, classroom teachers, and school administrators. We do not think it is a coincidence that this school system had one of the lowest rates of disengaged teachers as compared to other jurisdictions that we have studied.

In previous chapters we have frequently noted that trust is an important component for anything that happens in a school and especially for learning new practices or improving familiar ones. For most individuals in any organization, the challenge of fear and anxiety is always at least in the back of their minds if not front and center. People often feel vulnerable, unsafe, and inadequate when trust is not present. Furthermore, all learning involves risks and therefore some fear. Senge et al. (1999, pp. 244-250) outline a number of strategies for meeting the challenge of fear and anxiety in any attempt to move from where we are to where we might want to be. These include (a) starting small and building momentum before confronting difficult issues; (b) avoiding frontal assaults; (c) setting an example of openness; (d) using breakdowns as opportunities for learning; (e) ensuring that participation is a matter of choice and not coercion; (f) developing a common frame around vision and current reality; and (g) reminding people that fear and anxiety are natural responses. Bardick (1996) has developed a similar list. He notes that leaders create a cadre of committed individuals when they generate
- 'Confidence in people who were frightened
- Certainty in people who were vacillating
- Action where there was hesitation
- Strength where there was weakness
- Expertise where there was floundering
- Courage where there was cowardice
- Optimism where there was cynicism
- Conviction that the future will be better;' (p. 139)
 Taken together, these strategies can reduce the negative connotations typically associated with fear and anxiety and place these natural emotions into a context of trust and support. In developing trust with colleagues, it is important to understand that trust itself is as much an emotional response as are fear and anxiety. We trust some-

one because in our heart we feel we can depend upon that person. When fear and anxiety are framed in a relationship with trust and support, we can be less afraid or anxious about feeling afraid and anxious.

Shared Leadership and Shared Power: A Synthesis

Kouzes and Posner (1995) suggest that credible leadership based on shared values fosters stronger feelings of personal effectiveness, promotes positive work norms, fosters pride in the organization, fosters teamwork, and reduces job stress and tension. Their position is that learning can best occur under *credible* leadership. From our perspective, learning, and the development of a learning community, can best develop in an environment of *shared* leadership and shared power. These configurations of leadership and power increase the capacity within the school for people to identify gaps between existing conditions and desired realities, and to find effective and desirable ways to close at least some of those gaps. Figure 7.1 presents an image of how we see leadership and power flowing in a learning community. In this image, leadership and power are located within an environmental set of systemic, cultural, and political elements, and they serve to advance the tasks of influence, direction, and change. This configuration of leadership and power builds the capacity in a learning community for individuals to participate as a community of leaders and a community of learners.

Figure 7.1 Leadership and power in a learning community

In this chapter, we have tried to signify that, in any attempt to improve school operations or to enhance teaching and learning, the principal retains a crucial position. Even in the presence of shared leadership and inclusive practices, the principal still holds many levers with which to create an environment for continual renewal and knowledge generation. The principal can apply these levers in numerous ways: through investing in learning processes; through support and inquiry; through leadership example; and through fostering communities of learners. To foster a learning-oriented culture, principals and other leaders should understand that they do not need to have all the answers. Perhaps the most that can be expected of them is that they have some ways to find answers. For example, they might devote attention to mentoring, stewardship, and coaching; they might focus more on design than on decisions; and they might push decision making out into the school community. Principals, in particular, need to realize that they cannot do the job alone. And they need to feel comfortable with and capable of asking questions rather than providing answers because it is through questions that people arrive at inquiry and reflection. This question-asking stance positions the school principal as a learning agent who helps others to build the capacity to improve teaching and learning.

One of the challenges in writing this chapter has been the gap between the promise of shared leadership and the current reality of bureaucratic schools and hierarchical leadership. We have wrestled with the ways in which the administrators are positioned in contemporary schools. Much of what we have said about shared leadership and shared power is not immediately applicable in many schools. It takes considerable effort, attention, and commitment to move in the directions suggested in this chapter. Fullan (1999), for example, suggests that these sorts of profound changes can take as much as 10 years to bring to fruition. Nor is the process one of continuous forward motion. Instead, limits to growth always set in as people try to conserve particular aspects of the past and particular familiar practices (Senge et al., 1999). This should serve not as a reason to disengage from the journey but as a caution that, once on the path, one can expect to face some roadblocks, detours, breakdowns, and dislocations. In the end, however, we believe that the journey is worth the effort.

8

Organizational Capacity: Making it So

Saying that a learning community must be thus and so does not automatically make it so. We have stated several times in this book that the creation of a learning community is not an easy endeavor. It entails fundamentally different ways of thinking about teaching and learning and fundamentally different ways of being teachers and administrators. It asks educators to put their professional identities on the line, to admit they do not know everything, to expose their knowledge gaps to themselves and to their colleagues, and to reconstruct both their professional narratives and their professional identities. This is truly an awesome and frightening proposition. Having said that, we want also to emphasize that the task is not an impossible one. It is, rather, a developmental process that takes time, care, sustained attention, and commitment to make it so.

Because a learning community is a human system, it moves through cycles of progress and regress. At times people will move forward eagerly, but at other times they will push against the flow of the process. As Senge et al. (1999) point out, whenever something changes in a human system, the system will push back to seek equilibrium and to conserve certain aspects of the former condition. It is especially critical to remember this cyclic aspect during periods of regress. At such times, the benefits that have accrued from previous forward motions may be the only things that will sustain individuals' commitment to the process. And although the underlying *raison d'être* of a learning community is to enhance students' educational experience, considerable benefits are also in store for the professional staff. Lipman (1997) found, for example, that after a year's experimentation with team collaboration, teachers expressed 'appreciation for the mutual support, cooperation, and the "family atmosphere" of teams – in short, improvement in their professional lives' (p. 30). It is just such outcomes that can sustain commitment to the difficult processes even when momentum has slowed or stopped entirely.

In previous chapters we have provided a list of strategies for developing personal, interpersonal, and organizational capacity for building a learning community, but the ideas have been presented somewhat piecemeal. This is one of the unfortunate consequences of linear text. In this chapter, we hope to pull some of the pieces together by providing a framework for putting the ideas into practice. We do not expect that this framework will suffice in all contexts. It is, however, a framework that has worked well in our own experiments with learning communities. The framework begins with the administrators in a community (especially school principals), moves to the creation of sustainable conditions, then to the development of a learning architecture, and concludes with a discussion of some phases through which a learning community can be expected to pass. We see these steps as a developmental, ordered, cyclic series of moves that can lead to an organizational milieu that promotes sustained and sustainable capacity to bring about the profound improvement promised by the metaphor of the learning community.

Engaging the Administrative Cadre

Even though a learning community is characterized by shared power and ubiquitous leadership, the administrators play a critical role in whether or not a learning community will develop and, once established, whether or not it will continue. The administrative cadre includes the school principal and vice-principal, department heads, and system supervisors, and all of these people play a key role in the creation of a learning community. But even so, the school principal is the linchpin; without the active support and commitment of the principal, a learning community is unlikely to emerge in most schools. We have found this to be the case in every school that has worked on even some of the strategies we have presented in previous chapters, and our experience is not unusual. Hannay and Ross (1997), for example, have this to say: 'Our data suggest that this role is black and white rather than gray. The schools that were initiating changes had principals who acted collaboratively and engaged their staffs in collaborative decision making. In the schools that were waiting, the principal was either not engaged in the process or exhibited resistant behavior' (p. 586). It seems that the old adage is true: As the principal goes, so goes the school. The first step, then, is to engage the principal in the process of building a learning community.

This is not to say that the principal should control the process or dictate the outcomes. Quite the contrary. But it is to say that the principal needs to be a part of the process at every step. In the first instance, the principal needs to give clear signals that professional learning is important, that it has a high profile in school structures and priorities, and that it has sufficient time and dollar resources. One of the easiest ways to do this, of course, is to protect a professional development line item in the budget and to schedule professional development and collaboration time in the annual calendar and weekly schedule. But a more personal (and probably more sustainable) way is for the principal to model active professional learning and collaborative engagement. This sort of role-modeling can serve as a powerful signal that professional learning, both individual and collective, is the root improvement strategy for the school. These are just the strategies that Alan (who was first introduced in Chapter 2) used to engage the teachers in school-wide improvement efforts.

Alan was the principal of a small elementary school located in a poor inner-city neighborhood with a population of students who were at serious risk in the school system. For two years the staff had been trying to deal with serious behavior infractions and an impoverished learning environment and had subsequently instituted a school-wide behavior management program. In the first year of implementation, as teachers were actively learning about the philosophy and procedures of the program and as the troublesome behaviors decreased dramatically, there was considerable enthusiasm for the project. In the second year, as the results became less dramatic and the procedures more routine, commitment to the program began to waver. To keep the project alive and to move it to a new level of effectiveness, Alan and three of the staff members decided to investigate a positive reinforcement component that would help students to learn new interaction patterns, thereby reducing the need to 'manage' the students' behavior.

This search became the heart of Alan's professional growth plan for that year. He sought out various positive reinforcement programs and brought several ideas back to the staff. He facilitated a whole-staff reflection meeting that focused on their hopes, beliefs, and assumptions about student behavior and positive reinforcement, and he scheduled a school-wide professional development day for a more in-depth consideration of the philosophy that should direct the choice of a program. At that workshop, Alan participated as a co-learner with the rest of the professional staff. He made suggestions and asked questions, but he did not dominate the discussion nor did he exert pressure in any one direction. From the foundations laid during the reflection meeting and the workshop, the staff began to experiment with different configurations of positive reinforcement. When we left the school, they had not yet settled on any one program but were experimenting with a variety of strategies and had begun to develop a more inclusive and positive relationship with the students. Throughout the entire process, Alan demonstrated that he was learning along with the staff, and his efforts did not go unnoticed. One teacher, for example, said, 'Why do we have a learning staff? Because we have a learning principal.'

Alan's story gives some indication of the sorts of things that a principal can do to promote the development of a learning community, but it begs the question of how to get the principal engaged in a process of community building in the first place. In Alan's case, it happened from the 'outside-in' when we, two university researchers, approached him with the possibility of conducting an action research project on collective learning in his school. He had learned about collective learning processes in a graduate program in educational administration, he had already established a good working relationship with us, and he was in a school where there was a clear need to do things differently. These conditions made him a prime candidate for our project, and when we presented Alan with the opportunity, he was interested and eager. Once the staff expressed a similar interest, we began the experiment. Although Alan had no idea of what would transpire or how the process would unfold, he readily committed himself to the experiment, and we moved forward.

Engaging the principals can also happen from the 'inside-out' when they do it on their own. That is, principals can be intrinsically engaged when they have been exposed to the principles and practices of a learning community and believe in its potential to transform the school. This is what happened in Peggy's case (whose story is told in Chapter 3). Because of her previous work with sports teams, she saw her principal's role not as a leader but as a coach, and the idea of collective professional learning resonated with this view. She too had learned about the notion in graduate school and had immediately related it to her coaching experience. To Peggy, the notion of a staff learning together to improve teaching and learning was the same as a team practicing together to improve sports performance. At the first opportunity, she began to institute some collective learning practices in the school, and a learning community began.

A 'bottom-up' approach begins with individual teachers or with groups of teachers. This happens when the professional staff (or an individual teacher) sees a need for collective learning about some particular issue or concern in the school and enlists the principal's support for the project. We have seen numerous examples of this kind of engagement, with a host of initiatives such as, among other things, thematic teaching, new curricula, new reading programs, and school-wide events. The teachers' success in gaining the attention and the support of the principal has been somewhat mixed, in our experience, and we have yet to see a true learning community emerge from such initiatives. However, we have at least one example of a bottom-up initiative that came close to achieving this kind of school-wide focus on development and improvement.

In one rural kindergarten-to-secondary school, a small group of elementary teachers had a hunch that they could be doing things better. Most of these people were either new to teaching or new to the school, and they brought with them some novel approaches to teaching and learning. They convinced the principal to invest time and money in a series of investigations into school improvement programs. These resources enabled them to invite keynote speakers and workshop leaders to the school for school-wide professional development days, to visit other schools, and to purchase new teaching resources and educational materials. This small group of teachers initiated some school-wide planning sessions with colleagues in the elementary and secondary wings. Their efforts were consistently supported by the principal and were not opposed by any other sub-group of teachers in the school. Gradually, these small, early steps expanded into a full-blown school improvement project that engaged the commitment of all the professional staff. What kept them from being a true learning community, in the sense that we have described it in this book, is that the deconstruction and reconstruction of professional practice was achieved by only a handful of teachers. But the processes were in place, and this too could have transpired if key people had not left the school or if they had not been distracted by family obligations.

The degree to which a bottom-up approach engages the principal depends, to a large extent, on two things: the relationship between the principal and the professional staff, and the willingness of the principal to be an active learner. When the relationship is at least harmonious and when principals are committed to their own professional learning, the bottom-up approach works well. Under the opposite set of conditions, it is relatively ineffective. (The press of alternative demands appears to be an excuse rather than a reason for lack of engagement. With the other two conditions in place, we have seen some extremely busy principals get involved in projects initiated by the professional staff.) In spite of the equivocal outcomes, however, we have seen principals become engaged in collective professional learning where formerly they had seen that as the exclusive province of the teachers. Bottom-up approaches have been successful in highlighting issues in the school that demand or deserve sustained attention from the principal and from the rest of the professional staff. Although it has not always been easy for teachers to engage the principal, we have witnessed many cases where the teachers persisted until they achieved the desired results.

Perhaps a more typical (or expected) way of engaging the principals is from a 'top-down' approach. In this case, supervisory officers or other educational officials put collective learning expectations and structures in place and expect principals to implement them in their respective schools. In fact, many of the school improvement projects that we have studied have followed a top-down strategy. One particularly successful project occurred in a large suburban school division surrounding a university and government city. The system was comprised of four elementary schools, four secondary schools, and two kindergarten-to-secondary schools spread over a wide geographic area. In this case, the director of education was the key player in starting the process of school improvement, in developing mission statements and action plans, in promoting professional engagement, in collecting data in each school and in central office operations, and in celebrating successes. When we conducted interviews in the individual schools, educators expressed clear commitments to ongoing professional learning, instructional improvement, caring relationships, and student achievement. Invariably, the school principals expressed appreciation for the leadership of the director and for the commitment of the professional staff. The director of education consistently modeled professional learning and improvement of practice, and he invested his own personal time and considerable institutional resources in the professional development of the teaching cadre. This is probably the best example that we have seen of a successful top-down approach for initiating school improvement.

Although the top-down approach may be effective for initiating engagement and for directing action, it is a hierarchical strategy that is fraught with danger and that may not be in the spirit or interests of a learning community. Even (or especially) when engagement happens from the top down, there is a need to ensure that the learning is natural and organic rather than forced and mechanical. Furthermore, there is a clear need to honor the contextual and cultural conditions that shape the learning in each school and to recognize that any initiative will look different from school to school and from classroom to classroom. In other words, unless the top-down approach is handled with extreme sensitivity, it is not as likely as the other strategies to lead to commitment on the part of the principals and to profound improvement in the school. In any top-down initiative, it is essential for the initiating administrators to shift leadership functions and ownership to at least some of the professional staff (Hajnal et al., 1998). That is, unless a top-down approach facilitates the creation of a community of leaders, it is not likely to stand the test of time.

The four configurations – top-down, bottom-up, inside-out, and outside-in – means that different engagement processes will ensue depending on who, exactly, is trying to engage the principal and how, exactly, they are going about doing it. Each principal is likely to have different incentives and needs, different wishes and wants. Each principal dreams in a different way and has a different ultimate desire. Knowing these dreams and desires can lead to more effective engagement strategies because the incentives can be tailored to the dreams of the principal. Getting the principals onto the train of the learning community is a bit tricky, at least in part because of institutional inertia, but once they get onboard, institutional momentum and clear benefits can keep the train moving. The momentum can bring others onto the train, especially when the benefits appear to be well worth the effort. (Implicit in this discussion is the assumption that principals and other key leaders know about the principles and practices of a learning community. This will not always be true. It implies that, as the train chugs along, leaders will need to learn more about what a learning community is and how to go about creating one.)

Creating Sustainable Conditions

Having engaged and knowledgeable leaders is a necessary but not sufficient condition for the creation of a learning community. Conditions in the school must also support and sustain individual and collective professional learning. Because we have devoted a complete chapter to strategies for building cognitive and affective conditions, we do not go into a similar kind of detail here. In this chapter we want simply to point out the importance of creating group dynamics, communication patterns, and interaction patterns where people are safe from attack, where they feel supported and emotionally secure, where the difficult questions are welcome, where the status quo can be safely challenged, and where even the strangest ideas get a hearing. These are the conditions that are sustainable for the long term and that can sustain the interest, engagement, and learning efforts of all those who are part of the learning community.

Unfortunately, such conditions have not been typical of some of the schools we have observed. We have been shocked at the ways in which some educators treat one another. We have witnessed sniping, gossiping, rudeness, disrespect, negativity, and even open hostility. Perhaps an extreme example is what happened to Andrea, a Grade 5 teacher in a small, rural kindergarten-to-secondary school. The school was part of a school system that was shifting from a content-based to a process-based curriculum. The elementary teachers had embraced the initiative and had gone to a number of training sessions and professional development workshops. The secondary teachers, on the other hand, were resistant to any intrusions into their traditional content-based teaching. After Andrea had attended a weekend workshop on resource-based learning, she prepared a bulletin board in the staff room to highlight the key ideas from the workshop. A small group of secondary teachers was offended by the bulletin board and destroyed it after Andrea had returned to her classroom. They re-arranged the letters into profanities, they drew genitalia and body hair on the pictures, and they added obscene gestures to the backdrop. The message was clear: Anyone who dared to present new ideas in the staff room would not be treated kindly. Of course, Andrea was devastated by the incident. She said, 'I used my own time and money to make this bulletin board. Why did I bother? Why would anyone bother trying to do anything different when this is the kind of treatment they receive? From now on, I keep my ideas to myself.' She left the school the following year.

Andrea's story demonstrates that, in spite of what they teach the children in their classrooms, some adults do not always feel it necessary to control their own behavior in their interactions with colleagues. When collegial relations are strained, risk taking is at a minimum and trust is quickly broken. This is not to say that constant agreement, harmony, and pleasantries should characterize school conditions. These conditions cannot sustain professional learning any better than hostility can, because they usually serve to mask differences of opinion and sensitive issues that need to be aired. Conflict will always be part of any community, including a learning community, and the trick is to 'learn to confront the conflicts that inevitably arise as the community emerges' (Wineburg & Grossman, 1998, p. 353). Effectively confronting conflicts is one of the crucial conditions for sustaining professional learning and school development.

A useful framework for dealing with conflict is provided by Amason, Thompson, Hochwarter, and Harrison (1995). They distinguish between A-Type, or *affective*, conflict, and C-Type, or *cognitive*, conflict. A-Type conflict focuses 'on personalized anger or resentment, usually directed at specific individuals rather than specific ideas' (pp. 24-25). By contrast, C-Type focuses 'on substantive, issue-related differences of opinion' (p. 22). They make the point that C-Type conflict is a desirable aspect of team functioning because it opens spaces for divergent thinking, creativity, and open communication. Without this kind of conflict, teams do 'a poor job of managing and resolving their differences' (p. 21), and sensitive issues or divergent ideas tend to be masked or hidden in group discourse. According to these authors, successful teams are aware of the two types of conflict and are able to turn A-Type into C-Type conflict. This framework is enticing because, unlike most other available frameworks, it takes the spotlight off individual responses to conflictive situations and shines it on the nature of the conflict itself. This affords room to depersonalize a tense situation and to shift the conflict from a personal to a substantive frame of reference.

Creating sustainable conditions means, first, understanding the culture that exists in the school and, second, deciding on those norms and values that deserve to be retained and those that should be changed. In a learning community, all members of the school share the responsibility for creating, maintaining, and sustaining a culture of inquiry where risk taking is common and where the heroes, stories, myths, and metaphors revolve around learning and innovation. These are the conditions that make people excited about coming to school. Thus the second step in making it so is for everyone to share in the creation of sustainable and sustaining school conditions.

Developing a Learning Architecture

With engaged principals and sustainable school conditions, a staff is well positioned to build structures and strategies that facilitate and enhance professional learning. This is the learning architecture. According to Gozdz (1995), the learning architecture consists in 'the systems and structures that sustain memory and learning in the organization over time' (p. 61). He argues that the structures are both visible and invisible. From our perspective, the invisible structures consist in knowledgeable and engaged people and in sustainable and sustaining conditions. That is, if key people are knowledgeable about and committed to the learning community and if the conditions are sustainable for the long term and sustain professional learning, then the invisible structures support the learning community. Creating the visible structures constitutes the third step in the process of building a learning community.

In Chapter 6 we advocated the use of learning teams, and that is one of the first structures to be put into the learning architecture. In the schools that have been the most successful in generating sustained individual and collective learning, the teams have been configured in as many different ways as possible. Some teams have been comprised of teachers with similar teaching assignments and others with different assignments, some with single purposes and others with multi-purpose task sets, some for the short term and others for longer terms, some for classroom instruction and others for school-wide programs. Teams have been created to facilitate the implementation of new curricula, instructional strategies, student evaluation, and reporting procedures. Other teams have come together simply to reflect on current conditions and to envision new directions. In small schools, the same teachers have been members of several different teams and have transferred the learning from one team to another. In large schools, cross-team meetings have taken place to ensure that the smaller teams do not operate in isolation from one another. Throughout all of this, within-team and cross-team communication and problem solving conjoin to ensure an institution-wide community that aligns the learning and capitalizes on the growth happening in the teams. In short, many different configurations and purposes of teams are possible, and the ways in which they find their way into the learning architecture of any particular school is limited only by the contextual conditions and by the imagination of the staff. Our contention is this: the more learning teams that exist in a school, the more likely that professional learning is available to all staff members, that individual learning is accessible to other members of the team, and that the learning is directly connected to the issues and deep mysteries faced by the professional staff.

In conjunction with the learning teams, a structural element that we have found to be useful is that of a learning agent. This is an individual who opens spaces for collaborative learning, who facilitates connections with networks within and beyond the school, who structures learning opportunities for the rest of the staff, and who pushes the learning into deeper levels by asking key questions and by prompting teachers to conduct metacognitive reflection on and critical analysis of their educational beliefs and practices. We discovered this structure quite by accident in a number of collaborative research projects and consulting services with school staffs. Because of the learning and reflection tasks into which we were inviting the staff members, they were able to break through some of their deeply embedded assumptions, to ask different questions, and to begin the process of reconstructing their professional narratives. In that way, we inadvertently filled the role of a learning agent, and we have since come to believe that this is a key structure in the learning architecture. Lipman (1997), for example, has found that, without deep probing into embedded assumptions, collaborative processes reflect 'little real engagement of substantive issues' (p. 30). We believe that a learning agent is uniquely positioned to engage just such deep probing.

The question of who should serve as the learning agent is a tricky one. Our experience suggests that the learning agent should be someone who is familiar with school rhythms, is trusted by the staff, has daily non-instructional time available, and has excellent group facilitation skills. Although we have each served as external learning agents, that has been successful only after we have taken considerable time to familiarize ourselves with the operations of the school and to establish a trusting relationship with the staff. Because most external people do not have the luxury of that kind of in-school time, the external learning agent may not be the best solution. But positioning an internal staff member as a learning agent is equally challenging. In some cases of an internal agent, the school principals or vice-principals have taken on this role, but that has only been successful when power was distributed evenly between the administrative and professional cadres and when the administrators were not expected to serve control functions. In schools where administrators have had the task of conducting performance appraisals on teachers, the best learning agents have come from within the ranks of the professional staff. These people have been department heads, special education teachers, key opinion leaders, and regular classroom teachers. In other words, there is no one existing teaching assignment that is best suited for the tasks of the learning agent. What matters is that the individual has a commitment to professional learning, to the school, and to colleagues; is trusted and deemed credible by colleagues; and has both the time and the capacity to construct and facilitate a wide variety of professional learning opportunities.

Even with learning teams and a learning agent, of course, the critical structural element is institutional time in which to schedule sustained opportunities for educators to engage in professional discourse and personal learning. Time is needed to reflect on the professional narrative, to identify knowledge gaps, to seek out new ideas, to reflect on the results of experimental trials, and to reconstruct the professional narrative. This kind of time is seldom, if ever, available in contemporary schools, and the lack of time always haunts teachers' efforts to work on educational improvement. But Adelman and Walking-Eagle (1997) have shown clearly that extensive professional learning time, both individual and collective, is required at every step on the learning curve – at the beginning, at the middle, and at the end. School staffs have been quite imaginative in the ways that they have managed to wrest collaborative learning time from a busy schedule. They have met early in the morning, at noon, after school, in the evening, and on weekends. They have taken their planning time to meet, and they have used student mentorship and 'big buddy' programs to group classes together, thereby freeing one of the instructors. But ad hoc strategies serve only a small part of the purpose. In addition, some prime time needs to be devoted exclusively to professional learning. This means that, at times, students will need to be dismissed from class to provide opportunities for an entire staff to come together for in-depth professional workshops or reflection meetings. And this time investment needs to come not just from individual schools but also from entire school districts. Scheduling several professional development days into the annual district calendar is one of the best ways for school boards and supervisory officers to signal their commitment to professional learning.

A supporting structure that needs to be infused throughout the learning architecture is the presence of intensive and extensive feedback. The idea here is to build mechanisms that continuously foreground professional learning, highlight the gaps between actual and desired realities (Senge, 1990), and signal the presence of dynamic creative tension. Creative tensions can be found everywhere: between the desire for critical thinking and the press of routine action, between the interest in pedagogy and the focus on events, between the promise of change and the assurance of stability, and between the excitement of new ideas and the comfort of the familiar. By bringing the creative tensions to the foreground, feedback provides data about where past learning has occurred and where there is leverage for future growth. This database is useful for helping educators to understand prior experiences and to inform ongoing learning.

Feedback can come from many different sources, in many different ways, and through many different mechanisms. It might be something as formal as a checklist of learning goals or as informal as asking 'How are we doing, folks?' at a team meeting. It might take the form of direct observational data or of reflective or analytic questions. It might be the responsibility of the learning agent or school/team leaders, or it might be prepared by all staff members at different times. Feedback gives educators constant reminders about what is being sought, what has already been achieved, what learning is taking place, and what still remains to be done. It opens spaces for people to touch base on occasion, to find out how others are doing, and to share their own stories of professional mysteries, trials, and learning. And it affords opportunities to recognize and celebrate the positive outcomes of professional learning and to acknowledge and honor the contributions and gains made by individual members and by groups of dedicated professionals.

Experimenting with new practices and reconstructing the professional narrative are risky ventures that deserve to be valued by the institution as well as by the individual. From that perspective, organizational incentives and reward structures should be in place for individuals and teams who embark on professional learning enterprises. The incentives might be fully funded workshops, conferences, or other learning sessions outside the school; system-sponsored and system-financed professional development days within the school; or allocation of non-instructional time in the daily timetable. Reward structures might be public recognition, letters of acknowledgement, notes of gratitude, career advancement, advanced pay scales, extra remuneration for participation, or even a pat on the back. We acknowledge that this part of the learning architecture is a highly controversial subject because of an implicit assumption that teachers should engage in professional learning from intrinsic motivation and for intrinsic rewards. We agree, and we believe that the best learning happens when these conditions are in place. But we also know that teaching (and leading) school is an exhausting and time-consuming profession, and there is very little time or energy left after dealing with the demands of daily practice. Without incentives or external rewards, teachers may feel little desire (or need) to embark on another round of exhausting and time-consuming professional learning activities. Our point of view is that the controversial nature of incentives and rewards implies not an avoidance of such measures but a sensitive engagement with them. This means that the incentives must connect directly to professional learning that is meaningful and relevant for individual educators. It means that the reward structures must honor the process of learning as much as the ultimate outcomes. It means that educators should have considerable input into the kinds of incentives and rewards that are built into the learning architecture. Finally, it means that the structures must be flexible and diverse, for what is motivating to one person will not be so to another.

Learning teams, a learning agent, time, feedback, and incentives and rewards: these are at least some of the elements of a learning architecture. They are the elements that we have found to pave the way for individual and collective professional learning and for the creation of a learning community. These, of course, are not the only structures that can or should be part of a learning architecture. In other contexts, other individuals will find other structures that advance the learning in their school communities. That is as it should be. But regardless of how it unfolds, the development of a learning architecture is one of the critical steps in bringing a learning community to life.

Going Through Phases and Cycles

Even with knowledgeable and engaged leaders, sustainable and sustaining conditions, and a learning architecture, professional learning will not progress smoothly, evenly, or consistently. Instead, it is a cyclic process that moves through different phases and that proceeds in fits and starts. A professional learning community will, at times, charge full steam ahead and, at other times, it will wash up on the shore or founder on the shoals. This is perfectly natural. We are dealing here with a human phenomenon with all the foibles, idiosyncrasies, and emotions of the human condition. People are not machines that can be turned on and off at will. They have needs and wants and desires and frustrations and distractions that affect their level of participation in any project, even one that is yielding exciting outcomes. Recognizing the cyclic nature can help people to move gracefully through the down times, rather than to succumb to guilt or frustration.

Our own work with learning communities has demonstrated that the push and pull of a professional learning community advances through successive iterations of three learning phases: naming and framing, analyzing and integrating, and applying and experimenting (Mitchell & Sackney, 1998). These three phases are not isolated, independent, or linear. Instead, they represent three mutually influencing and overlapping categories of learning through which educators move, with the ascendant phase at any given time being deeply influenced by particular circumstances, conditions, and histories. Movement through and with the phases is a circular and iterative process, and people may be learning in all three phases at the same time with different content. We do not want to leave the impression that we think this is the only or the best phase framework. Others have been defined in the past, and probably are as useful as this one. This, however, is the framework with which we have had experience and that we can illustrate with examples.

Naming and framing involves the development of personal and shared understandings and the creation of a school culture that supports professional learning. It is in this phase that individuals begin to describe and to discuss their professional narratives, to sort out what they know and what they think they know. This is the time for people to talk about their assumptions and beliefs about old practices and to consider what they think and believe about new ones. Naming and framing is typically characterized by story telling, detailed descriptions, and advice giving. This is the 'I remember when . . .' and 'I know what . . .' and 'You might try . . .' and 'To me, this means . . .' period. It is at this phase that the personal narratives that are (at times implicitly) guiding individual and group practice get put on the table for all to see. From that foundation, individuals can hash out how the stories and details mesh or collide and then construct shared understandings of common phenomena. And it is also during this phase that the interpersonal affective climate is built, for without trust and mutual respect, no one is likely to expose innermost beliefs and assumptions. There's just too much risk of being shot down in flames. But with sufficient interpersonal capacity to affirm one another and to listen respectfully to colleagues' stories and details, personal understandings can be revealed, and shared understandings can be reached.

Analyzing and integrating involves deep reflection and critical analysis of professional narratives and the integration of new insights into personal and collective professional narratives. It is here that the construction of knowledge and the reconstruction of the professional narrative begins. This is the time for 'I see that we usually . . .' and 'Why did we . . .?' and 'What were we thinking of when . . .?' and 'How did I . . .?' and 'What else could we . . .?' These sorts of comments and questions engage critical analysis and metacognitive reflection, and the insights gained from such discourse can be used to reconstruct the professional narratives of individuals and of the group. This is when the interpersonal cognitive climate becomes important, for without the critical questioning and deep probing from colleagues, it is all too easy for individuals to hold fast to unspoken assumptions, unarticulated beliefs, and familiar practices. But with the interpersonal capacity to think and analyze together, educators can find their way past outdated assumptions or practices and come to grips with alternative ways of thinking, doing, and being.

Applying and experimenting is the phase where actual changes occur. It involves active experimentation with new practices, new ideas, and new ideals, as educators move to the action part of action research. This is where new ideas are tested in classrooms, staff rooms, and meeting rooms to see if they address better than old ones a deep mystery or tough problem of teaching and learning in a specific context. This is where we hear 'What happened when . . .?' and 'What if I tried . . .?' and 'What might work for . . .?' and 'How could we . . .?' Through the applying and experimenting phase, some new ideas will prove to be worth further development and ultimate inclusion in the professional repertoire, but others will not stand the test. Some old practices will end up being abandoned, but others will be reaffirmed. Throughout this phase, assumptions and practices ebb and flow, and there is a natural and ongoing reconstruction of the professional narratives that guide individual and collective action.

The mutuality of the phases becomes evident when one thinks about how the sequence is likely to unfold in real time. For example, even as applying and experimenting is going on, people will still be developing personal and shared understandings (naming and framing) about different aspects of the trials, and they will be continuously assessing the new practices for efficacy and institutional fit (analyzing and integrating). That is, the phases represent inclusive and overlapping categories of learning more than they represent a linear sequence of learning. We have also observed people moving through the phases on a broken front, where they operated at one phase in relation to one initiative at the same time as they were at another phase with something else. For example, in one school the teachers were experimenting with alternative classroom management strategies but were still analyzing student assessment and reporting structures and still developing personal and shared understandings about conflict resolution. In this school, the three different phases were all in ascendance at the same time with three different initiatives.

Our approach to the learning community implies that any practical model is likely to be a recursive one, with multiple interdependencies, feedback loops, and cycles of progress and regress. In any human system, the press for equilibrium will eventually set in and growth will slow. During those times, it is natural to think that the learning has stopped or that the trial has failed. But that is not necessarily the case. More likely, it simply signals that the new practices or new ideas have come up against some long-standing issue or unarticulated belief. Rather than give up or get frustrated, the people who are at the center of the project need to step back and reflect on what is happening. This is the time to consider what people are trying to conserve (Senge et al., 1999) and to critically assess the value of their position. If it is worth conserving, then steps should be taken to protect it explicitly. If not, then steps should be taken to provide opportunities for everyone to discuss the conserving trend and the ultimate conse-quences of retaining this particular practice or belief. If a period of regress has shone the spotlight on some particular institutional roadblock (such as lack of time, au-tonomy, or efficacy), then steps need to be taken to clear out the blockage. In both cases, critical and metacognitive reflection can help to break through the conserving tendency or the slowing trend and move the learning forward. Assuming that periods of regress will never happen is a naïve approach, for when they do occur, individuals are not equipped to manage them. By contrast, assuming that periods of regress will happen and then planning for and taking an active problem-solving orientation to them when they appear gives educators strategies, hope, and leverage for moving forward with grace, dignity, persistence, and efficacy.

Building the Capacity for a Learning Community

In this chapter we have been discussing some strategies for bringing a learning com-munity to life. The mechanisms we have presented help to synthesize some elements of the model with which we began this book. That is, the development of personal capacity, interpersonal capacity, and organizational capacity are all at issue through the engagement of key leaders, the creation of sustainable and sustaining conditions, the development of a learning architecture, and the movement through phases and cycles. Although in this chapter we have positioned these four elements as aspects of organizational capacity, we are sure that they sounded familiar to the readers. This is to be expected because they were also a part of previous chapters. Our position is that personal, interpersonal, and organizational capacities enmesh with one another as school people come to deeper understandings about the mysteries, perplexities, and problems of teaching and learning. Trying to keep specific aspects isolated from one another is not only impractical, it is actually quite impossible and completely undesir-able.

In Figure 8.1, we embed the four elements from this chapter with other elements that we have discussed previously. This figure represents a synthesized view of key elements in each of the three spheres of capacity. This is not to denigrate the impor-tance of other elements that have been presented in foregoing chapters but that have not been included in the figure. It is, rather, to foreground those elements that we have found to be helpful in leading toward profound improvement in teaching and learning.

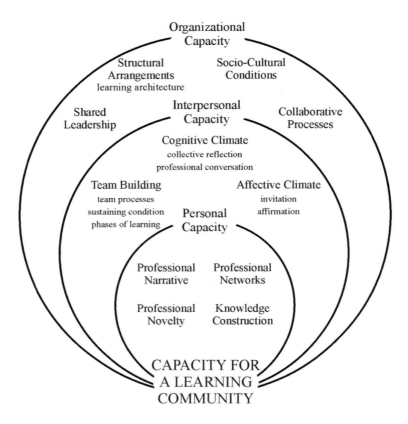

Figure 8.1 Key elements in building the capacity for a learning community.

The elements and issues that we have discussed throughout this book are fundamental to the capacity that locates in the hearts and minds of people and in the visible and invisible structures of a school. Elements that have an impact on the capacity to improve teaching and learning include anything that shapes how people do their work in a school. They are the things that affect how people interact, how they react, and how they act in their relationships with one another, with teaching and learning, and with improvement in their practice. What we have been talking about in this chapter and in the rest of the book are some elements that can support the search for profound improvement in teaching and learning and that can move schools and school people closer toward realizing the goal of a learning community. This is the heart of what we envision as a curriculum of capacity building.

9

The Learning Community: Retrospect and Prospect

The notion of the school as a learning community represents a fundamental shift in the ideology that shapes the understanding of schools and of professional practice. The traditional view of schools is grounded in a mechanistic worldview, which is associated with a positivist epistemology and rationalist methodology. From this perspective, control and power reside at the top of the school organization, and roles, responsibilities, and spheres of decision making are clearly delineated. A fundamental assumption of this worldview is that there is one best way to do certain things and that this best way can be discovered through experimentation and disseminated through direct instruction. Recent investigations of human development have shot gaping holes through the mechanistic view. These investigations have demonstrated that there is never just one way or even one best way. Instead, alternative voices and understandings are not only possible but are always present. This view of human development is turning attention toward a new worldview for education, one that is grounded in a wholeness worldview and that is associated with a constructivist epistemology and an interpretivist methodology.

The wholeness worldview, especially when it is premised upon ecological models, positions schools and learning as generative rather than instrumental, insomuch as learning is an organic aspect of the human condition and schools are structured to facilitate human learning, regardless of the direction that the learning takes. This worldview foregrounds the notion that, through their interaction patterns and organizational structures, people construct dominant organizational narratives that henceforth shape thinking and learning and limit professional practice and discourse. Intepretivist methodologies work to expose and to critique those narratives so that, if necessary, they can be modified to honor the generative nature of learning. These notions, and the wholeness worldview, lie at the heart of everything that we have talked about in previous chapters. Even though we have presented our ideas in chunks and pieces, these chunks are not separated from one another in our own minds. Instead, they are all mutually influencing and deeply embedded constructs that, together, constitute the ecosystem of a learning community.

In this final chapter, we take a retrospective and prospective view of building a learning community. The retrospective view gives us an opportunity to explore the ways in which learning (individual as well as collective, professional as well as student learning) has typically been constructed in schools. This allows us to consider some of the more common configurations of or assumptions about learning and learning communities. This retrospective view suggests to us that past practices have created a host of troublesome but largely unarticulated (and usually unacknowledged) barriers to learning. Our position is that the barriers derive from implicit but powerful assumptions, belief systems, and embedded practices that are grounded in the traditional mechanistic worldview and that will continue to limit learning as long as they remain untested and unchallenged.

The prospective view gives us an opportunity to explore the promise of the learning community when it is grounded in a wholeness perspective. The metaphor of the learning community has enticed educators and energized educational discourse for some time now, but it remains more of an idea than a reality. Our position is that the concept of the learning community will only fulfil its promise of educational growth and renewal if it is grounded in a wholeness worldview. This perspective allows for the profound changes in understandings, beliefs, and practices that comprise the heart of the learning community metaphor. Our prospective look at the learning community offers some of the insights we have gained when we have begun to think about the metaphor from a wholeness perspective. It is our contention that this way of configuring the learning community enables school people to acknowledge, challenge, and overcome at least some of the barriers. This kind of engagement serves as a basis for building personal, interpersonal, and organizational capacity to enhance school effectiveness and bring to fruition school renewal.

Retrospect

Our primary contention here is that schools, schooling, teaching, and learning are currently constructed in accordance with the assumptions and belief systems of a mechanistic worldview and a bureaucratic mode of organization. This social construction has sought to render the people and processes predictable and therefore controllable. In this kind of environment, teachers teach, administrators lead, students learn, and parents pay. There is a place for everyone, and everyone stays in that place. In the classroom, the teacher is considered to be the fount of all knowledge and the solver of all problems. Information is given by the teachers and received by the students. This information is based on a curriculum that has been developed outside the school. Tests are given (many of which are standardized and nationally normed), and if students can recite what has been taught, learning is said to have taken place. The amount of learning that is demonstrated on the test is a measure of the success of the school, the teacher, and the student. If the measurement is problematic, then corrective interventions are expected to be implemented. All of these practices support and sustain what Sergiovanni (2000) calls the 'systemsworld' (p. 4). The systemsworld consists in management designs and protocols, strategic and tactical actions, policies and procedures, and efficiency and accountability measures, and these are the issues and concerns that dominate the contemporary educational arena. It is, at the core, a clockwork model of schools and of schooling.

What this means is that the systemsworld drives almost all educational assumptions, goals, and practices. In recent years, this has been most evident (and most troublesome) in the host of accountability measures that have taken education by storm right across the English-speaking world (and probably beyond). It is not so much the existence of accountability measures that is a problem, but there certainly is a problem with the ways in which accountability is being enacted. The sorts of accountability that are being emphasized take the form of standardized testing with centrally determined questions. In some jurisdictions, test results are used to determine the ways in which resources are distributed across schools. Furthermore, in some cases, comparative test results are published in the local media (e.g., league tables in England and Wales). These conditions cause teachers to teach to the test so that the school will 'look good' in the media and so that additional resources will accrue to the institution. Teaching and learning, then, are instrumental. They are not directly connected to the deep mysteries and the recurring issues in the lives of teachers and students.

From a mechanistic perspective, learning is viewed as an individual activity. The emphasis is on the *gesellschaft* or the *I* rather than on the *gemeinschaft* or the *We* (Sergiovanni, 1996, pp. 49-50), and there is little if any attention paid to the ways in which the social group or structural arrangements enhance or limit the ability of people to learn. Classrooms, especially in secondary schools or in large elementary classes, are largely arranged to keep students separated from one another, and activities are largely structured for individual learning. This reduces the mechanisms by which students might gain support and assistance from their classmates. Furthermore, schools are largely arranged to keep teachers separated from one another, and teaching tasks are largely structured for individual teaching. As with the students, this reduces opportunities for teachers to learn with and from one another. These conditions are seen to be essential for controlling the work of the teachers and evaluating the learning of the students because they make it possible to attach particular learning or teaching outcomes to particular individuals.

This kind of education assumes that every student learns in the same way and that every teacher can teach in the same way. It assumes that every student needs and can learn the same set of knowledge and skills and that every teacher can teach this set to every student. Learning is viewed as a rational process in which the student absorbs the information and applies it in an appropriate way. Students are assumed to arrive at school without sufficient knowledge and skills and are thus viewed as deficient. It is the role of the teacher to teach the student so as to eliminate or reduce the deficit. If students do not learn, then they are assumed to be even more deficient and they need to be 'fixed.' If teachers are unable to teach particular groups of students, then the teachers themselves are perceived to be deficient and in need of repair. From this perspective, idiosyncratic or serendipitous styles and outcomes of teaching and learning are not considered to be appropriate, and people are positioned as means to achieving particular educational ends rather than being ends in and of themselves.

Language patterns, common words, and typical metaphors found in most schools reflect this mechanistic and instrumental relationship between people and learning.

With respect to language patterns, teachers predominantly speak to students and students predominantly listen. Teachers give instructions and students follow them (at least, that is the intention). With colleagues, teachers swap stories and recall events – usually about problem students, trivial events, or everything except professional practice. Terms such as *problems, needs, intervention, horror story, scope, sequence, standards, mine, my, lack, fail, pass, no, don't,* and *can't* are frequently heard in the classrooms, hallways, and staff rooms of most schools. Typical metaphors used to describe students are *scattered, gifted, capable, lazy, focused, unprepared, inattentive, disabled,* and *challenged.* These language idiosyncrasies reflect a comparative view of learning (poor, good, and indifferent learning) and a deficiency view of students who are falling at the 'poor' end of the learning scale. This dominant view has a profound impact on the ways in which teachers and students view themselves, their work, and their efficacy.

Within a mechanistic worldview, power flows up the hierarchy and blame flows down. In relation to schools, this has meant that teachers and school people have little autonomy over what happens in the educational domain and yet they are the very people who are held responsible for all sorts of educational woes. For example, most decisions about educational goals, curriculum, and student assessment mechanisms are usually made outside the school and teachers are expected to enact these elements, even if they have little relevance for the students in their classrooms. Furthermore, schools and teachers are frequently blamed for students' leaving their educational experience unable to read or write well or to think creatively or critically. Assigning blame in this way fails to take into account the larger societal and economic conditions within which schooling is embedded. The school is not the sole influence on the lives of the students, and what happens in the school and the classroom is deeply affected by what happens on the streets and in the governments of the day and the homes of the students. When responsibility for learning rests exclusively (or largely) with teachers and schools, these influences are not acknowledged and teachers are unfairly blamed, and when most of the key decisions are made elsewhere, teachers have little room for enacting solutions that make sense in their context.

These conditions have led to a popular view that the educational system is failing and to subsequent demands for educational reform, but the arena of educational change and improvement has also been dominated by the systemsworld. For the most part, initiatives are developed elsewhere and imposed on teachers and schools by power elites from outside the school, such as ministries of education, reform consortia, central office administrators, and organized parents' groups. Teachers are seldom included in defining the issues requiring (or deserving) change or in offering ideas for new initiatives. Because many different initiatives are developed in many different places and imposed with little regard for what is currently happening in specific classrooms and schools, what ends up being enacted in schools is often fragmented and piecemeal. When new programs or curricula hit the school, teachers are given little, if any, training before they are expected to implement the new ideas and, in many cases, before they are evaluated on their ability to do so. Their participation in the change process is passive and instrumental; they are simply the tools by which other people's agendas and wishes are enacted. That is, change is something that has been done *to* teachers rather than something that has been done *by* teachers.

All of these conditions reflect a mechanistic worldview of education insomuch as they increase the ability of teachers to control students, of administrators to control teachers, and of politicians to control administrators. We have painted a rather bleak picture in the foregoing paragraphs, and we do not want to leave the impression that all schools are like this or that people do not rise above these conditions. We have seen some fine examples of schools that are constructed quite differently and of educators who do not live by this narrative. What we argue, however, is that the mechanistic worldview inscribes a complex set of assumptions, beliefs, values, practices, and understandings that are embedded so deeply into the collective psyche that many people in the educational world simply do not see any alternatives. It is not that people intend to brutalize students or to demoralize teachers. It is that the implicit and explicit structures and the cultural scripts are so powerful and so compelling that they do not afford any way to do otherwise.

The mechanistic worldview has also found its way into some of the early works dealing with collective learning and learning communities. We have found metaphors of hierarchy, control, instrumentality, and deficiency in some of what we have read, and, to our great chagrin, we have from time to time found them creeping into our own thinking and writing. The tone in at least some of the literature is structural, functional, and mechanical in tone; teachers, students, and learning are positioned as instruments of educational improvement; and the principal is positioned as the key person in building a learning community. In some cases, collective learning and/or the learning community are positioned as the 'one best way' to achieve improvement or the 'final answer' to any number of educational woes. Now, we do not want to imply that these sorts of writings are without merit. On the contrary, they are raising some interesting issues, presenting some critical insights, and providing some useful frameworks. But they still reflect a mechanistic worldview, a dominant systemsworld, and an intact hierarchy. If this trend continues, the prospect of realizing the potential of a learning community will, in our view, be diminished.

Support for this position can be found in the events that transpired in an independent elite school. On the request of the headmaster, we had worked with a small cadre of teachers for one school term on some principles and practices of collective reflection and group learning. At the end of the term, the teachers commented that they were surprised at how much they had learned about and from one another and they expressed a desire to expand the collective learning to the rest of the instructional staff. The following year, the headmaster retired and a new person arrived to take the helm of the school. When we met with the new headmaster, he listened politely to our description of the previous year's activities and to our hopes for the coming year and then, even more politely, told us that he did not see the need for further exploration along the lines of a learning community. He had other professional development ideas that he planned to pursue with the staff. He thanked us for our time and our service to the school and ushered us out the door. Subsequent conversations with teachers from the school indicated that the head master was in firm control of the professional development and that the teaching staff was not in a position to debate or to contest the chosen direction. The headmaster was able to exercise such tight control over the process because of the rigid hierarchy and the dominant systemsworld operating in that school.

Prospect

As we have configured it in this book, the metaphor of the learning community is based on a social constructivist view of human development that is rooted in postmodern and critical theory ideologies. Our position is that both postmodernism and critical theory present part of the picture but that the learning community is always more than any particular ideological position. It transcends theoretical and ideological boundaries because it deals with a fundamental aspect of the human condition. That is, it places the 'lifeworld' (Sergiovanni, 2000, p. 4) at the forefront of educational matters. This sort of focus on the people, their purposes and dreams, their rituals and traditions, their norms and beliefs, their actions and interactions, and their ways of being leads directly toward a wholeness worldview for schools and schooling and for teaching and learning. A wholeness worldview assumes that everything is intimately connected with and embedded in everything else, that different elements are unique manifestations of the same underlying reality, and that any change in one element eventually leads to some sort of change in many other elements (and probably in all elements) (Bohm, 1980, 1985). This is an ecological perspective of education and of teaching and learning.

From this perspective, organizational arrangements are flexible and fluid, and differences in roles do not imply differences in status. In relation to schools, this means that principals, teachers, students, and parents may take on different functions in a school but that none is more important or more highly valued than any other role. There is no one 'best place' for the individuals who serve in the various roles, and the efforts of all people meld together in the process of learning and growth. This perspective positions visible and invisible structures at the service of learning, regardless of who is learning, who is teaching, and who is leading at any given moment. At times, students teach teachers as much as teachers teach students; teachers lead leaders as much as leaders lead teachers; and parents teach and lead as much as anyone else in the school. Knowledge resides throughout the community, and all people join together as a community of learners, a community of leaders, and a community of practice.

In this kind of learning community, there is still a need for accountability, but this becomes a collective and responsive enterprise. When the focus of accountability is on teaching and learning (and on human growth and development), the focus is placed squarely on the child, not on the test. Measuring devices (sometimes tests, but also many other strategies) are developed in response to a particular child's developmental process. There are no standardized tests nor are there any normed measures because people (children and adults alike) are neither standard nor average. All people are unique. All students develop on their own timeframe and in their own way, and teachers, parents, administrators, and students together figure out the accountability measures for any specific student or context. Together, these people evaluate what has already been accomplished by the student and by the school, and what is important to be provided in subsequent learning episodes. Warranted practice emerges from the intense focus on the learning of particular students. Accountability from this perspective is organic, and it will look different in different contexts, for different students, and for different learning episodes. This kind of accountability still informs parents about their children's learning, and it does so not from any comparative standpoint but from a standpoint that honors the unique ways in which specific children learn, grow, and develop.

Such accountability derives from a capacity-building model of learning rather than from a deficit model. The assumption is that any individual (child and adult alike) comes to the school with a rich knowledge base and skill set that provides a solid foundation for subsequent learning. Gaps in knowledge and skills are expected and desirable. They are not viewed as deficiencies to be eliminated but as opportunities around which to construct a new phase of growth and development. Learning paths and learning outcomes are always diverse, usually idiosyncratic, and often serendipitous. They are seldom uniform, controllable, or predictable. It may be possible to construct learning opportunities that engage a number of people in the same learning event, but the process by which people move through the event and the learning that emerges from the end of it will be quite different for each individual. This phenomenon is evident each time a teacher, at the end of a lesson or instructional set, asks students what they have learned. Different students always remember different things, and they are not always the sorts of things that the teacher had anticipated would be remembered. From a wholeness worldview, these sorts of discrepancies are not problematic. Instead, diverse learning paths and learning outcomes enrich the capacity of the whole.

Paradoxically, although learning is unique and individual, organizational arrangements in a learning community recognize and accommodate social constructions of knowledge. That is, there is a clear understanding that, even though they will construct their own understandings, many people learn well when they engage in learning activities with others. Sense-making, then, is at the same time individualistic and influenced by others. Furthermore, learning is more than a rational activity; it also has an emotional dimension and is driven as much by intuition and hunch as by cognition and logic. And emotions are more quickly engaged when people are in contact with other people than when they work in isolation. These sorts of social constructions are important not just for students but also for educators, and constructivist ways of knowing have been evident in recent emphases on teacher collaboration as a form of teacher learning and teacher professionalism. Learning, then, for students and educators alike is a collaborative process whereby people come together to learn from and with one another. Through the social arrangements and the academic discourse in the school, the people come to develop a sense of interdependency, mutual obligations, shared commitments, and common understandings that are juxtaposed with individual perspectives, personal understandings, and unique knowledge bases and skill sets. When learning is positioned and valued as an ongoing, active, collaborative process, this encourages dialogue and it recognizes the value of others. This foundation is helpful in generating a love of learning that can then permeate the entire school environment.

In this kind of environment, the language will be quite different from that in a mechanistic environment. Instead of metaphors of need, deficiency, and control, the language would be permeated with metaphors of growth, development, and empowerment. Instead of saying, 'You can't do that,' people might say, 'How could you do that otherwise?' Teachers and students talk with one another rather than at one another, and there is as much conversation among students as between students and teachers. Collegial conversations focus on matters of teaching and learning as much as on recreational topics. From a wholeness worldview, comparative learning is irrelevant because students are seen to be progressing at a unique pace and learning unique things, and differences in scope or speed of learning are therefore inconsequential. This eliminates the urge to speak of gifted, disabled, or challenged students, and it eliminates the tendency to speak of needs or interventions. A learning problem is only considered to be problematic if it is so designated by the student. That is, the student would be the one to say, 'This is a problem. Can you help me?' While teachers might shape particular learning opportunities, they are not expected to shape the learning outcomes and therefore have no need to identify any particular outcome as a problem. This kind of discourse shapes a craft environment that is validating and affirming for students and educators alike.

This environment places individuals in control of their own learning and teaching outcomes and gives them power over their own learning and teaching processes. It is postmodern in the sense that it acknowledges the deeply embedded nature of power and knowledge (power is knowledge and knowledge is power). And it is postmodern in that it recognizes multiple constructions of power and knowledge through multiple views of reality, of learning, and of life. This view is also in tune with critical theory in that it recognizes the contested relationship between knowledge and power (does knowledge lend power to? power over? power with? power for?). By vesting power and control in the hands of the learner, this view advances a critical theory agenda of equity and democratic values. Even if schools continue to be organized vertically, this view takes control and power away from a hierarchical flow. Instead of power flowing up the channels, the channels serve to facilitate the activities of individual students, teachers, school administrators, and other partners in the educational enterprise. That is, control functions are replaced by facilitative functions, and decisions are made at the level where they will be enacted – in the home, the school, the classroom, the executive suite, or the board room, depending on who will carry the responsibility for bringing them to pass. 'Problem solving' (itself a contested notion from our perspective) is a collaborative process among the interested parties in an educational event, including parents, students, classroom teachers, school administrators, supervisory officers, and others. Thus the principle of subsidiarity is enacted at all levels of the school system.

This implies, of course, that educational change and school development are organic processes that emerge naturally from the discourse among partners in the light of general and particular outcomes. Change is not something that is done to teachers, to students, or to schools. It is something that is always and already a part of the educational world because it is always and already a part of the human condition. Educational change happens as people change; people change as they grow and develop. New ideas come from new networks and relationships; the impetus for seeking out new ideas comes from deep mysteries or stubborn problems that occur to specific people in specific contexts at specific times. New initiatives might be introduced wholesale into various contexts at the same time, but they will take on very different configurations in each context, depending on the natures and histories and current conditions and learning patterns of particular people. None of this is controllable or predictable. None of it can be modeled or molded or manipulated to serve any pre-determined goals or expectations. Educational change, like any human process, is fundamentally paradoxical, ambiguous, multi-layered, and evolutionary. Although it certainly can (and probably should) be influenced by particular forces or nudged in particular directions, it cannot be forced into unnatural shapes or prodded in unnatural directions. It is a life force and, like any other life force, it will flow as it should, given sufficient support and sustenance to do so.

Central to these conceptions of schools and of teaching and learning is the notion of community. In particular, schools with these sorts of constructions constitute a learning community, a place where students and adults alike are engaged as active learners in those things that matter to them and where everyone encourages and helps others to learn. A learning community is a place where there are communities of leaders, where students, teachers, non-instructional staff, parents, and administrators share the opportunities and responsibilities for decision making. It is a place of reflection, inquiry, discourse, sharing, and risk taking, where its participants engage in these processes from a desire to learn and to seek better ways of doing things. This kind of school is a place where people are continually enhancing their capacity to confront the deep mysteries of their lives, to create the sorts of places they want to create, and to develop the skills and conditions that enable them to produce the results that matter – to them. A learning community is one that promotes and values individual and collective learning for all members of the community, and people in the community are interested in improving the quality of learning and life for all.

This conception of schools and of teaching and learning is not intended to imply that the learning community is 'the best' or 'the correct' way of doing things. It is not intended to subjugate or to override other ways of getting at school development nor is it intended to answer all educational woes or solve all problems. In fact, we do not intend to position the learning community at the *service* of school development at all. Instead, our intention is to offer a different way of looking at and thinking about education in its broadest sense. The learning community, as we have configured it in the previous paragraphs and chapters, acknowledges the organic nature of learning for educators and for students, and it positions educational improvement as a natural consequence of a natural view of a natural process. It represents an alternative set of assumptions, beliefs, values, practices, structures, and understandings that, if held by enough people and supported in enough places, could break the iron cage of the mechanistic worldview.

Managing the Transition

But the iron cage of a mechanistic educational system is strong, and the transition to a different sort of worldview is not easy. Barriers exist on at least three levels: the individual, the group, and the organization. At the individual level, of course, we have all been educated in school systems that reflected the mechanistic set of assumptions (or at least most of us have), and we have all internalized these assumptions. They are so deeply embedded in cognition and practice that they are seen not as assumptions at all but as reality itself. Furthermore, if the education has gone according to plan, people are likely to have a low sense of empowerment, little propensity for taking risks, and a preference for working alone. Previous experiences with change may also be a drawback to new constructions because *plus ca change, plus la même chose*. Moreover, any new construction entails loss as well as gain, and knowledge or ways of doing things that are grounded in a wholeness perspective are quite likely to be incompatible with prior understandings and prior practices. In a change of this magnitude, self-efficacy will be threatened, emotions will clamor for attention, and people may back away from conditions that appear to be emotionally laden. All of these conditions serve to limit the capacity of individuals to engage in reconstructing the educational world from a wholeness perspective.

At the group level, the conditions that derive from a mechanistic worldview tend to separate people from one another, to compare them to one another, and to place them in competition with one another. This is more likely to generate distrust and isolation than caring and teamwork. Poor communication and a lack of commitment to a common vision or a shared purpose contribute to contested values and strategies and discourage collective learning (as well as individual learning). Many schools have in-groups and out-groups, and the issue of power is seldom resolved. In most groups, deviant behaviour (which will always occur, and usually sooner rather than later) is often the target of gossip or hostility, but it is generally not addressed openly or resolved satisfactorily (Mitchell, 1999b). If the members of a group do not like each other, opportunities for coming together in authentic interaction and deep collective learning are unlikely to emerge. Furthermore, if the group is event-oriented, then individuals remain mired in the events of the day (or week) and fail to consider larger pedagogic or philosophic issues. Such conditions reduce the opportunities for group members to engage in effective teamwork or to begin the deep dialogue that can serve to deconstruct current conditions or to reconstruct conditions that promote community building.

At the organizational level, institutional conditions influence the degree to which people are willing to take the risks that a new construction entails. Tight control mechanisms, stressful school circumstances, and weak or rigid leadership are common to many schools, and these conditions do not open spaces either for deconstruction or for reconstruction (Mitchell, 1999a). In addition, if there are limited resources for professional development or if there is an inadequate learning architecture, then there is little support for the sorts of learning that educators will need to engage in if they are to come to grips with a new worldview for education. Other organizational barriers include inappropriate (or nonexistent) reward and recognition systems, unarticulated or unshared vision and mission, and few structured opportunities for groups of teachers and others to meet in deep academic discourse (or in any sort of discourse). Furthermore, the culture of most schools is unlikely to sustain deep learning. A culture that is open, honest, and communicative; that honors difference and divergence; that embraces conflict and emotion; and that fosters inquiry and reflection is more supportive of learning than one that is not (Mitchell, 1999a). Unfortunately, these are not common norms in most schools. This implies that the ways in which a school is structured and organized are important considerations in whether or not people will be able to bring to pass the conditions that reflect a wholeness worldview.

Although such individual, group, and organizational barriers certainly present deep challenges to the development of a learning community that is grounded in a wholeness worldview, they should not be seen as deterrents to the process. Instead, they indicate that people who wish to begin the journey will need to expend some special efforts in making the transition between the old and the new. Bridges (1997) argues that transitions always entail some sort of loss, and grief over what is ending exists alongside excitement over what is beginning. But there is often some confusion as to what is *ending* and what is *beginning*. Most educators, when they hear a call for educational change, assume that they will be expected to give up everything they have done in the past. This is absolutely not the case. Even though the transition to a wholeness worldview is a radical shift, it does not necessarily mean an end to all past practices. Many educational practices have served teachers and students well, and these need to be honored and validated. This kind of validation treats professional practice with respect and gives dignity to educators. In a learning community, a critical discourse often reveals tried and true as much as it does a need for new.

But in spite of the past goods, new beginnings do signal the end of something. When educators (or parents or students) give up something that they have held on to for a long time, they will suffer a loss, and they will grieve (Bridges, 1997). Bridges contends that such losses should be acknowledged openly and sympathetically, and people should be allowed space and support to grieve. Instead of suppressing or discouraging these emotions, the grief process should be honored and validated. People (leaders and followers alike) can bring closure to old ways through celebration of what has been accomplished in the past and through recognition of the foundations for new beginnings that were laid in past practices. These strategies recognize the human impact of change and allow people to move gracefully through their own process of coming to terms with different ways of being, doing, and thinking.

Transition management also means moving beyond the endings to attend specifically and directly to the new beginnings. This stage of transition can be (and has been) designed from any number of approaches. Bridges (1997), for example, contends that leaders should design strategies around four Ps: the purpose, a picture, the plan, and a part to play. His point is that participants need to be clear about the purpose of the new way of doing things, and this needs to be communicated often and clearly. They need to have a picture of what the new beginning looks like, they need to see the plan, and they need to understand the part they are to play in the plan. This approach, however, places a strong focus on leaders and it puts people in a somewhat passive (and instrumental) role in the process. Although leaders may need to 'get the message out' and to build momentum, continued reliance on a few strong leaders to manage the transition does not particularly resonate with the sorts of conditions that typically characterize a learning community.

The notion of transition from old to new is one that has been addressed implicitly in a number of works related to learning communities or learning organizations, even though the term *transition* is seldom used. These discussions have often focused on the ways in which organizational structures increase the capacity of people to engage in deeper levels and different ways of learning. For example, Senge et al. (1999) contend that the community's ability to learn depends on coaching capacity, permeability of organizational boundaries, information infrastructure, and a learning culture. Similarly, Marks and Louis (1999) identify the dimensions of school capacity for organizational learning as structure, shared commitment and collaborative activities, knowledge and skills, leadership, and feedback and accountability. Furthermore, Lambert (1998) positions leadership as the central structure for creating a learning community, with appropriate leadership identified as broad-based skillful participation in the work of leadership, roles and responsibilities that reflect broad involvement and collaboration, and a leadership norm of reflective practice and innovation. Together, these works provide some interesting insights into some organizational conditions that can support the transition from a mechanistic worldview to one based on an appreciation of wholeness.

Rather than attempting to prescribe any one particular transition path, our position is that, if the ultimate goal is a community of learners and a community of leaders (for which we have argued throughout this book), then the process of managing the transition belongs to the people in the educational community. They are the ones who, alone and together, sort out what conditions limit their capacity to grow and what conditions support it. They are the ones who, together, hammer out the paths they will follow, alone and together, in their search for new ways of constructing the school. They are the ones who, together, decide who does what, when, and how. Even though the leaders might initiate the process, they do not determine its direction or force its flow. That is the business of the members of the community. The leaders certainly can suggest and advise, but their role is to facilitate the process, not to control it. They support the transition and they encourage it, but they do not manipulate it.

The model that we have articulated in this book implies that a number of individual, group, and organizational elements are likely to find their way into transition processes. One individual element that we expect to emerge is the notion of *self-efficacy*: people with a high sense of self-efficacy view themselves as having the power to produce the desired results and seek solutions that will facilitate those ends (Ashton & Webb, 1985). A further individual element is *emotion*: moving into unfamiliar territory is always more than a rational activity, and learning is as much about intuition and emotion as it is about cognition and logic (Lang & Newtion, 1997). Another is *knowledge and skill development*: reconstructing a worldview can only occur if individuals extend their professional narratives to include new ideas and a new knowledge base (Marks & Louis, 1999). Yet another is *critical reflection*: by reflecting on what they do and how they think, on what effects are produced and what they had hoped for, and in what ways they might change their thinking and their practice, educators engage more critically with the narratives that construct their worldview.

Group elements that find their way into a transition process might include *authentic relationships*: when relationships are based on trust, caring, and mutual respect, people have a safe foundation for moving into strange terrain, and learning is facilitated. Another group element is *professional networks*: the existence of networks and interrelationships inside and outside the school gives people a context for exchanging information and for discovering new ideas. A third element is *communication*: reconstruction is encouraged when people know what information is relevant and know how to present it so it will be heard; and it is encouraged when new ideas are communicated from networks beyond the boundaries of the community. Another is *shared commitments*: a shared purpose shapes the commitments of those working in the school and it extends the capacity to create common understandings about the desired reality. Still another group element is *collaborative activity*: when educators share practices, discuss curricula, use reflective dialogue, pose questions, talk openly about their work, and take collaborative action, they learn alternative ways of viewing reality, of solving problems, and of confronting deep mysteries. This sort of collaboration opens personal and shared mental models to a process of deconstruction and reconstruction.

In relation to organizational elements, a key element is that of *infrastructure*: resources (time, personnel, and money), policies, and work arrangements should bring people together and further the work of learning, and ideology and mission should convey the importance of community building. Marks and Louis (1999), for example, argue that 'removing structural impediments may be more critical to the success of the program to improve performance than adding new resources' (p. 713). Another organizational element is *leadership*: transformative, empowering, facilitative, and decentralized leadership provides direction for the process of transition and a safe ground for experimenting with new configurations of the organizational narrative. Another is a *learning agent*: transitions are supported when there is an individual who encourages the search for new knowledge, skills, information, practice, and theory, and who fosters a culture of inquiry. Still another organizational element is *feedback*: when school people pay attention to learning outcomes, they have greater capacity for learning and can use that capacity to expand and enhance what they hope to accomplish or to create. This allows them to develop accountability standards that resonate with their context and that improve their professional practice (Newmann, King, & Rigdon, 1997). Such feedback is critical in any attempt to reconstruct the organizational narrative.

With these lists of elements, we do not mean to imply that they are the only ones or even the best ones. They are elements that we have found to be important in our own work with learning communities in schools. Our point here is that the process of managing the transition from a mechanistic to a wholeness worldview deserves some careful and explicit attention to creating a setting wherein both the individual and the group benefits. Learning communities, especially ones grounded in a wholeness worldview, do not develop by accident. They develop because a decision has been made to move in this direction. Consequently, a new ideology needs to be built into the structure of the school, its mission and vision, its staffing, its professional development, its policies, and its structural arrangements.

The sort of transition that we have been describing in this chapter has profound implications for people at all levels of the educational system, but especially for administrators and politicians. These are the individuals who have benefited most from a mechanistic educational order because they are the ones who have held the most potent levers of power and have wielded them to maintain control over the educational system. As an example, we remember one retired supervisory officer commenting that the new director of education in a large urban school system, who had tried to create a more responsive and open school system, had 'lost control of her organization.' This kind of assumption is common to many administrators and politicians, but it does not support the development of a learning community nor does it reflect a wholeness view of education.

Many classroom teachers (and some school administrators) already know and believe much of what we have presented in this book, but they feel unable to make these sorts of changes. In many jurisdictions, the policy environment places a heavy emphasis on accountability to externally determined measures and leaves school people with little autonomy or leverage to make any real changes in the way that schooling is enacted. In many cases, educators' efforts to change the educational system have been stymied by power relations and political agendas operating in their schools, school systems, and state or provincial departments, and many of our professional colleagues have admitted to feelings of intense helplessness and victimization in light of the conditions within which they work. Because of the place that administrators and politicians hold in the power hierarchy, they will have to take first responsibility for creating a policy environment that can support the shift that we have described in this chapter. These are the individuals who probably will have the most to give up in any move from a mechanistic worldview, and they are the ones who perhaps will need to take the first steps toward reconstructing the metaphors upon which the narratives of schools and school systems are constructed.

Profound Improvement: Building Capacity for a Learning Community

The view of the Earth from space has brought forth an entirely new set of images for grounding the metaphors of the social order and it has sparked at least the beginning of a deep shift in human understanding, one that honors the wholeness of the planet. According to O'Sullivan (1999), these new images demand a whole new set of sensibilities that are grounded on an appreciation of diversity and complexity, of connections and interrelationships, and of wisdom and creativity. He contends that old sensibilities are both seductive and addictive and they saturate the consciousness so deeply that they appear to be unassailable. But he believes that the old ways of thinking, being, and doing ignore the organic nature of human processes and lead to soul-destroying structures. This condition is not sustainable for life, nor is it sustainable for learning. It is our belief that the notion of the learning community holds at least some promise for lifting education out of the grips of mechanistic structures to the higher ground that is suggested by a wholeness perspective of the world. This is what we believe can lead to profound improvement in teaching and learning.

The kind of learning community that we have described in this book implies a deep change in the views of professional practice, of people, and of school organizations. The view of professional practice (of teaching and learning) holds continual learning for students and for educators at the heart of everything that goes on in and about a school. It holds knowledge and skill gaps as natural aspects of the human condition and as opportunities to grow and develop. It holds learning as natural and organic and deeply connected to the lives and realities and mysteries of the people who are part of the community – students, teachers, parents, administrators. This view of professional practice asks educators to open their practices to their own critical scrutiny and to the scrutiny of others. It asks them to invite others into their professional spaces, to try out new ideas and be not afraid to make mistakes. It recognizes the deep emotion that new learning involves, and it asks all people in the community to make the emotional investment in their own learning and in the learning of other community members.

The view of people (of the self, of colleagues, of students, of parents) holds different people as unique expressions of one interconnected life force. It recognizes the deep interrelationships even among people who are in fundamental disagreement with one another, and it honors the deep value of every human soul. This view holds that when we direct negativity toward another person, we are injecting it into our own lives, and when we respect others, respect shall return to us. This view of people recognizes diversity as essential for sustaining life, health, and learning. Differences are inevitable, necessary, and desirable. In this view, people are not means to any end. They are human beings who deserve care, respect, and regard for their unique abilities, capacities, desires, and dreams – regardless of how nonconformist they might be.

The view of school organizations holds that leadership, power, and structures are all in service of teaching and learning. The organization is there to increase the capacity to bring about human growth and development. It is there to provide the means to get things done. Leadership is enacted throughout the system, and leadership and followership are two parts of the same process. Differences in position or role do not imply or lead to differences in status or worth. The environment within the school affirms and invites reflection, inquiry, experimentation, facilitation, risk taking, autonomy, and diversity. It places teaching and learning at the center of the challenges, stimulation, support, encouragement, and reward systems that make up the organizational context.

With this book, we do not intend to situate the learning community as yet another recipe with some strategies for tinkering at the margins of what we already do. It is a way of being and a way of living. We are not presenting these ideas to convince the reader that we have the answers or that we want to change everything in all schools. This is definitely not in the spirit of a learning community or in the reflection of a wholeness worldview. We present these ideas to encourage readers to reflect on their own contexts. The ideas we discuss in the pages of this book are the ideas that have made sense for our professional and personal questions. They are not necessarily the answer for other questions that should be posed in other contexts. Instead, they are some of our own frameworks and insights that we share in the hope that they might spur some musing and pondering about the tough problems and deep mysteries in other contexts.

In a learning community, no one can tell people what to do. They have to be allowed to get to where they are going on their own. Profound improvement happens from within, from a deep internal search for meaning, relevance, and connection. It is a search for those things that will make one's life more authentic and purposeful, and it emerges naturally when one sees a new destination and then sets out on the journey. Bridges (1997) says, '[leaders] forget that while the first task of change management is to understand the destination and how to get there, the first task of transition management is to convince people to leave home' (p. 32). We hope that, through the pages of this book, we have given you an incentive to leave home.

References

Adelman, N.E. & Walking-Eagle, K.P. (1997). 'Teachers, time, and school reform'. In A. Hargreaves (Ed.), *Rethinking educational change with heart and mind: 1997 ASCD yearbook*, pp. 92-110. Alexandria, VA: Association for Supervision and Curriculum Development.

Amason, A.C., Thompson, K.R., Hochwarter, W.A. & Harrison, A.W. (1995). 'Conflict: An important dimension in successful management teams'. *Organizational Dynamics*, 24 (2), 20-34.

Anderson, T. & Klinge, E. (1995). 'Developing a regenerative community'. In K. Gozdz (Ed.), *Community building: Renewing spirit and learning in business*, pp. 351-359. San Francisco: New Leaders Press.

Argyris, C. (1993). *Knowledge for action: A guide to overcoming barriers to organizational change*. San Francisco: Jossey-Bass.

Argyris, C. & Schon, D. (1978). *Organizational learning: A theory of action perspective*. Reading, MA: Addison-Wesley.

Ashton, P. & Webb, R. (1985). *Making a difference: Teachers' sense of efficacy and student achievement*. London: Longmans.

Aston, M. & Hyle, A.E. (1997, October). *The impact of social networks and teacher beliefs on educational change*. Paper presented at the annual meeting of the University Council of Educational Administration, Orlando, FL.

Bakkenes, I., de Brabander, C. & Imants, J. (1999). 'Teacher isolation and communication network analysis in primary schools'. *Educational Administration Quarterly*, 35 (2), 166-202.

Barth, R. (1990). *Improving schools from within*. San Francisco: Jossey-Bass.

Beck, L.G. (1994). 'Cultivating a caring school community: One principal's story'. In J. Murphy & K. Louis (Eds.), *Reshaping the principalship: Insights from transformational reform efforts*, pp. 177-202. Thousand Oaks, CA: Corwin.

Beck, L.G. (1999). 'Metaphors of educational community: An analysis of the images that reflect and influence scholarship and practice'. *Educational Administration Quarterly*, 35 (1), 13-45.

Beck, L.G. & Foster, W. (1999). 'Administration and community: Considering challenges, exploring possibilities'. In J. Murphy & K.S. Louis (Eds.), *Handbook of research on educational administration*, 2nd ed., pp. 337-358. San Francisco: Jossey-Bass.

Berger, P.L. & Luckman, T. (1966). *The social construction of reality*. New York: Anchor.

Bohm, D. (1980). *Wholeness and the implicate order*. London: Routledge & Kegan Paul.

Bohm, D. (1985). *Unfolding meaning: A weekend of dialogue with David Bohm*. London: Routledge & Kegan Paul.

Bredeson, P.V. (1993). 'Letting go of outlived professional identities: A study of role transition and role strain for principals in restructured schools'. *Educational Administration Quarterly*, 29 (1), 34-68.

Bredeson, P.V. (1999, April). *Paradox and possibility: Professional development and organizational learning in education.* Paper presented at the annual conference of the American Educational Research Association, Montreal, QC.

Bredeson, P.V. & Scribner, J.P. (2000). 'A statewide professional development conference: Useful strategy for learning or inefficient use of resources?' *Educational Evaluation and Policy Analysis*, 8 (13). [On-line]. Available: http://epaa.asu.edu/ epaa/ v8n13.html.

Bridges, W. (1997). *Managing transitions: Making the most of change.* London: Nicholas Brealey.

Brooks, M. & Brooks, J.G. (1999). 'The courage to be constructivist'. *Educational Leadership*, 57 (3), 18-24.

Brown, J., Collins, A. & Duguid, P. (1989). 'Situated cognition and the culture of learning'. *Educational Researcher*, 18 (1), 32-42.

Carr, W. & Kemmis, S. (1986). *Becoming critical: Education, knowledge and action research.* London: Falmer.

Conley, D. (1993). *Roadmap to restructuring.* Eugene, OR: Eric Clearinghouse in Educational Management.

Crow, G. (1999). 'Implications for leadership in collaborative schools'. In D. Pounder (Ed.), *Restructuring schools for collaboration: Promises and pitfalls.* Albany, NY: SUNY. (draft)

Cuban, L. (1988). 'A fundamental puzzle of school reform'. *Phi Delta Kappan*, 69 (5), 341-344.

Darling-Hammond, L. & McLaughlin, M.W. (1996). 'Policies that support professional learning in an era of reform'. In M.W. McLaughlin & I. Oberman (Eds.), *Teacher learning: New policies, new practices*, pp. 202-218. New York: Teachers College Press.

Deal, T.E. & Peterson, K.E. (1998). *Shaping school culture: The heart of leadership.* San Francisco: Jossey-Bass.

Deal, T. & Peterson, K. (1994). *The leadership paradox: Balancing logic and artistry in schools.* San Francisco: Jossey-Bass.

Dixon, N.M. (1997). 'The hallways of learning'. *Organizational Dynamics*, 25 (4), 23-34.

Douglas, M. (1986). *How institutions think.* Syracuse, NY: Syracuse University.

Elmore, R.F. (1992). 'Why restructuring alone won't improve teaching'. *Educational Leadership*, 49 (7), 44-48.

Fang, Z. (1996). 'A review of research on teacher beliefs and practices'. *Educational Research*, 38 (1), 47-65.

Firestone, W.A. (1996). 'Images of teaching and proposals for reform: A comparison of ideas from cognitive and organizational research'. *Educational Administration Quarterly*, 32 (2), 209-235.

Firestone, W.A. & Louis, K.S. (1999). 'Schools as culture'. In J. Murphy & K.S. Louis (Eds.), *Handbook of research on educational administration*, 2nd ed., pp. 297-322. San Francisco: Jossey-Bass.

Foster, W. (1989). 'Toward a critical practice of leadership'. In J. Smyth (Ed.), *Critical perspectives on educational leadership*, pp. 39-62. London: Falmer.

Fullan, M. (1992). 'Visions that blind'. *Educational Leadership*, 47 (5), 19-22.

Fullan, M. (1997). 'Broadening the concept of teacher leadership'. In S. Caldwell (Ed.), *Professional development in learning-centered schools*, pp. 34-48. Oxford, OH: National Staff Development Council.

Fullan, M. (1999). *Change forces: The sequel*. London: Falmer.

Fullan, M. & Hargreaves, A. (1996). *What's worth fighting for in your school*. New York: Teachers College Press.

Fulmer, R.M., & Keys, J.B. (1998). 'A conversation with Chris Argyris: The father of organizational learning'. *Organizational Dynamics*, 27 (2), 21-32.

Gardner, H. (1983). *Frames of mind: The theory of multiple intelligences*. New York: Basic Books.

Gherardi, S. (1999). 'Learning as problem-driven or learning in the face of mystery?' *Organization Studies*, 20 (1), 101-124.

Gitlin, A. & Margonis, F. (1995). 'The political aspect of reform: Teacher resistance as good sense'. *American Journal of Education*, 103 (August), 377-405.

Gozdz, K. (1995). 'Creating learning organizations through core competence in community building'. In K. Gozdz (Ed.), *Community building: Renewing spirit and learning in business*, pp. 57-67. San Francisco: New Leaders Press.

Gronn, P. (1998). *Life in teams: Collaborative leadership and learning in autonomous work units*. Hawthorn, Victoria, AU: Australian Council of Educational Administration.

Guskey, T.R. & Peterson, K.D. (1996). 'The road to classroom change'. *Educational Leadership*, 53 (4), 10-14.

Habermas, J. (1984). *The theory of communicative action:* Volume 1. Boston: Thomas McCarthy.

Hajnal, V., Walker, K. & Sackney, L. (1998). 'Leadership, organizational learning, and selected factors relating to the institutionalization of school improvement initiatives'. *Alberta Journal of Educational Research*, 44 (1), 70-89.

Hannay, L.M. & Ross, J.A. (1997). 'Initiating secondary school reform: The dynamic relationship between restructuring, reculturing, and retiming'. *Educational Administration Quarterly*, 33 (Supplement), 576-603.

Hargreaves, A. (1991). 'Contrived collegiality: The micropolitics of teacher collaboration. In J. Blase (Ed.), *The politics of life in schools: Power, conflicts, and cooperation*, pp. 46-72. Newbury Park, CA: Sage.

Hargreaves, A. (1993). 'Individualism and individuality: Reinterpreting the teacher culture'. In J.W. Little & M.W. McLaughlin (Eds.), *Teachers' work: Individuals, colleagues, and contexts*, pp. 51-76. New York: Teachers College Press.

Haskins, M.E., Liedtka, J. & Rosenblum, J. (1998). 'Beyond teams: Toward an ethic of collaboration'. *Organizational Dynamics*, 26 (4), 34-50.

Hoffman, J., Sabo, D., Bliss, J. & Hoy, W. (1994). 'Building a culture of trust'. *Journal of School Leadership*, 4, 484-501.

Hudson, J. (1997). *Dynamic harmonization in a school restructuring endeavour*. Unpublished doctoral dissertation, University of Saskatchewan, Saskatoon, SK.

Isaacs, W. (1999). *Dialogue and the art of thinking together*. New York: Doubleday.

Janov, J.E. (1995). 'Creating meaning: The heart of learning communities'. *Training and Development*, 49 (5), 53-58.

Kanter, R.M. (1978). 'Power failure in management circuits'. *Harvard Business Review*,57 (4), 65-75.

Kemmis, S., & McTaggart, R. (1988). *The action research planner* (3rd ed.). Victoria, AU: Deakin University Press.

Kouzes, J., & Posner, B. (1995). *The leadership challenge: How to keep getting extraordinary things done in organizations*. San Francisco: Jossey-Bass.

Lakoff, G. & Johnson, M. (1980). *Metaphors we live by*. Chicago: University of Chicago.

Lambert, L. (1998). *Building leadership capacity in schools*. Alexandria, VA: Association for Supervision and Curriculum Development.

Lang, S. & Newtion, J. (1997). 'Educating the gut: Socio-emotional aspects of the learning organization'. *Journal of Management Development*, 16 (4), 284-301.

Lawrence-Lightfoot, S. & Davis, J. H. (1997). *The art and science of portraiture*. San Francisco: Jossey-Bass.

Leithwood, K. (1992). 'The move toward transformational leadership'. *Educational Leadership*, 49 (5), 8-12.

Leithwood, K. (1999, October). *Accountability for what? Community vs. instrumentality*. Panel conversation presented at the annual conference of the University Council for Educational Administration, Minneapolis, MN.

Leithwood, K. & Duke, D. (1999). 'A century's quest to understand school leadership'. In J. Murphy & K.S. Louis (Eds.), *Handbook of research on educational administration*, 2nd ed., pp. 45-72. San Francisco: Jossey-Bass.

Leithwood, K. & Jantzi, D. (1990). 'Transformational leadership: How principals can help reform school cultures'. *School Effectiveness and School Improvement*, 1 (4), 249-280.

Leithwood, K. & Louis, K. S. (1998) (Eds.). *Organizational learning in schools*. Lisse, NL: Swets & Zeitlinger.

Leithwood, K., Jantzi, D. & Fernandez, A. (1994). 'Transformational leadership and teachers' commitment to change'. In J. Murphy & K.S. Louis (Eds.), *Reshaping the principalship*, pp. 77-98. Thousand Oaks, CA: Corwin.

Leithwood, K., Jantzi, D. & Steinbach, R. (1999). *Changing leadership for changing times*. Buckingham, UK: Open University Press.

Lieberman, A. & Miller, L. (1990). 'The social realities of teaching'. In A. Lieberman (Ed.), *Schools as collaborative cultures: Creating the future now*, pp. 153-163. New York: Falmer.

Lieberman, A. (Ed.). (1990). *Schools as collaborative cultures: Creating the future now*. New York: Falmer.

Lieberman, A., & Miller, L. (1990). 'The social realities of teaching'. In A. Lieberman (Ed.), *Schools as collaborative cultures: Creating the future now*, pp. 153-163. New York: Falmer.

Lipman, P. (1997). 'Restructuring in context: A case study of teacher participation and the dynamics of ideology, race, and power'. *American Educational Research Journal*, 34 (1), 3-37.

Little, J. (1982). 'Norms of collegiality and experimentation: Workplace conditions of school success'. *American Educational Research Journal*, 19, 325-340.

Little, J. (1990). 'The persistence of privacy: Autonomy and initiative in teachers pro-fessional relations'. *Teachers College Record*, 91 (4), 509-534.

Little, J.W. & McLaughlin, M.W. (Eds.). (1993). *Teachers'work: Individuals, colleagues, and contexts*. New York: Teachers College Press.

Little, J.W. (1993). 'Teachers' professional development in a climate of educational reform'. *Educational Evaluation and Policy Analysis*, 15 (2), 129-151.

Louis, K.S. (1994). 'Beyond "managed change": Rethinking how schools improve'. *School Effectiveness and School Improvement*, 5(1), 2-24.

Louis, K.S., Kruse, S.D & Bryk, A.S. (1995). 'Professionalism and community: What is it and why is it important in urban schools?' In K.S. Louis & S.D. Kruse (Eds.), *Professionalism and community: Perspectives on reforming urban schools*, pp. 3-22. Thousand Oaks, CA: Corwin.

Louis, K.S., Toole, J. & Hargreaves, A. (1999). 'Rethinking school improvement'. In J. Murphy & K.S. Louis (Eds.), *Handbook of research on educational administration*, 2nd ed., pp. 251-276. San Francisco: Jossey-Bass.

Louis, K.S., Kruse, S., & Associates. (1995). *Professionalism and community: Perspectives on reforming urban schools*. Thousand Oaks, CA: Corwin.

Louis, K.S., Kruse, S., & Marks, H. (1996). 'Teachers' professional community and school reform'. *American Educational Research Journal*, 33 (3), 719-752.

Manchester, W. (1992). *A world lit only by fire: The medieval mind and the Renaissance*. Boston, MA: Little and Brown.

Marks, H.M. & Louis, K.S. (1999). 'Teacher empowerment and the capacity for organizational learning'. *Educational Administration Quarterly*, 35 , 707-750.

Marquardt, M. (1996). *Building the learning organization*. Toronto, ON: McGraw-Hill.

McLaughlin, M.W. (1990). 'The Rand Change Agent study revisited: Macro perspectives and micro realities'. *Educational Researcher*, 19 (9), 11-16.

Merz, C. & Furman, G. (1997). *Community: Promises and paradoxes*. New York: Teachers College Press.

Mitchell, C. (1999a). 'Building learning communities in schools: The Next Generation or The Impossible Dream?' *Interchange*, 30 (3), 283-303.

Mitchell, C. (1999b, June). *Problems of organizational learning*. Paper presented at the Annual Conference of the Canadian Society for the Study of Education. Sherbrooke, QC.

Mitchell, C. & Coltrinari, H. (In press). 'Reflective journal writing: Encouraging critical reflection in adult education'. In T. Barer-Stein & M. Kompf (Eds.), *The craft of teaching adults*, 3rd ed. Toronto, ON: Culture Concepts.

Mitchell, C. & Hyle, A.E. (1999, October). *Reconstructing capacity: A model for school improvement and school assessment*. Paper presented at the annual meeting of the University Council of Educational Administration, Minneapolis, MN.

Mitchell, C. & Sackney, L. (1998). 'Learning about organizational learning'. In K. Leithwood & K.S. Louis (Eds.), *Organizational learning in schools*, pp. 177-203. Lisse, NL: Swets & Zeitlinger.

Murphy, J. & Louis, K.S. (1999). 'Introduction: Framing the project'. In J. Murphy & K. S. Louis (Eds.), *Handbook of Research on Educational Administration*, 2nd ed., pp. xxi-xxvii. San Francisco: Jossey-Bass.

146

Newmann, F. & Wehlage, G. (1995). *Successful school restructuring*. Madison, WI: University of Wisconsin.

Newmann, F.M., King, M.B. & Rigdon, M. (1997). 'Accountability and school performance: Implications from restructuring schools'. *Harvard Educational Review*, 67 (1), 41-74.

Noddings, N. (1992). *The challenge to care in schools*. New York: Teachers College Press.

Osterman, K.F. (1990). 'Reflective practice: A new agenda for education'. *Education and Urban Society*, 22 (2), 133-152.

O'Sullivan, E. (1999). *Transformative learning: Educational vision for the 21st century*. Toronto, ON: University of Toronto Press.

Parker, G.M. (1994). *Team players and teamwork*. San Francisco: Jossey-Bass.

Perkins, D. (1999). 'The many faces of constructivism'. *Educational Leadership*, 57 (3), 6-11.

Phelan, A.M. (1996). '"Strange pilgrims": Disillusionment and nostalgia in teacher education reform'. *Interchange*, 27 (3), 331-348.

Pounder, D., Ogawa, R. & Adams, E. (1995). 'Leadership as an organization wide phenomena: Its impact on school performance'. *Educational Administration Quarterly*, 31, 564-588.

Prawat, R.S. (1999). 'Dewey, Peirce, and the learning paradox'. *American Educational Research Journal*, 36 (1), 47-76.

Prawat, R. & Peterson, P. (1999). 'Social constructivist views of learning'. In J. Murphy and K.S. Louis (Eds.), *Handbook of research on educational administration*, 2nd ed., pp. 203-226. San Francisco: Jossey-Bass.

Prestine, N. & LeGrand, B. (1991). 'Cognitive learning theory and the preparation of educational administrators: Implications for practice and policy'. *Educational Administration Quarterly*, 27 (1), 61-89.

Redding, J. & Catalanello, R. (1994). *Strategic readiness: The making of the learning organization*. San Francisco: Jossey-Bass.

Richardson, V. (1990). 'Significant and worthwhile change in teaching practice'. *Educational Researcher*, 19 (7), 10-18.

Roemer, M.G. (1991). 'What we talk about when we talk about school reform'. *Harvard Educational Review*, 61(4), 434-448.

Rosenholtz, S. (1989). *Teachers' workplace: The social organization of schools*. New York: Longman.

Rost, J. (1991). *Leadership for the twenty-first century*. New York: Praeger.

Sackney, L. & Dibski, D. (1994). 'School-based management: A critical perspective'. *Educational Management and Administration*, 22 (2), 104-112.

Sackney, L., Walker, K., & Hajnal, V. (1998). 'Principal and teacher perspectives on school improvement'. *Journal of Educational Management*, 1 (1), 45-63.

Schlechty, P.C. (1991). *Schools for the 21st century: Leadership imperatives for educational reform*. San Francisco: Jossey Bass.

Schon, D.A. (1983). *The reflective practitioner: How professionals think in action*. New York: Basic Books.

Scribner, J.P. (1999). 'Professional development: Untangling the influence of work context on teacher learning'. *Educational Administration Quarterly*, 35 (2), 238-266.

Senge, P.M. (1990). *The fifth discipline: The art and practice of the learning organiza-tion*. New York: Doubleday.

Senge, P.M. (1995). 'Creating quality communities'. In K. Gozdz (Ed.), *Community building: Renewing spirit and learning in business*, pp. 49-55. San Francisco: New Leaders Press.

Senge, P.M., Roberts, C., Ross, R., Smith, B. & Kleiner, A. (1994). *The fifth discipline fieldbook: Strategies and tools for building a learning community*. London: Nicholas Brealey.

Senge, P.M., Kleiner, A., Roberts, C., Ross, R., Roth, G. & Smith, B. (1999). *The dance of change: The challenges to sustaining momentum in learning organizations*. New York: Doubleday.

Sergiovanni, T. (1996). *Leadership for the schoolhouse*. San Francisco: Jossey-Bass.

Sergiovanni, T. (2000). *The lifeworld of leadership: Creating culture, community, and personal meaning in our schools*. San Francisco: Jossey-Bass.

Shields, C. (1999, October). *Accountability for what? Community vs. instrumentality*. Panel conversation presented at the annual conference of the University Council for Educational Administration, Minneapolis, MN.

Shulman, L. (1987). 'Knowledge and teaching: Foundations of the new reform'. *Harvard Educational Review*, 57 (1), 1-22.

Smith, S. & Scott, D. (1990). *The collaborative school*. Alexandria, VA: ASCD.

Smylie, M., & Hart, A. (1999). 'School leadership for teacher learning and change: A human and social capital development perspective'. In J. Murphy & K.S. Louis (Eds.), *Handbook of research on educational administration*, 2nd ed., pp. 421-441. San Francisco: Jossey-Bass.

Speck, M. (1999). *The principalship: Building a learning community*. Upper Saddle River, NJ: Prentice-Hall.

Stamps, D. (1998). 'Learning ecologies'. *Training*, 35 (1), 32-38.

Starratt, R.J. (1996). *Transforming educational administration: Meaning, community, excellence*. New York: McGraw-Hill.

Starratt, R.J. (1999, October). *Accountability for what? Community vs. instrumentality*. Panel conversation presented at the annual conference of the University Council for Educational Administration, Minneapolis, MN.

Swieringa, J. & Wierdsma, A. (1992). *Becoming a learning organization*. Amsterdam: Addison Wesley.

Tartar, C., Sabo, D., & Hoy, W. (1989). 'School characteristics and faculty trust in secondary schools'. *Educational Administration Quarterly*, 25 (3), 294-308.

Tell, C. (1999). 'Renewing the profession of teaching: A conversation with John Goodlad'. *Educational Leadership*, 56 (8), 15-19.

Walker, K., Shakotko, D., & Pullman, E. (1998, October). *Towards a further under-standing of trust and trustworthiness*. Paper presented to the Values and Educa-tional Leadership Conference, University of Toronto, Toronto, ON.

Weick, K. (1995). *Sensemaking in organizations*. San Francisco: Sage.

Wenger, E. (1998). *Communities of practice*. New York: Cambridge University Press.

Whitney, R.V. (1995). 'Caring: An essential element'. In K. Gozdz (Ed.), *Community building: Renewing spirit and learning in business*, pp. 199-207. San Francisco: New Leaders Press.

Wignall, R. (1996). 'Funding teacher education in the postmodern world: A view from Canada'. In B. Jeans & K. Rebel (Eds.), *Issues in teacher education: Policy and practice* (Vol. 1) (chap. 14). Victoria, AU: Felicitas Academic Press.

Wineburg, S. & Grossman, P. (1998). 'Creating a community of learners among high school teachers' *Phi Delta Kappan*, 79 (5), 350-353.

Wirth, A.G. (1989). 'The violation of people at work in schools'. *Teachers College Record*, 90 (4), 536-549.

Wyatt, S. (1997). 'Dialogue, reflection, and community'. *The Journal of Experiential Education*, 20 (2), 80-85.

Zemke, R. (1996). 'The call of community'. *Training*, 24-30.

Index

150

156

CONTEXT OF LEARNING
Classrooms, Schools and Society

1. Education for All. Robert E. Slavin
       1996. ISBN 90 265 1472 7 (hardback)
            ISBN 90 265 1473 5 (paperback)

2. The Road to Improvement: Reflections on School Effectiveness.
    Peter Mortimore
       1998. ISBN 90 265 1525 1 (hardback)
            ISBN 90 265 1526 X (paperback)

3. Organizational Learning in Schools.
    Edited by Kenneth Leithwood and Karen Seashore Louis
       1999. ISBN 90 265 1539 1 (hardback)
            ISBN 90 265 1540 5 (paperback)

4. Teaching and Learning Thinking Skills.
    Edited by J.H.M. Hamers, J.E.H. van Luit and B. Csapó
       1999. ISBN 90 265 1545 6 (hardback)

5. Managing Schools towards High Performance: Linking School
    Management Theory to the School Effectiveness Knowledge Base.
    Edited by Adrie J. Visscher
       1999. ISBN 90 265 1546 4 (hardback)

6. School Effectiveness: Coming of Age in the Twenty-First Century.
    Pam Sammons
       1999. ISBN 90 265 1549 9 (hardback)
            ISBN 90 265 1550 2 (paperback)

7. Educational Change and Development in the Asia-Pacific Region:
    Challenges for the Future.
    Edited by Tony Townsend and Yin Cheong Cheng
       2000. ISBN 90 265 1558 8 (hardback)
            ISBN 90 265 1627 4 (paperback)

8. Making Sense of Word Problems.
    Lieven Verschaffel, Brain Greer and Erik de Corte
       2000. ISBN 90 265 1628 2 (hardback)

9. Profound Improvement: Building Capacity for a Learning Community.
    Edited by Coral Mitchell and Larry Sackney
       2000. ISBN 90 265 16347 (hardback)